# TAROSOPHY SQUARED

## MARCUS KATZ

First English edition published 2021 by Forge Press (Keswick).

Cover art 'Temperance' by Janine Hall, back cover 'The Sun' from the *Tarot of Everlasting Day* (2021), www.janinehallstudio.com.

ISBN: 9798744043025

# DEDICATION

This book is dedicated to Alexander Chaphino.

*In Memory*

Stuart R. Kaplan.

April 1, 1932 – February 9, 2021.

"The sun, which shines behind him, knows whence he came, whither he is going, and how he will return by another path after many days."

- A. E. Waite on the 'Fool'.

And finally, but above all, to:

Anistita Argenteum Astrum,

The Priestess of the Silver Star,

She whose light leads the way to the Arcanum Arcanorum, the Secret of Secrets,

Vos Vos Vos Vos.

V.V.V.V.

# CONTENTS

# CHAPTER II: ARCHETYPES, SYMBOLS & LANGUAGE

# CHAPTER III: THE 21 PRINCIPLES OF TAROT

# CHAPTER IV: FOUNDATIONAL CONCEPTS

# CHAPTER V: SKILL DEVELOPMENT EXERCISES

# CHAPTER VI: KABBALAH

# CHAPTER VII: NLP SKILLS & TALISMANS

# CHAPTER VIII: THE MAJOR ARCANA

## CHAPTER IX: TAROT INCANTOS

## CHAPTER X: THE MINOR ARCANA

## CHAPTER XI: COURT CARDS

## CHAPTER XII: TAROT FOR ALL SEASONS

## CHAPTER XIII: PRACTICAL METHODS & SPREADS

CONCLUSION

BIBLIOGRAPHY

Also by Marcus Katz

# ACKNOWLEDGMENTS

My thanks to Soror C. L. and Soror R. for initial reading and comments.

My thanks also to Janine Hall for the Tarot of Everlasting Day.

# DON'T BUILD DOORS OUT OF KEYS

What the Major Arcana say about the concerns that may hold back your tarot reading, starting with the Magician, then the High Priestess, all the way through the twenty-two cards to the World.

And what the Fool answers at the end. That.

I don't have the skill,
I don't have intuition,
I don't have experience,
I have no power,
I don't know the rules,
I don't love tarot enough,
I don't go far enough,
I am frightened,
I am alone,
It goes round and round in my head,
I am unbalanced,
I can't read reversals,
I'm scared of the Death card,
The Spirits do not talk to me,
People think it's the work of the Devil,
I keep learning then it all falls apart,
I'm hopeless,
I am not deep enough.
I am not bright enough,
Everyone will judge me,
I am not as good as/like everyone else,

You know what, says the Fool, I have no care,
Just Read Your Tarot.
For they are the Keys to Your Freedom,
Not more locked Doors.

*The tarot is the door between the Fool and the World, and its key.*

# - I -
## TAROSOPHICAL TAROT

This book further develops Tarosophy, the unique approach to tarot, cartomancy, and divination, which was first presented in the original book *Tarosophy*, published in 2011.[1] In the decade since *Tarosophy* was published, much has happened to open the world of divination, cartomancy, and esotericism to a larger audience, particularly through social media.[2] This present book provides the main developments of Tarosophy over that time and is the second of a trilogy of books, the third of which will likely be published in 2031.

This book should be considered as an intermediate book, requiring some experience and knowledge of both tarot and Tarosophy. It is recommended that the reader is familiar with the first *Tarosophy* book, although both books are written to stand alone in their presentation of tarot and divination. In this second book we will provide many new practical methods, spreads, and skill development exercises. We will also re-examine the foundational concepts of Tarosophy, given as the twenty-two Tarot Principles.

I will also share several examples of *Tarot Incantos* - poetry or prose based on the sequences of tarot. We will look at new ways of working with the Majors, Minors and Court cards in further split-deck methods, first

---

[1] Throughout this book, Tarosophy refers to the subject and *Tarosophy* (italicised) refers to the first book.

[2] As social media is entirely a visual medium and much of the content is interpretation (i.e., creating dance moves to existing music) or re-presentation and curation of images to tell (or sell) a narrative, tarot is an ideal artefact for this purpose, used authentically or otherwise.

introduced to Tarot in the original *Tarosophy*.[3]

As with the first book, the reader is encouraged to recognize the various models employed in the methods, such as NLP, Kabbalah, and esoteric correspondences, and learn the cards as their own language, ultimately finding their own oracular voice. I will provide further reading in each of these subjects.

We will begin with a re-statement of the basics of Tarot from a *Tarosophical* perspective, in the form of questions and answers.

## 1. What is Tarot?

The Tarot is a realized dream of reality – like all experience – in a recognized pattern of seventy-eight entities. The template of this pattern is twenty-two Major Arcana, sixteen Court cards and forty Minor cards in four Suits, usually termed Pentacles, Swords, Cups and Wands.

This pattern is usually (but not always) demonstrated in the form of art upon cardboard, a deck of tarot cards. This pattern has correspondence – *resonance* – with many other models of the universe.

## 2. How Does Tarot Work?

The Tarot works by arising in the same interface (between our sense of Identity and our sense of Universe) as all our experience of reality.

It exists as a stabilized and tested representation through iteration and evolutionary processes. As a reasonably congruent, consistent, and comprehensive map of experience, it functions to partially reflect our engagement with the Universe. As such, it also provides a blank bible for personal philosophy.[4]

In the shuffling of a deck of tarot cards, we recognize the interplay of the Universe and the resulting chosen cards – images – can be *interpreted* as modelling that relationship, in an unbound manner. This unbound manner is partially a-temporal, non-spatial, and non-linear, whilst being represented in a unique moment of space-time.

As a result, the images can provide illustration of events, advice, probabilities, possibilities, and states of mind - whether past, present, future, historical or imagined, present or distant - that are uniquely accessible through this process, which we call *divination*.

---

[3] I use the term "we" to refer to myself as author and yourself as reader, exploring the contents of this book together in a spirit of mutual enquiry.
[4] The powerful notion of tarot as a personal and "blank bible" comes from my co-author of other works, Tali Goodwin.

### 3. What is Tarosophy?

Tarosophy is *the living wisdom of the tarot*; in the main formulation that we use *tarot to engage life, not escape it*. It arises from an attitude of curiosity that generates techniques for every oracular moment. We hold two further important determinators; that *there is no such thing as an accidental oracle* and *the oracular moment is sacrosanct*.

Tarosophy has a character that can be recognized by experimental, enthusiastic, and open play with the limitless opportunities of tarot – or any other form of cartomancy, divination, or magical practice. It recognizes a *full deck of possibilities* and celebrates the diversity of divination.

### 4. What are the three key tenets of Tarosophy?

The World is Bound by Invisible Knots - You either Speak with Honey on your Lips from the Book of Clouds, Echoing the Voice of Living Fire in the Trembling Darkness, or you Do Not. There are no half-way Oracles.

### 5. What is the Aim of Tarosophy?

The aim of Tarosophy is to make accessible the language of tarot prior to delivering the journey into the place in which that language is spoken. To teach tarot as a symbolic system in preparation for initiatory, mystical, and magical experience in the Western Esoteric Initiatory System.[5]

### 6. What is the heart of Tarosophy?

The heart of Tarosophy is the embodiment in the practitioner of the living wisdom of tarot – an applied philosophy mediated by the structure and images of the deck.

The heart of Tarosophy was developed from long-term systematic observation and encounter with hundreds of tarot readers over three decades and comprehensive review of published and unpublished material over the last three centuries.

Tarosophy uniquely bridges academic appreciation of tarot and allied subjects with long-term experience to deliver a powerful revisioning of tarot.

It focuses on teaching *correspondence, incorporation,* and *utilization* to move the practitioner into the oracular moment – to go from nothing to here, to go from knowledge and experience to intuition and inspiration.

---

[5] See Marcus Katz, *The Magicians Kabbalah* (Keswick: Forge Press, 2015).

In summary:

- Tarosophy teaches *correspondence* to empower elegant readings and prepare the practitioner for work in the Western Esoteric Initiatory System if they pursue that path.

- Tarosophy teaches *incorporation* to ensure that readings work with the client's issues and language, not the readers – whilst leaving space for the original interpretation and oracular nature of the reader.

- Tarosophy teaches *utilization* to emphasize the readers own skills and allow them to develop their diverse methods in an accelerated and flexible manner.

## 7. What is the Ambition of Tarosophy?

The ambition of Tarosophy is to remove the barriers to entry for all who seek to learn tarot – whether it be for self-development, divinatory and oracular purposes, or fortune-telling. We recognize that there are many gates and many paths, all of which lead to one destination.

## 8. How Does Tarosophy Teaching Differ from other Deliveries of Tarot?

Tarosophy teaching separates "skills" and "methods" to provide accessible and accelerated training. It teaches from the destination backwards; understanding how readers read after thirty or forty years and reverse engineering those skills to be taught to beginners.

It has also asked systematic questions of contemporary readers (taking advantage of social media) and derived answers that are unique to Tarosophy and have led to the development of hundreds – if not thousands – of new methods.

## 9. What are the Unique Foundation Methods of Tarosophy?

There are hundreds of unique methods in Tarosophy; the most prominent are teaching tarot in three minutes and teaching tarot in ten minutes; *split-deck methods*; standing methods (such as "Finding Hope"); pinpointing and bridging; chunking to apply any card to any question; the *keyword kaleidoscope* to generate personal keywords; real-time construction of spreads based on a client's metaphor; tarot *gated spreads* (such as *Tarot Life*) and countless other innovative methods.

The three-minute method uses the three interpretative lenses of resource, challenge, and lesson, for each card, providing three core components of narrative structure. The ten-minute method uses the structure of Kabbalah to formulate a simple mapping of any easily described creative act in the life of the student to the structure of the tarot. These two methods have been refined over many hundreds of hours teaching to provide the fastest and easiest way to learn tarot from its own foundation.

In this sense, our teaching methods refer to the principles of learning a game like Chess, where the rules can take less than an hour to learn, the common patterns may take years to learn and practice, and mastery is the work of a lifetime.

## 10. How do I engage with Tarosophy?

The primary book for Tarosophy is the book of that title, *Tarosophy*, (2011). There are seventy-eight new methods of Tarosophy in *Tarot Twist* and the absolute beginner's booklet, *Tarot Flip*.

To understand some of the oracular nature of Tarosophy, refer to *Tarot Inspire*. The Gated Spread experiences are to be found in *Tarot Life* (in twelve booklets), and others such as *The Gates of Valentine*, *The Garden of Creation*, *The Ghost Train* and *The Resurrection Engine*, etc.

The Western Esoteric Initiatory System is explored in the *Magister*.

The reader will note, as with much of the work of Tarosophy, that the ten statements above are mapped to the *Sephiroth* of the Tree of Life from *Kether* to *Malkuth*. The first Tarosophy book introduces the importance of the Tree of Life as a lens through which tarot is seen as the language of initiation and the structure of its mysticism. In all that follows, assume that any material given in sets of twenty-two, twelve, ten, four, etc., has correspondence to the Major Arcana, the Zodiac, the *Sephiroth*, the elements, etc. These correspondences should be studied until they become a natural expression of the practitioner.

We will now look to responding to many of the first questions that arise from work with divination, both from readers themselves as they dive deeper into their practice, and by others who may be critical of the practice of divination.

## Why Read Tarot?

I read Tarot because ...

In frivolity there is freedom,
To say what must be said,
To know what can be known,
To grow what can be grown,
To own what must be owned,
To teach what can be taught,
To love what cannot be fought,
To go where we can go,
To fight what can be fought,
To atone when we are alone,
To sail the seas of destiny,
To right the injustice we see,
To turn things on their head,
To leave things rarely unsaid,
To speak with angels pure,
To keep the devil at the door,
To know more than we can say,
To seek an everlasting day,
To face fear as a way to pray,
To meet the light upon our way,
To resurrect ourselves anew,
To do all that we can do.[6]

## Why So Many Decks?

As we saw in *Tarosophy*, the average reader at that time who was invested in tarot sufficient to be a regular at the Tarot Association TarotCon conventions, or on the social media platforms, would have - on average - around **forty** different decks. At the time we did not expand on this observation, other than to say that more than forty made you officially a collector.

The usual external observation on this phenomenon, i.e., that a tarot reader will have many decks, is that there appears to be no requirement for a

---

[6] As with most prose and poetry in this book, the words, lines, or verses will follow a tarot sequence such as the Major Arcana, or the structure of the Tree of Life. In this poem, for example, we have produced a keyword for each of the Major Arcana and presented it as a teaching aid in two forms, such as "teach" and "taught" for the Hierophant.

reader to purchase more than one deck, as they can read with one. However, whilst the decks may be tools of utility, they are also tools for accessing wholly different states and each deck is tuned to different purposes.[7]

Similarly, given the complex nature of the universe, which may indeed be a 'simple rule repeated an almost infinite number of times', the cards themselves are merely components of a vast algorithm.[8] Another component of that algorithm is the reader, and another is time – a particular deck may suit a particular reader at a particular time. Also, a deck is time-bound (culturally-bound) to its own time, whether it is 'mainstream' or 'rebellious' to the cultural norms in which it arises. A gardener is now more likely to use a lawnmower than a scythe; although the latter may still be useful sometimes.

We can also answer this question with the response; "why are there so many books, they're all just based on just the same 26 letters?" (at least as far as all books written in English).

The answer is also that different decks are based on different principles, themes, and utilisation. As 'mere' artwork, they are also all different expressions.

The more we study and use tarot, the more these differences are useful; and the more we study and use tarot, the most wonderful and powerful is the diversity. At the end of the day, as readers, we love to experience the worlds of more than one book or one deck.

And we should never find ourselves in the same position as someone who is listening to their favourite tracks of music, and suddenly hears the devil whisper in their ear, "You know, all it does is go up and down".

## Elevator Pitches for Tarot Decks

A useful exercise for the Tarosophist is to develop and maintain "elevator pitches" for various aspects of cartomancy, i.e., stock answers that can be recalled and delivered as succinctly as possible, conveying the most important material in the least amount of time. In the following examples, we have our preferred elevator pitches for four of the main lineages of tarot decks.

---

[7] We looked at this same thing from the perspective of the question asked by a client, in *Tarosophy*, under the section on "tuned and attuned decks".

[8] Beyond the scope of this present work is the comparison of divination and cartomancy with the Stephen Wolfram physics project. In that project, an attempt is being made to represent the simplest laws of relationship in the universe capable of generating a model that resembles – not most unlike to – our present universe. In the comparison, cards can be seen as elementary particles, presented as localised persistent states (in a reading, bound with time and space) from which emerges a spatial hypergraph of meaning through interpretation.

## The Tarot de Marseille (c. 15th C.)

The Tarot de Marseille was designed as a living allegory of the triumph of virtues and a reliquary of Christian and mystical teaching.

## The Tarot of the Golden Dawn (c. 1888 onwards).

The Tarot designed by the Golden Dawn was never produced as a deck but copied by hand in notebook diagrams between members of the order to convey illustrations of the initiation system and the Tree of Life teachings taken from Kabbalah.

## The Thoth Tarot (1938 - 1943)

The Thoth Tarot was designed to function as an atlas of the universe through hieroglyphs depicting the doctrine of scientific illuminism. It also serves as a pantacle of thelema built from the bricks of the Aeons.

## The Waite-Smith Tarot (1909-1910)

The Waite-Smith Tarot was designed as a rectification of the power of symbolism to provide universal access to a hidden sanctuary of mystical experience, created by a Bohemian Catholic artist and a Catholic mystic, presented through the Theatrical tradition.

The reader will discover, throughout the original *Tarosophy* and this present book, sections which can provide or provoke elevator pitches for other common questions such as "how does tarot work?", "do you believe in tarot?" and similar enquiries of our art and science.

**The Tarot Expects a Reader to Know…**

In Tarosophy we look at the tarot deck as a living language which has emerged and stabilised in manifestation as a means of communication between aspects of presented reality. As it arises in the same manner as all things, it is ultimately a-temporal and non-spatial, and as a result can connect with aspects of manifestation that are apparently (in the true sense of the word) distanced from the present moment in time, both "past" and "future". It also allows us to divine – see beyond the normative world – events apparently disconnected and distant in space.

When we look at the tarot deck like this, we can also utilise it in a meta-manner, beyond itself, and the usual practices that have so far been accorded to it. One common method in Tarosophy is to use the Major Arcana as a set structure (as corresponding to the Tree of Life in Kabbalah) for formulating any pattern of existence – and thus providing an instruction manual, question set, or expectation set for any situation or artefact of existence, including itself. As Eliphas Levi (1810 - 1875) remarked:

> A prisoner devoid of books, had he only a Tarot of which he knew how to make use, could in a few years acquire a universal science, and converse with an unequalled doctrine and inexhaustible eloquence. The oracles of the Tarot give answers as exact as mathematics and measured as the harmonies of nature. By the aid of these signs and their infinite combinations, it is possible to arrive at the natural and mathematical revelation of all secrets of nature.[9]

If, for example, we wanted to know what we were expected to know so we can best utilise tarot, we can see that already presented to us in the Major Arcana. When we interpret the cards in this manner, we allow the tarot itself to tell us something about the tarot – or our best approach in using it. Here is what the tarot might expect a reader to know, then, in twenty-two responses following the numerical order of the Major Arcana:

1.  The Magician: How to divine and communicate clearly.

2.  The High Priestess: How to access your intuition.

3.  The Empress: How to acknowledge that nature and nurture have a role in the situation of the client.

---

[9] Éliphas Lévi, *Transcendental Magic: Its Doctrine and Ritual* (London: George Redway, 1896), p. 103.

4. The Emperor: How to empower the client, not yourself.

5. The Hierophant: The History of our sacred art and science.

6. The Lovers: Enough about relationships to answer 3 out of every 5 questions you will face which will always be on relationship.

7. The Chariot: When to use logic to go forwards and when not.

8. Strength: How to gain rapport with the client no matter their state towards you.

9. The Hermit: When to take time to yourself before you give it to others.

10. The Wheel of Fortune: The difference between fate and destiny, and the role of free-will.

11. Justice: How to measure up the cards with impartiality and recognise the presence of bias.

12. The Hanged Man: How to read reversals if they are one of the third of readers who read them.

13. Death: About death, dying and grief. Also, life.

14. Temperance: How to create a space for change not only during the reading but thereafter.

15. The Devil: How to recognise and work with the shadow, projection, and transference – and all the blocking mechanisms of depression, repression, etc. Also, how to know what you do not yet know.

16. The Blasted Tower: How to elegantly incorporate and utilise significant life events for positive outcome.

17. The Star: How to set realistic expectations and orient the client to the future.

18. The Moon: About walking into the dark places and speaking the symbols of dream.

19. The Sun: How to work with the inner child.

20.   The Last Judgement: How to use the cards for their own calling and to discover the true calling of the client.

21.   The World: To establish and maintain clear boundaries and a professional business, understanding finances, contracts, terms and conditions, personal ethics, and a code of good practice and conduct.

0.   The Fool: But most of all, the tarot expects a reader to be brave enough to walk in emptiness.

If the reader also places these responses on the Tree of Life according to any common pattern of correspondence, they will see the way these activities connect the *Sephiroth* of the Tree of Life. In doing so, we discern which aspects of the utterly unknowable universe we are experiencing and activating in each practice. If, for example, we are developing our work with the Inner Child, corresponding to the Sun, we are working on the path of *Resh*, between Hod and Yesod; the "splendour of the foundation". In doing so, we come to activate that 'splendour' – the patterns of our own childhood in conscious thought (Hod), re-connected to their earliest origin (Yesod). In this, we bring them into the front of our mind, or head, the literal meaning of the letter *Resh*. We also come to see how the universe is its own splendour of the foundation, in that the patterns of existence from its original point are still present in all manifestation, i.e., as light, symbolised by the Sun.[10]

---

[10] The word splendour (a translation of the Hebrew word, *Hod*) derives from the Latin, *splendere*, meaning 'to shine' which in turn may derive from the root *splnd, 'to be manifest'.

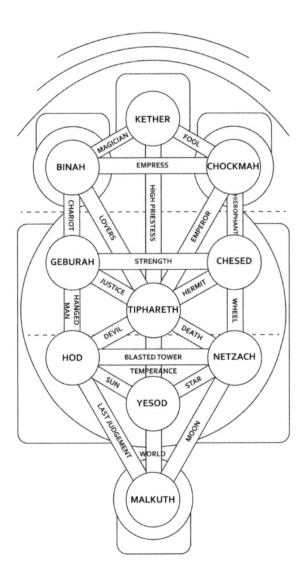

*Illus. The Tree of Life with Tarot Correspondences.*

## A Tarot Reader

In attempting to define what a tarot card reader is, or what they do, it is important to keep it simple. I always state that I am a "tarot card reader" so I "read the tarot cards". I am paid to read the cards. If I read the cards, that is what I am paid to do and the service I offer. My experience is in reading tarot cards, usually the deck or decks that I use to conduct the reading.

I may be a reader who is well-studied, highly intuitive, a good people-reader or a master of the secret Arch of Shamballah. I might be able to channel Zathras of the Fortieth Aethyr or my most illustrious Ancestors. I may be able to go into a trance and divine from Apollo himself, or use the deepest symbolism of alchemy to produce a stone of philosophy. These are all interesting, useful, or weird and curious, depending on our beliefs. However, if I am a tarot card reader then I will read tarot cards; everything else is something else.

I do also try and communicate what I have read to my client. This is far further towards personal experience and skill, natural or learnt – or both – than the actual interpretation of the cards, their "reading". The communication of the reading is a separate thing and thus one that can be separately developed.

However, as I could never guarantee such a complete mastery of communication and the client's ability to appreciate and integrate any particular message, I do not offer the communication of the reading as an entirely infallible part of my service. I guarantee that I will read the cards.

Usually, I read the cards and tell the client what I read, and it is useful to them. Often, it is a powerful and moving experience - or a hilarious one - that gives them information that might prompt change in their life. Sometimes, it does not appear to be, even though I have read the cards, as I always do when I am paid to read the tarot for someone:

What are your fees?" inquired Guyal cautiously. "I respond to three questions," stated the augur. "For twenty terces I phrase the answer in clear and actionable language; for ten I use the language of cant, which occasionally admits of ambiguity; for five, I speak a parable which you must interpret as you will; and for one terce, I babble in an unknown tongue.[11]

I am, after all, simply a tarot card reader. One who reads tarot cards.

---

[11] Jack Vance, *Tales of the Dying Earth* (London: Mayflower, 1972), p. 99.

## Aspirations

As we have seen, the approach of Tarosophy encourages readers to use their deck to answer or provide a framework for any situation. If we were to ask the deck what it inspired in people, either ourselves or our clients, we can discern the answers in the Major Arcana as we can to any other question. A Tarot Reader should aspire themselves and their clients to be:

> Free, Magical, Mysterious, Nurturing, Empowering, Wise, Loving, Active, Strong, Self-Aware, Connected, Fair, Radical, Transformative, Creative, Physical, Striking, Visionary, Reflective, Demonstrative, Decisive, and Present.

Just like the Major Arcana, from the Fool to the World.

When we have these answers, we can pull a Major Card for ourselves and the card will suggest to us which aspiration we can work towards that day.

## Do Not Pay Me

There are some readers – and many clients – who have a somewhat strange (and deliberately so, in the case of prospective clients) view of tarot and payment. Some readers, increasingly few in proportion during the present expansion of interest, claim that you can only give readings for "free" as it is a "spiritual" practice. Whilst I would accept that divination is a spiritual practice, I personally do not accept that time and attention in the linear realm should not be fairly compensated. Similarly, I believe that a client should be aware of exactly what they are being asked to purchase, which is far more beyond the hour and the cards that a reading might appear.

In response to this matter often being raised on our social media platforms, I wrote the following personal pitch for myself, and would encourage every reader to fully evaluate their own unseen capital.

Do not pay me for this hour of tarot reading.

*Instead, pay my dad for allowing access to an early photocopier in his company, so I could photocopy a set of 22 cards from a book that I had loaned from the grown-up section of the library - and the librarian for letting a 13-year old borrow the book.*

Do not pay me for what I will tell you about your situation based on these cards.

*Instead, pay me for a thousand or more hours that first year being obsessed with the cards, reading them for schoolfriends, visualising them every night, stepping into them in dream so that I could meet them as living things in my own life every hour of every day.*

Do not pay me for any new insight I might offer from this reading.

*Instead, pay me for all the thousands of books I purchased and hundreds of courses I took over thirty years so I could prepare for this moment with you.*
*All the books on therapy, communications, business practice, astrology, tarot, psychology, history; all the courses on business, marketing, customer service, finance, alchemy, and kabbalah.*

Do not pay me for opening solutions from the deck that you could not get anywhere else, despite how much you paid them.

*Instead, pay me for six years of my life costing tens of thousands of pounds, studying western esotericism at a university 346 miles away, and flights to conferences in Europe and America, taken to Masters and PhD levels to ensure a comprehensive understanding of the context of these cards.*

Do not pay me for interpreting any of several quintillion possible combinations of cards that you will see on the table in a moment.

*Instead, pay me for purchasing hundreds of decks, reading with them for thousands of people, in public and in private, for all the multitude of questions that have been brought to oracles since the beginning of time.*

Do not even pay me for the cost of this deck, this room, this light, this time.

*Instead, pay me for every second I risked my livelihood to devote myself to a passion, to write books with little return, to organise events just because it was important, to spend time learning, teaching, and sharing every moment I could, when I could have been doing something else.*
*Pay me for the online negativity I had to learn to ignore - particularly from others 'in tarot' for the first five years before they realised I wasn't going to go away, and the death threat (from another 'tarot person') I had to report to the police.*

And certainly, do not pay me for laughter, tears, sudden revelations, or a slowly dawning appreciation of what you can do next to resolve your situation.

*Instead, pay me for choosing to devote myself to something ridiculed by most, seen as an idle curiosity by others, a futile occupation by even those who were once friends, and yet here we are.*
*You and me.*

*And these cards.*
*So, do not pay me for this hour of tarot reading.*

Pay me for everything I have done to this moment so we can get on with something that might just be useful to you.

In summary, I believe someone is paying me for thirty years' experience and practice, and the risk I take in offering them insight from the entire universe, transcending all known notions of time and space, by uttering inspired and oracular words - in a manner that could potentially change their entire life - based on a single layout of one of 1.4 quintillion combinations of seventy-eight historical and arcane images that correspond to every psychological, practical, emotional, intelligible, situation that any human being has ever experienced, is experiencing or ever will likely experience.

And my fee for doing such a thing is stated on my website.

## Facts and Fallacies

In *Tarosophy*, we dealt with several facts and fallacies about tarot, and the history of the deck as far as it is currently known. We will now delve deeper — perhaps, pedantically - into several narrow fallacies. It is unfortunately necessary as there are so many online sources still alleging that the tarot was invented by the ancient Egyptians, or that you should only be gifted your first deck, and worse fallacies.

## The First Illustrated Pips

There is a fallacy that the Waite-Smith Tarot (1909) was the first deck to use "illustrated pip cards". It is often conflated with another fallacy that this accounted for its success and enduring popularity. Unfortunately, neither of statements are entirely true. There were many other card decks which used illustrated scenes on the pip cards, the most notable cartomantic example being the *Sola Busca* deck. It was this deck which Waite and Colman Smith viewed in the British Museum, when images from it were loaned from the Italian family which owned the deck at that time. We can see the equivalent images in several of the Waite-Smith cards, such as the Three of Swords.

In a sense, every card deck has "illustrated" pips, even if they are merely seven cups to show that card as the Seven of Cups. The phrase might be better as "scenically or character-based interpretations" for the pip cards, such as a group of people using the five wands on the Five of Wands to fight each other playfully rather than them being illustrated as a broken tower of sticks.

Many antique playing card decks prior to tarot had "scenically or character-based interpretations" for the pip cards, often presented as 'morality' or 'teaching' decks to avoid tax or religious censure. Some also had key-phrases, short poems or couplets, biblical phrases, and even speech bubbles to denote the message of the card.

## Your First Tarot Deck

There is a sometimes-repeated fallacy that a reader must be "gifted" their first tarot deck. Despite research, the first publication of this idea has yet to be discovered. It is also an extra layer of problematic answer to say that this was introduced to stop non-readers buying their own deck and putting fortune-tellers out of business. It is certainly nice to be gifted your first deck, as it will be a source of nostalgia in future, particularly if it is a unique situation or someone special to you who presents the gift. It is nice to make your own first deck. I did, and several other readers I know did likewise. It is also nice to purchase your first deck in the most ordinary of situations and then discover how extraordinary your experiences become with it.

## Bonding with Your Deck

Another fallacy and a question asked most on social media and according to our Tarot Association website hits is that a reader must place their deck under a pillow and sleep on it to bond with the deck - or perform some other act of bonding. In ritual terms, this would be considered a "consecration", a dedication of an object to a specific purpose.

I would counter-propose that a tarot deck is consecrated to its purpose of divination by its use - the performance of shuffling, sorting, and selection into a spread is a ritual of itself. Further, we could suggest that each deck and reader would be better served by what we call an *attuned* consecration. This means that we would consecrate a *Tarot of the Moon* deck on a full moon night, with white wine and silver candles being part of the dedication. The Thoth Tarot we would consecrate by the recitation of an Ancient Egyptian verse or Thelemic ritual. The Druidcraft Deck we would take to a stone circle, or grove, etc.

Whilst sleeping with a Tarot Deck under our head may consecrate it to speak to you unconsciously or through dream, this might not specifically serve you in a wide-awake reading with a real person.

## Storing Your Deck

Whilst it may be good to store your deck in silk, each reader should find personal and effective ways to store their decks. My two most personal and favorite containers for tarot are a hand-made cork box cut perfectly to size for my old Waite-Smith deck and hand-painted with the Golden Dawn symbol, and an old sackcloth coffee-grind bag in which I carried my hand-made tarot cards when I was young.

**Natural Gift or Learnt Skill?**

It is sometimes implied that one must have a "natural gift" to read Tarot, or that you cannot be "taught" to read Tarot, or "learning from books" is not a way to learn tarot. There is no one way of learning tarot being "better" than another, or the only way of learning. However, it can certainly be taught, be improved, and some people also have a natural gift to particular ways of reading. And that is all for the good.

**Reading for Yourself**

Some find it difficult to read for themselves, and others say it is impossible. Some people only ever read for themselves. Again, it is all good. Whilst it may be challenging and require more objectivity there are no more problems in reading for oneself than reading for someone else. When we read for others, we still project, have potential bias, and there can be transfer and counter-transfer. Our own state of mind also influences a reading whether for ourselves or others. There are many methods we can use to read for ourselves that make it easier.

**Tarot in Antiquity**

As mentioned at the start of this section, fallacies continue regarding the history of tarot as being mysterious or unknown, when it is neither. Tarot appeared first in 15th Century Italy. The origin of the word "Tarot" is, however, unknown, appearing only almost a century after the first decks to describe the game, and in Italian, as "Tarocchi". They were earlier referred to as a "Game of Triumphs", or "carte da trionfi".

There are many ideas that the Tarot embodies hidden, even ancient wisdom, deliberately or through universal patterns, etc. There are ideas that the Tarot was 'carried' by 'gypsies' and originated in 'ancient Egypt'. None of those ideas has any solid proof, in an academic or historical sense, i.e., primary, or even secondary source material, such as a set of twenty-two images carved in a pyramid that exactly relates to the modern tarot, in the same way that the "Game of Hope" cards match the "Lenormand" cards, separated by only 50 years.

The first evidence we have of these more 'esoteric' ideas appears in Court de Gebelin's *Le Monde primitif*, volume 8, in 1781. There is no written or recorded evidence prior to that date of any connection of Tarot to ancient Egypt, Kabbalah, secret teachings, Freemasonry, or any other system.

## Tarot is Evil

It may be superstitious, but some believe that the tarot "is evil" or that "it opens you up to evil spirits". In my personal experience, I have had no evidence of this. The only evil I consider that tarot can promote is a dependence or avoidance of responsibility when consulting the cards. That is why we say, "tarot to engage life, not escape it".

## Tarot is just Cold Reading

Critics argue sometimes that reader do not read anything at all from the cards, we simply 'read' clues from the body-language, dress, or behavior of the client, and from what they say to us. This of course does not explain how many readers offer email readings - but that we will cover again with the next fallacy which is "you have to make a physical connection with the client".

I personally would never deny that when in-person or by telephone, Skype, etc. I do not pick up anything from the client in terms of their tonality, metaphors, and non-verbal language, but this simply adds to the reading and I neither deny it nor do I rely on it. Sometimes the cards tell a completely different story to the one as presented by the person in front of me.

At the end of the day, we read the cards.

## Connection to Clients

Although it is less common these days since the internet, some believe that you must physically connect with your client, or the cards must be held (or never held) by the client.

My only rule on this is that there are some decks I would not have my clients shuffle because I use them purely for my own magical workings, dream work or personal readings, and some decks that I have as "collectors' items" and never - or rarely - work with.

I also offer online readings, email, and telephone readings, Skype, etc., so I believe from experience there is always a connection in the moment of reading, which transcends a physical necessity.

## Tarot and Fortune Telling

Even in divination circles, there is an argument that you *cannot* use tarot for fortune-telling, or you can *only* use tarot for fortune-telling. This is a strange yet profound subject, because it rests on our experience of time and free-will

– of our own understanding and beliefs of our everyday state of existence as a "being in time and space":

- Do we believe the future is singular and has already been set in motion, like it is "determined"? If so, how does that give context to our readings?

- Do we believe that time is unwritten "in the future", so can be "changed" by a reading or any other action? How does that speak in our readings?

- Do we believe that fortune-telling is more like a "forecast" than a "prediction"?

Have you ever "told a fortune" so clearly that it surprised even yourself – and then it turned out to happen – or not happen – and why do you think so, in either case? Basically, this simple question or fallacy about tarot being one thing or another, or a tool only capable of one thing or another, or whatever, is a question about how reality works for us.

The reader is encouraged to answer all these fallacies with their own experience and have an answer to each, as they are common. What do you think? How does time work? Do we have free will? If so, what is it and what does it mean for "fortune-telling"?

## Tarot on the Edge or Mainstream

As we will see in the conclusion of this present book, there is a fallacy - or argument perhaps - that tarot should be on the edge of society, and those who read it are "weird", or, alternatively, that tarot should be mainstream – or would be ruined by being "mainstream".

Firstly, we should question what does "mainstream" mean, or, for that matter, "weird". Consider the rise of "geek" or "nerd" culture, with shows like the *Big Bang Theory*. The game of *Dungeons and Dragons* was considered virtually "demonic" at one point, and now some old-time gamers complain about the way it has become 'watered-down' by being popularised.

Tarot has been promoted and sold in vast quantities to buyers at *Urban Outfitters*, although one wonders how many buyers just have it on a shelf as an esoteric ornament. Does a Gummy Bear tarot deck devalue the art, or elevate it? Or make no difference at all?

Perhaps it is at least better than Tarot always being evil and surrounded by superstition, when we see it on prints and designs on fashion runways in Paris and Milan. Or do we want to keep it mysterious? Powerful and Profound?

Away from the masses? Is there a middle-ground? Will it indeed, always protect itself from being "ruined" in any way? This argument is an old one and a continuing one - and is likely to prove even more challenging in the future, to which we will return at the conclusion of this book.

## Tarot & Superpowers

We might see the prevalence of superhero movies and extended story arcs in streaming services as the latest emergence of ancient mythic and epic story telling. In the same manner that the phases of "wild west" and "cop" narratives answered an ineluctable social and psychological privation, superhero stories provide a child-like escapism and a form of modern theology. The identity-process of the ego is assuaged by momentary and transitory identification with the protagonist of genre movies. The fragmented and flawed parts of the psyche are to be found to be ultimately healed in the third act of "buddy-cop" movies or the "team event" of superhero narratives. Our superego wishes to be nothing more than more than nothing – and in so, we all carry a secret identity, even a secret flaw and villainous side that must eventually be exposed to complete our journey to true heroism – and our necessary sacrifice.

Yet we do not need to go epic to realise our own heroic journey. Our life is already such a journey, for it is to what we identify writ large-scale in any fictional narrative. As such, we can reflect on our own personal journey through the multi-dimensional liminality of the tarot.

Consider something you do very well, or other people tell you that you do.

It can be anything from knitting to looking after people, from party-planning to keeping things tidy. Anything, no matter how big or small, that you do well enough that it is common knowledge to others.

Consider that, and ask the cards, "what is the essential secret to my skill?"

Take a deck, shuffle, and pull a card.

What does this tell you about one of your own super-power? It might be an expression of a specific aspect of yourself (a Court card) or be part of a bigger pattern in your life (Major Arcana) or be a skill that has different manifestations in your life (Minor Arcana).

Repeat this question for several times, each with a different skill that you exhibit, until you have drawn several cards, denoting the secrets of your powers. Arrange these cards into a narrative as follows:

- Court cards: Superheroes in the story.
- Major cards: Villains and challenges in the story – also their ultimate lesson to the hero(es).
- Minor cards: Events that reveal the characters of the hero(oes).

Identify these cards with existing fictional heroes, or even better, make them up for yourself.

## Who Not To Read

There are lists of contra-indicated clients for certain therapies, even if they are not always agreed upon by the profession. Hypnosis is contra-indicated for schizophrenia, for example, and not recommended as effective for those with a short attention span or disorder in which this arises. However, there are sometimes variations of an approach that can work with such indicators, i.e., *Vogt's Fractionation* method of inducing a trance-state in ever-increasing chunks, which works effectively with those who are experiencing a noticeably short attention span.

In Tarosophy, there is almost no-one for whom we would not read, even the "cynics" or "glare and stare" types of personality. We would rarely read for those who appear to be intoxicated or obviously on drugs, for their altered state is not one easily tracked, and to which can be reliably communicated without skill or experience.

We would certainly not read for those who have not requested it unless they were part of a situation in which we were reading for our own context. If a King of Swords turned up as an immediately identifiable person in a reading for oneself, and we drew a clarifier card or two which investigated their motives or actions, it would still be within the context of a reading for oneself.

We read for the person *inside* the presented person, the person who has brought the outer person to our table. We read for the person in the future; the person this person can be, once they recognise from the reading that their story is connected to everything and everyone, even their future self.

We can read for the bully with compassion, for the cynic with open-mindedness and for the scientific, with curiosity. We can read for the lost with a sense of freedom and for the constrained with a sense that with each card, a brick is being removed. We can read for the guilty with innocence and for the shamed without judgement. We can read for the powerless with respect and the powerful with honesty. We can read for the exhausted with compassion and for the terrified with courage.

The cards will not only tell us what to read but – if we look another layer in – how to read it.

A spread with many Swords tells us to cut to the chase, be precise, break our reading into smaller points. A reading with many Pentacles might indicate to provide concrete examples and actions. A prevalence of Cups may suggest a poetic delivery and a stack of Wands a reading delivered as a motivational speech.

When we read the cards, we are giving them voice – let them tell you how to read for the real person in front of you, not the one they have presented to your table.

## Three Questions You May Not Ask

In this section, I would like to share three questions that you may not think to ask your cards, particularly when reading for yourself. A tarot deck can provide us provocative answers and help us think outside our own usual patterns, particularly if we ask it provocative questions.

Here are three questions you may not think to ask your cards. Perhaps one, two or all three of them may prove relevant or useful to a situation you might put to your deck.

## 1. What Question Have I Not Asked?

The first question you may not always think to ask your deck is to help you with the question itself. We are often drawn to ask a question which seems most reasonable, and this may not always be the question that provides the most useful or easily enacted response.

Ask your deck "What question have I not asked?" and draw two cards. If one or either are a Court Card, this indicates aspects of yourself (or if immediately obvious, another person) which should be questioned. If one card was the Queen/King of Swords, for example, the new question should involve asking about "where can I be ruthless?" or however you read that card.

If a card or both are Majors, these can be considered to indicate big patterns that need to be in the question. If you had the Wheel of Fortune card as one of the two cards, it would suggest asking "What is going around again in this situation – how can I get off?"

Of course, you may read the card differently when reading it with the other card to make a question.

If a Minor card, or both are Minors, these can be seen to provide a fairly direct question about what angle of activity or response should be questioned. The 8 of Wands suggests asking more about "What can be rapidly moved on?" whereas the 10 of Pentacles says to ask more about "What can be settled?"

Using this approach, we might have a situation where we were going to ask, "How can I get the most out of the forthcoming trip?" and instead, first, draw two cards for the unasked question.

These two cards might be Temperance and the 10 of Wands. This would suggest we ask instead, "In the forthcoming trip, what might I hold back which will actually lead to a personal struggle?"

*Illus. Temperance and the Ten of Wands indicating an Unasked Question.*

This might prove a far more interesting question to ask the deck.

## 2. How Will I Describe This in the Future?

Instead of asking the deck – which we already accept can transcend time in some way – about the present or future, why not ask it to consider the future from a further future, as the past?

That is to say, why not ask your spread to describe not the future but how it will be seen from an even further future?

In framing the question this way, we can perhaps tap into a far more intriguing way of reading tarot as if we are looking constantly at our own present from the future.

You can perform any spread with your situation framed this way, although a three-card reading will be sufficient to provoke insight.

Some spreads might need tweaking if they have fixed positional meanings such as "past" and "future". In this case, simply see the "past" card as referring still to the future of the present, and the future card referring to an even further future, from the future position.

Again, a three-card spread might be better for the first time you use this approach. If I asked this question of a situation and drew Judgement, the Page of Cups and the Six of Pentacles I might say:

*In the future, I will look back at this situation and know that it was part of a greater calling, surprising me in how creative I became and eventually it did lead to a better way of me seeing my finances.*

## 3. What is the Smallest Thing About This?

We always ask the big questions, so why not ask the small ones? We sometimes do not think to ask a little question, something trivial, that might be something we can do.

Ask the deck "What is the smallest thing about this situation?" with a mind to receiving a simple answer that tells you something small which is manageable, maybe obvious, or something you can easily change by action, decision or looking at things differently.

I might ask the deck, "What is the smallest thing about this [hugely important] situation?" and receive the 2 of Swords. I see this as 'conformity' regarding my question, and it shows that the smallest thing is about conforming to something – and this is something I can see as being not so important.

There are probably a lot of questions you may not ask the tarot and I trust in this section we have opened a few new avenues of questioning to which your deck may be very enthusiastic in response.

## The Tarot is Dangerous

The Tarot is dangerous and like any tool must be used correctly to avoid harm.

The danger of tarot is **not** that it contacts evil spirits, **not** that it shows your imminent doom in the Death card, and **not** that it attracts the curses of the dead upon you, but something far more common and even worse than any curse – the danger of *laziness*.

We know that generally, half of people think that tarot is negative in some way. However, the reason they give is not because of the aforementioned idiocies but actually for a very good reason. They know, as some tarot enthusiasts online may seem to be forgetting, exactly why the tarot is dangerous.

In 2001, a public survey was conducted in the UK on behalf of the Independent Television Commission (ITC) and the Broadcasting Standards Commission (BSC). It aimed to survey public attitudes to subjects such as astrology, tarot, and psychic phenomena and its results were used to establish all regulation on the broadcasting of such subjects in the UK. Whilst I looked at this survey in detail in *Tarot in Culture Vol. I,* I would like to return to it briefly, in that it showed one thing; tarot was seen by the audience as **positive** when it offered "positive, comforting information and generic advice," but **negative** when it produced personal information that "delved into a person's consciousness".[12]

Whilst experienced readers saw the immediate misunderstanding of Tarot here, I would argue that many actual tarot readers are falling under this same spell.

There is a growing trend amongst tarot enthusiasts to simply put across their own thoughts using a tarot card or spread as illustration of the message they wish to convey.

I would argue they do this to give implied authority to their words, which otherwise would be more simply, "their opinion" or "their belief". The danger is that they may even believe that this is the case, that the tarot is supporting their belief, their opinion.

This is self-hypnosis of the worst possible kind, in that appears benign and supportive. Whilst at times we may all do so, whilst at times it may be difficult to be courageously responsive to our cards, we should at the very least not fall into the laziness of turning our tarot into a deck of confirmation.

When people create a meme, an inspirational message with a tarot theme, or add text to a set of tarot cards, they are often using the tool of tarot to convey their own message – a message that is independent of the cards and to which the cards are forced into servicing.

This arises in two ways, and both are dangerous.

The first is that the archetypes behind the tarot images have simply swallowed the conscious considerations of the user. They have allowed themselves to become overwhelmed by their unconscious (and often shadow) content, by opening to that content through the cards. Their conscious and reasonable mind – common-sense – has surrendered to the uncommon power and energy of the unconscious, which is comparatively all-powerful in this context.

The second way is that the person has shut down any communication from the tarot to themselves, denies it and projects it outwards. This causes mental instability (or arises from it, as the person seeks to protect themselves) and results in the cards being used in increasingly strident ways to the point of obsession.

Whilst this may manifest in seemingly gentle, apparently positive, and generally harmless ways; everyone sharing the meme, everyone "liking" the post, or most just scrolling by it, there is a growing danger that the tarot is being diluted, even entirely uprooted from its own source of power.

---

[12] Marcus Katz, 'Tarot on the Threshold: Liminality and Illegitimate Knowledge' in Emily E. Auger (ed.), *Tarot in Culture Vol. I* (n.p.: Valleyhome Books, 2014), pp. 272-3.

At least this will protect it, if not the users. It is like unplugging a toaster – no-one will be able to electrocute themselves with it, or set fire to anything, but they may smash their toes by trying to use it as a hammer. The toaster may still survive until it gets back into the hands of someone who knows it needs plugging in and wants to make toast for themselves – or their family and friends.

The Kabbalists understood this process, too, much earlier. They said of *gematria*, the numerology of Kabbalah, that one should never use *gematria* to prove something that one already knew.

As an example, I saw someone recently go through quite a significant downfall, which was made public by them - as the situation unfolded from their happy launch to their eventual loss. They were expecting the project to go very well, and it failed. They then "pulled" (I suspect 'chose') and posted online the "Wheel of Fortune" card for the event, to explain it away, with appropriately soft-focus image of the Wheel and a friendly font.

Most importantly, they wrote something that they could have more easily written **without** the card. They wrote what they wanted to write about having to now be patient, their time was not yet, one day they would succeed, karma, etc.

The card indeed provided them a lot of comforting advice. It was advice they wanted to hear. However, if you "plugged in" that card, it would be actually and truly dangerous – it might tell you, perhaps, that what was actually required of you was a **revolution**. A revolution of your thinking; what you thought was up should be down, and what you dropped down should now go up. The card might tell you to push harder, go round the wheel again, get off your bottom and head back to the top, to do the opposite of what you just done, swallow your pride, realise that we are all on a cycle, grab somebody else's hand to help lift you up, etc., etc.

It is a card of a major turning-point, the point of the Fool's journey where everything is seen in one whole - ahead of a final realisation at the World.

It is not a pretty picture to tell yourself what you want to tell yourself. It is a tarot card.

It is dangerous. It will delve into your consciousness and tell you to change it – and tell you how.

Tarot is dangerous – and you should let it be so, but not by telling yourself what you already know.

I admit there is a scale between "I am making this up without any reference to the cards in front of me" to "The cards told me to jump off a bridge, so I did" and the art I think is allowing the cards the most appropriate and effective impact on changing our perspective - and resultant action.

The tarot is a fable of the singular fallacy of your soul; that there is something between you and the world.

## Timing and Tarot

There are many proposed methods for "timing" in Tarot, such as the correspondences of the Court Cards to the seasons (four seasons, four suits, etc) or the obvious correspondences such as the Sun (one year), the Moon (one month), and the Blasted Tower (very soon) or the Wheel (forever).

I personally use the Minor Arcana for an indication of how far the situation is along the cycles of manifestation, and in which worlds. This always tells me the likely outcome in time.

If we have a reading with ten cards and there are a lot of "Sevens", "Eights" and "Nines" in it, all in Pentacles and Cups, then basically, it is quite far along already, but getting stuck in the mud (Earth and Water) so needs a big push to get it to the "Ten" stage of completion. I'd look to the cards in the reading that stuck out from this, such as maybe the Ace of Swords or The Blasted Tower and their positions would indicate from where that push, or shock would come.

If we had a lot of mixed cards all over the place; Sevens, Fours, a Three and a Ten, then I would look at the middle card in that pattern, such as the "Four" and see what that meant – and how that related to time; such as the Four of Pentacles might indicate that "until the savings run out" or "until the contract is released".

Often, I ask for the range of timing from the client, i.e., "any time between a month at shortest and a six-month period at most, certainly not a year", and then roughly apply the balance of Minor cards as a percentage of that time, so if I had all Tens, it would be at the far end of that range, and all Aces, Twos and Threes, at the earliest time likely in the client's estimation.

This is a bit of an art, comes with practice, and you must ask the client for their likely timings even if that is between "now and never". That is still a time period.

That method can be done purely mathematically if you want to try experimenting with precise timing.

## Teaching Tarot

The first thing to teach is that "we read the cards. We are tarot card readers. The clue is in the title". Whenever we get stuck, there is no stuck – we have pictures, we have cards, we have illustrations and symbols. First, teach people to say what they see – "a man", "a skeleton", "a tower". Never be afraid of saying what you see, that is always going to be true.

Then, never teach that tarot is difficult to learn. It is easy to learn. We teach it in three minutes – or ten for non-scenic decks – but, like chess, we then recommend a thirty-year period of practice and study to get better at it and deepen your experience of it, and life itself as a result.

They say that a skill takes 10,000 hours of practice to become a "master" at it.[13] That is 10,000 readings – so start practising right away. Be honest that you are just learning. Use a book. Use books. Use your head. Use your notes. Use everything.

Then, teach that tarot is deeper than even you know, so the student doesn't learn your boundaries, or theirs, or anyone else's.

Teach the scene in *Rambo III* (dir. Peter MacDonald, 1988), where the Colonel tells Rambo:

> Let me tell you a story, John. There was a sculptor. He found this stone, a special stone. He dragged it home and he worked on it for months until he finally finished it. When he was ready, he showed it to his friends. They said he had created a great masterpiece, but the sculptor said he hadn't created anything. The statue was always there, he just chipped away the rough edges.

Be delighted that your students have their own way, their own voice, and their own manner.

## Connecting Cards

As we have seen, most tarot card and many oracle cards are not *symbols* but *metaphors* – a complex of several symbols. They are also *multivalent*, in that they can have any number of meanings. A specific card is "closer" to a specific theme or range of meanings than another, for sure – but they can potentially mean anything, such as the Death card heralding "love" depending on the question, the context, the other cards and the particular moment and inspiration of the reading. The oracular moment is sacrosanct.

Connecting cards is done through the process of constructing a narrative, like a story. It is done by taking one card and its metaphor in the reflection and relationship of another card. One card – one theme – two cards, a mix of those themes.

If we had the Hermit and the Four of Pentacles, that would be a "loner" and "someone saving", so "a loner saving" which might mean "a man keeping himself to himself". It would not be a "good" story.

Then, we can connect cards by pinpointing a specific symbol and bridging it to another symbol in another card. We weave a web of meanings, like sentences, to construct the whole story. We might see the sea in the background of the Two of Swords and bridge it to the sea in the background of the Two of Pentacles and say, "when you hold making a decision, nothing

---

[13] See Malcolm Gladwell, *Outliers* (London: Penguin, 2008), the 10,000 hour rule being based on a study by K. Anders Ericsson (1947 - 2020).

happens, but when you start to juggle it for real, you'll make waves".

Do not be afraid of making a new metaphor from the cards, and then applying it to the question.

## Tarot and Shakespeare

There is no explicit reference to tarot cards in the plays of Shakespeare, although there are references to alchemy and the practice of witchcraft as it was seen at the time. There are further suggestions of a popular knowledge of freemasonry, in the description, for example, of honeybees with "the singing masons building roofs of gold".[14] However, we now know that his plays were the source of much of Pamela Colman Smith's designs for the Waite-Smith Tarot, particularly the Minor cards.[15]

Tarot (as cards or a playing card game) was not widely known in England at the time of Shakespeare (1564 - 1616) having only arisen in Italy during the mid-1400's. It was not associated with cartomancy until around the mid-1700's. When the Golden Dawn mentioned it in the late 1800's, they had to import or source decks from Europe, mainly France and Italy.

However, as the main design for tarot at present remains the Waite-Smith Tarot, it is useful for readers to have knowledge of the plays - and in particular - the characters of Shakespeare, to deepen their connection with the Waite-Smith designs, especially the Minor Arcana. In studying Shakespeare, alongside the Golden Dawn *Book T*, the reader will unlock most of the designs and intent of that foundational deck.

## Tarot and Connection

> Only connect! That was her whole sermon. Only connect the prose and the passion, and both will be exalted, and human love will be seen at its height. Live in fragments no longer. Only connect, and the beast and the monk, robbed of the isolation that is life to either, will die.

> - E. M. Forster, *Howards End* (1910).

In a sense, everything is in relationship and therefore connection. The universe arises from one thing that is really no thing, as it contains everything – even all time. Plato called time the "moving likeness of eternity" and it is within the eternal moment that we are all moving – including the tarot.

---

[14] Henry V, Act 1, Scene 2.
[15] See Tali Goodwin & Marcus Katz, *Secrets of the Waite-Smith Tarot* (Woodbury: Llewellyn Publications, 2015), p. 81.

When we divine with cards, they are as subject as we to the connection of every past event to every future event. Nothing is without cause, and everything trembles the world-wide web of creation. When we shuffle, and read our cards for ourselves or a client, we are not connecting, but re-cognising the existing connection. We are reminding ourselves of what is always already the case.

The Greeks called this *anamnesis*; the loss of forgetfulness of the soul. In performing a tarot reading we have an opportunity to remind ourselves and our client that they are part of the story, they are connected. The congruence of the reading to their life is demonstration of this connection.

Our job then is to open an inspired dialogue – with the client, ourselves, the divine connection, the relationship of symbol and reality; it is a multifaceted dialogue that in part is mysterious even unto ourselves, and it from this mystery that we best speak when we are fully oracular.

As the three tenets of Tarosophy has it, "The World is Bound by Invisible Knots – You either Speak with Honey on your Lips from the Book of Clouds, Echoing the Voice of Living Fire in the Trembling Darkness, or you Do Not. There is no such thing as a half-way Oracle".

## Tarot and Geography

I have always wondered about the Golden Dawn system of attributing the stellar constellations to world geography and hence nations - a process generally referred to as locational astrology or *astrogeography*. There is also a form of creating a world map with planetary lines, *astrocartography*, based on the birth time of an individual, showing where certain places might be located worldwide for the benefit or detriment of that person.

As a result of correspondence, and "as above, so below", that means that the zodiac corresponds to nations. Other astrologers have assigned such signs to the "birth" of nations, or to their general characteristics. Then, from there, we can then make the regular correspondences of astrology to the tarot cards, either the Decans (Minor Arcana) or the Majors. That might give us, for example, the Emperor (Aries) for Senegal or the Five of Cups (1st decan of Scorpio) for the Atlantic Ocean, depending on your chosen system to correspond astrology to geography. Similarly, the position of Court Cards in the map of the heavens (minus the Pages) would also indicate corresponding earthly locations.

As different systems of astrology hold different sets of correspondences, as ever, it is better to choose one and modify it over time than try and pick and mix from a variety of systems. The following list, with some outdated names and geographic descriptions, comes from William Lilly, *An Introduction to Astrology* (1852, first published in 1647 as *Christian Astrology*).[16] I have added the Tarot card correspondences to the twelve zodiacal Major Arcana:

### The Emperor (IV)/Aries

- Countries: England, Germany, Denmark, Lesser Poland, Palestine, Syria, Naples.

- Towns: Florence, Verona, Padua, Marseilles, Burgundy, Saragossa, Bergamo.

### The Hierophant (V)/Taurus

- Countries: Ireland, Persia, Great Poland, Asia Minor, the Archipelago, and the southern parts of Russia.

- Towns: Dublin, Mantua, Leipsic, Parma, Franconia, Lorraine: also, the islands of Cyprus and Samos, and the port and vicinity of Navarino.

### The Lovers (VI)/Gemini

- Countries: North America, Lower Egypt, Lombardy, Sardinia, Brabant, Belgium, West of England.

- Towns: London (especially), Versailles, Mentz, Bruges, Louvaine, Cordova, New York, and Nuremberg.

### The Chariot (VII)/Cancer

- Countries: Holland, Scotland, Zealand, Georgia, and all Africa.

- Towns: Constantinople, Tunis, Algiers, Amsterdam, Cadiz, Venice, Genoa, York, St. Andrews, Manchester, New York, Bern, Lubeck, Milan, and Vicentia.

---

[16] CHAPTER XV. THE NATURE, PLACE, COUNTRIES, GENERAL DESCRIPTION, AND DISEASES SIGNIFIED BY THE TWELVE SIGNS.

## Strength (VIII)/Leo

- Countries: France, Italy, Bohemia, Sicily, Rome.

- Towns: Rome, Bath, Bristol, Taunton, Cremona, Prague, Apulia, Ravenna, and Philadelphia; also, the Alps and the ancient Chaldea, as far as Bussorah [Basra].

## The Hermit (IX)/Virgo[17]

- Countries: Turkey in Europe and Asia, Switzerland, Mesopotamia, or Diarbed; all the country between.

## Justice (XI)/Libra

- Countries: China, Japan, parts of India near them; Austria, Usbeck in Persia, towards India; Upper Egypt, Livonia, the vicinity of the Caspian Sea.

- Towns: Lisbon, Vienna, Antwerp, Francfort [Frankfurt], Spires, Fribourg, Charlestown in America, and its vicinity.

## Death (XIII)/Scorpio

- Countries: Barbary, Morocco, Norway, Valet the Catalonia, Bavaria, and the ancient Cappadocia.

- Towns: Francfort on the Oder [Frankfurt], Messina, Ghent, Liverpool, which is especially ruled by the 19th degree.

## Temperance (XIV)/Sagittarius

- Countries: Arabia Felix, Spain, Hungary, parts of France near Cape Finisterre, Dalmatia, Istria, Tuscany, Moravia, Sclavonia [Slavonia].

- Towns: Cologne, Buda, Avignon, Narbonne, Toledo.

---

[17] The Hermit, perhaps unsurprisingly, has no corresponding towns.

## The Devil (XV)/Capricorn

- Countries: India, Greece, parts of Persia about Circan, Macran, and Chorassan; Lithuania, Saxony, Albania, Bulgaria, Stiria, Mexico, and parts about the Isthmus of Darien, Santa Martha, Popayan, Pasta, etc.

- Towns: Mecklenburgh, Hesse, Oxford; and also, the Orkney Islands.

## The Star (XVII)/Aquarius

- Countries: Arabia the stony, Russia, Tartary, Prussia, parts of Poland, Lithuania and Muscovy, Lower Sweden, Westphalia.

- Towns: Hamburgh, Bremen, Piedmont; also, Affghaunistan, and other parts of Asia bordering on Persia; and this sign has rule over the affairs of state in England, especially the 13th degree.

## The Moon (XVIII)/Pisces

- Countries: Portugal, Calabria, Normandy, Galicia in Spain, Cilicia.

- Towns: Alexandria, Ratisbon, Worms, Seville, Compostella, Tiverton.

The reader is encouraged to experiment with using these twelve cards as locational devices, even if only to consider their next vacation.

## Waite-Smith Tarot (WST) Prevalence

Since the publication of the original *Tarosophy*, the growth of independent deck designers, particularly alongside increasing accessibility of print-on-demand or small print-run printers, has led to a dizzying and increasing range of published decks. In the previous ten years to this current work, the Waite-Smith template has been either diluted or entirely dissolved by radical new designs. In our social media platforms, we have been surveying the prevalence of the Waite-Smith deck and will continue to do so in the coming decade. Will it remain the most popular favourite, or be entirely replaced and forgotten in a sea of new designs?

We asked readers whether they only used the *Waite-Smith* deck or whether they never used it, i.e., they used a Waite-Smith Variant such as the *Aquarian Tarot*, or totally different designs such as the *Wild Unknown Tarot* by Kim Krans. We also asked if readers used a range, for example, they might read with the *Thoth Tarot* and the *Waite-Smith Tarot*. We also enquired as to the prevalence of those readers only using antique decks such as the Tarot de Marseilles, Sola Busca reproductions, Etteilla, etc.

By Waite-Smith we mean a deck that is either explicitly the Waite-Smith or virtually identical in design; so, a Waite-Smith deck design with cats replacing people is not counted, but a 'Universal Tarot' or '1909 Original' deck which is another artist who has re-drawn the Waite-Smith deck would be counted as Waite-Smith.

Here are the results from our survey of 2020. Interestingly, there was an increase in the number of people *mainly* using Waite-Smith from 2019, perhaps due to the number of beginners new to tarot during the pandemic who were usually starting with a Waite-Smith Tarot:

| | |
|---|---|
| Waite-Smith Mainly | 44% |
| Waite-Smith and Others Equally | 29% |
| Never use the Waite-Smith | 22% |
| Waite-Smith Only | 3% |
| TdM and Antique Decks Mainly | 2% |

## Above the Head

The Kabbalist Isaac Luria (1534 – 1572) was said to be a skilled practitioner of Metoposcopy.[18] This is the practice of physiological divination based upon the discernment of Hebrew letters in the lines of a person's forehead. Whilst we may not be as conversant with Hebrew letters as much as this, we are conversant with tarot cards, which correspond to Hebrew letters. As a result, we can try an interesting experiment; the next person you meet, imagine a tarot card appearing above their head, which answers the question "what has this person to teach me about life?"

## Different Voices

In Tarosophy we consider that different decks have different voices, as if they were a broad group of friends, each with their own opinion and experience. And, like people, they have their own unique quirks; so, the *Thoth Tarot* card of the Moon is by far more negative than the *Waite-Smith Tarot* Moon or the *Motherpeace Tarot* Moon.

At the same time, like friends, we might go to the *Thoth* knowing that we are better served by that friend rather than the *Motherpeace* - or vice-versa.

---

[18] See Lawrence Fine, 'The Art of Metoposcopy: A Study in Isaac Luria's Charismatic Knowledge', in Lawrence Fine, *Essential Papers on Kabbalah* (New York City: NYU Press, 1995), pp. 315-37.

## Bonding with a Deck

Whilst we looked at some of the fallacies of bonding with a deck, one early method I employed still proves useful with getting to know a new deck. Before sleep, with my eyes closed, I would visualise every card in order as much as I could, starting with the Majors, then the Suits, from Ace to Ten and the Courts (in order, for me, Pentacles, Swords, Cups, Wands).

I try and run through the whole deck, even if I get blanks or fuzzy images for some of the cards - or even a lot of them - I carry on until I get to the last card of the deck in this order, the King of Wands. In the morning I compare what I can remember from my imagination to any of the cards which I felt did not have enough detail or I had forgotten what they looked like. I then look through the physical deck at least once or twice during the day and notice a few more details, colours, patterns, symbols, etc. and repeat the process each night. I keep repeating the process for a week or two until I can shuffle the entire deck in my mind, pull three random cards, and see the detail of those three cards enough to do a reading in my imagination.

This may be a useful method for other readers to improve their bonding with a deck.

## Brings and Leaves

In this exercise, we look at the cards with an important and useful filter, which assists us unconsciously when we conduct a reading. This exercise also provokes a new way of viewing reversals as what the card is *taking away* from the situation, whether for good or bad.

1.      Take any card from the deck.

2.      Consider how it both *brings* its nature into the world, and what it also *leaves*.

3.      Use the sentence structure "It brings ... but it leaves ..."

## Examples

- Ten of Swords: It brings a stop to all those plans, but it leaves no room for doubt.

- Queen of Cups: She brings depth but leaves insecurity.

- The Hermit: Brings solitude but leaves company.

*Illus. Ten of Swords, "it brings an end to plans, but leaves no doubt".*

## Reversals

If all the cards are reversed in a reading, or a majority, and we definitely shuffled them, we can tend to assume the cards are telling us we need to ask the reverse of the question we asked or look at the situation in a totally opposite manner and ask a new question to the deck.

If there are just one or two cards not reversed out of several, we might consider that the spread is telling us that the answer is "what do you need to do to turn these cards on their heads, and the other cards are the consequences - that is my answer, now go do it".

If we take this to mean that the question is upside down, it is not the reading, which is just trying to do its job. We either turn every card the other way around (including upright cards which then become reversed) and read it, or we put the cards back in the deck and shuffle again, asking a new question which is totally the opposite of the one we thought originally to ask.

We then read the new reading to the new question, even if it still has a lot of reversals, which strangely enough does not seem to often happen.

## The Hanged Man Reversed

When beginners get the Hanged Man for the first time, they sometimes turn the card around because it looks upside-down, which is of course the very nature of the card. I used to find this card the most difficult to read when I first started reading, whether upright or reversed.

*Illus. The Hanged Man (reversed).*

It is an upside-down card, right-way up. It is all about being reversed, seeing things the wrong way up and differently to everyone else. What might it mean when we get the card reversed?

The little but powerful book, *Tarot Flip*, co-authored with Tali Goodwin, took the words of hundreds of real tarot readers and looked at what readers unconsciously think about card meanings from actual experience.[19] This allowed us to create sentences for each card as if a real reader was talking about it to a client, not what a reader might tell you "about" the card – which is also useful, but not the full picture.

These "tarot tellings" rather than "tarot meanings" were often surprising

---

[19] Tali Goodwin & Marcus Katz, *Tarot Flip* (Keswick: Forge Press, 2010).

but made sense on further contemplation; the Magician was not about 'skill', 'resources' or 'channeling' but about 'success'. That is, no matter what a reader says when that card turns up, in terms of the reading, it means essentially, 'success' - even if that success is as a result of 'skill', 'resources', etc. Similarly, the Sun turned out to hold the unconscious keyword of 'demonstration', which is illustrated by the little child on the horse, but also the sun itself - it can only burn, it cannot hide its own light. This is the essential placeholder meaning of that card, no matter how it is spoken of in the context of the reading and the situation. Death, as another clear example, was not about 'death' in readings but about 'life'. The World was about 'beginnings' and not 'endings'. This is because a reader takes the essential meaning of the card and then further interprets it. They may say 'death' with the Death card, but then they talk about transformation and living life.

Often these 'over-the-table' words are what follows the usual book keywords, so the Sun in a reading is really about 'demonstration' rather than what the books say about 'positivity' and 'radiance'.

When a real reader talks to a client about the Sun, they might encourage the client to demonstrate their self-worth or demonstrate by taking positive action, etc. They will not simply say out of context the words "positivity and innocence" as if they were a programmed robot.

When we look at the upright Hanged Man, the unconscious keyword for the card is not 'sacrifice' but rather 'surrender'. It is the surrendering to our highest values, what is most important to us, which can often turn our world upside-down, particularly if we have been living a lie or a make-do situation.

The Hanged Man is surrender in giving up to what is real and right above us. The symbol shows that the Hanged Man is fastened to the above and not the below – he is glowing because he is true to himself.

When we looked in the *Tarot Flip* project at the reversed meaning of the Hanged Man using the unconscious key-words of tarot readers, we got something that is not often given in books but is obvious when we think about it – struggle.

The Hanged Man (reversed) signifies a struggle. It is a struggle to put things the right way up, in the same way that we sometimes turn the card the wrong way up because we think it is wrong when it is right, so to speak – it is confusing and a real struggle.[20]

The unconscious keywords take our real experience when we see the card, as when we think "oh no, that's the Hanged Man reversed, that's really confusing, and I struggle to read it" and incorporate that response in what we

---

[20] I was recently taken by reader and Tarosophy Tarot Certificate graduate Dave Kim's interpretation of the reversed Hanged Man as self-denial, as in someone who does not even begin to think that the problem is with them, not someone or something else.

say. When the card comes up in reverse, feel that feeling and simply apply it to the reading, for example in a future position for a work situation; "You will struggle if you take this way, it will be very confusing, and you will not know which way is up".

In the same situation, if the Hanged Man card was the right-way up, we would say "You should be true to your highest principles even if you have to give way (surrender) and let something else happen".

The Hanged Man is a challenging card, but it should be a card of challenge, not challenging to read. The fact that you think it might be is the very way to easily remind you of what the card is all about.

The Hanged Man, as we might say, carries itself.

## Reversed Majors

In reversing the Major Arcana, we can look at their meaning as a hesitation to act on the impulse of the energy embodied by that archetype. This can be applied - as we see in the example list below - to everyday hesitations, such as the reason someone might lurk on a social media group and hesitate from engagement and action.

If the reader - or their client - is hesitant about some action or another, simply draw one reversed Major Arcana from a split-deck of Majors (or a Major-only deck) and read the reversal as follows:

0.   Fool: You don't want to be considered a Fool, so you don't leap in.

1.   Magician: You are waiting for magick and have yet to see that it is everywhere.

2.   High Priestess: You don't trust your intuition and feel like you're waiting for a sign.

3.   Empress: You don't feel as if you have enough experience, but you are wise with life.

4.   Emperor: You don't feel that you own your own power - but you do.

5.   Hierophant: In a world full of experts, you don't know what to trust, so why not ask and test the answers?

6.   Lovers: You find it difficult to choose between approaches, so you never end up fully committing.

7.  Chariot Everyone else seems driven, but you can't motivate yourself to engage.

8.  Strength: You're frightened of loudmouths and know-it-all's, but you can block from your life those whose bark is worse than their bite (or, perhaps, whose reason is less than their roar).

9.  Hermit: You're a bit solitary, but this gives you a unique way of looking at things - why not share it?

10. Wheel: You have a busy life of ups and downs at the moment, but you could make a still centre for one moment and do something to centre yourself.

11. Justice: There's always an argument for not taking time to do something that matters to you.

12. Hanged Man: You're often suspended in indecision, even about something important to you.

13. Death: There's a fear that if you say something, things might have to change.

14. Temperance: You don't like conflict, so it's often better not to get involved in something.

15. Devil: For some reason, tarot frightens you a little at some level - or maybe you always feel like you just don't know enough?

16. Blasted Tower: There's something holding you back, like everything might come toppling down if you open your mouth. Perhaps you can take out one brick at a time?

17. Star: It always seems hopeless, and things sometimes don't work out the way you envisioned them? But oftentimes we must wait for the dark to see the stars.

18. Moon: There's a fear of the unknown. But what's the worst that can happen, other than embark on an incredible new adventure?

19. Sun: You have an honest innocence to things but can get hurt. Maybe time to recognise how much you've already grown?

20.  Last Judgement: You haven't yet found your calling, so never go for anything. Maybe just go for anything - something - different, and go from there?

21.  World: There always seems too much to learn, and you can't see the point of it. So perhaps, start with what is in front of you.

One interesting side-effect of this reading in practice is that sometimes the client (or oneself) will read the card and suggest it does not fit with them. Sometimes they will be suppressing this reaction, even in the face of the reading, and sometimes they will immediately say, "It's actually more like …" and come to an actual realisation about their hesitation.

## On Death and Transformation

For those who have trouble dealing with the Death card in a reading, here is a tarosophical suggestion, based on the word most used by actual readers when they do not want to simply say 'death'.

*Illus. Death.*

Tarot readers often talk about the card as "transformation" and we can dig deeper into this generally recognised keyword for the card by considering the root of the word. The word 'trans-formation' comes from two Latin words, *trans-* and *form*, meaning 'across' and 'shape'. It literally means 'to change something from one shape to another', i.e., a change of appearance or structure without changing the actual component undergoing transformation. A useful example is coal, which is transformed plant-material, although it is not coal (as is sometimes popularly thought) that is transformed into diamonds, even though diamond is an allotrope of carbon. It is then transformed - technically, *transmorphed* - by heat into ash, sulphur dioxide, carbon dioxide, methane, and other by-products. All of these are (in part) within the existing material or created by a reaction of released materials with other chemicals, gases, etc., in the environment.

Water undergoes a similar transformation when subjected to a change of temperature (energy) - it transforms from a liquid to a gas when we boil it, but it is still the same molecules, just in a different state. This process of transformation is the same one being attributed to the Death card.

The card is saying that wherever it appears in the spread is *where we need to change the shape of things*; not add something or take it away but work with what we have got. The Death card is saying you can only change things around, there is nothing new to come, or anything of which you should get rid.

In the past position of a reading, Death tells us that we must change the shape of our *memories*. We cannot add anything into the past nor take anything away. In a practical sense, we could perhaps make some memories bigger than others by recalling them as more important and positive.

However we might think about the past, we have to change the *shape* of it, as another example, stretching a bad memory further back or bringing a good memory from childhood closer towards us.[21] We can massively change that landscape, even if we cannot add or remove anything from what has already happened.

In the future position, Death tells us that we might want to stop trying to find something new and start to simply *re-arrange what we have already*. In a practical sense, it is making changes in the workplace without looking (yet) for a new job, or similarly in a relationship. Whatever it is that we want in the future, the card is telling us that before we go there, we must transform what we already have in the present.

Strangely, that often opens new opportunities in the future, by simply re-organising the present.

In the present position, Death tells us that we are already being changed, but because it is not dramatic (as illustrated by the Tower), or subtle (the High Priestess), we probably will not see it yet. It tells us in the present that

---

[21] Marcus Katz, *NLP Magick* (Keswick: Forge Press, 2020), pp. 281-90.

we are changing the shape of our relationship to everything, and this is always inevitable and always happening, so if anything, we should simply *be patient and let it happen*. In a practical sense, Death in the present is a card that tells us to notice what is "the same, but different" and in doing so, realise how far we have come, and how far we might yet go.

## Turn a One-Card Reading into a Spread

In the fractal approach common to many Tarosophy methods, we can 'drill down' into the detail of a single card reading to provide further detail, making it either a deeper reading or even a new spread for four or more further cards.[22] If we take this method to an extreme, we can then repeat the process with any further cards, until we have exhausted the entire deck and reached the closest attractor point which represents the absolute answer.

This method also works best with complex designs and overloaded symbolic decks, which can assist the reading of a deck that might otherwise prove difficult to read.

It also works to go further into a single card in a larger spread, which might be proving curious or difficult to read - or one for which the client requests more information.

First, we draw a single card as we would do usually with a one-card reading - or select a card from a larger reading we wish to explore.

We then mentally divide the card into three to four sections, e.g., into four squares or two vertical or horizontally split rectangles, three corners, etc. depending on the design.

We then choose the main symbol (as we learnt in pinpointing cards) in each section of the card and use that symbol to suggest a theme as if it were a position in a new spread. If there appears to be no symbol in that section, the colour itself, even a plain blue sky or yellow floor, is a symbol; "your highest aspiration" or "means of grounding", for example.

We can then simply lay out a new card for each of those positions and read further into the card.

## Example

To explore the Empress, either as the result of a one-card reading or in a ten-

---

[22] In part, this method is based on the "Orchard" method in Kabbalah, wherein each Sephirah contains a full Tree of Sephiroth, and each Sephirah within that Tree contains another Tree. In this method, we can speak about the "Tiphareth of Netzach of Yesod". If we astrally travel to these locations, we can experience visions unique to the place, such as did the Golden Dawn by scrying combination of elemental Tattvas, such as the "Air of Earth".

card reading, in the position "What to Do".

In a single-card reading, we might read that card as 'let things take their natural course' but this might not be very practical, useful, detailed, or deep advice.

We can now divide the card into four sections and see that we have clear symbols in those four locations to which our intuitive eye might be drawn:

- SCEPTRE + TREES + SHIELD + WATERFALL.

*Illus. Empress Divided for One-Card Reading.*

We then imagine these are positions in a new four-card spread:

- Sceptre: What to do to take control.
- Shield: What to do to protect yourself.
- Trees: What to do to rise steadily.
- Waterfall: What to do to find the best flow.

We quickly draw four cards and place them around the Empress in those positions and read further into the card.

And as we have seen, we can then repeat the same method for any of those cards in a fractal reading, such as if we drew the Four of Swords for the Shield location of the Empress, which would answer "withdraw" to "What to do to protect yourself". We could then further dive into the Four of Swords and explore the exact steps to "withdraw". We might divide the card into a triangle of protection with three sections:

- PAX WINDOW + CARVED SWORDS + TOMB.

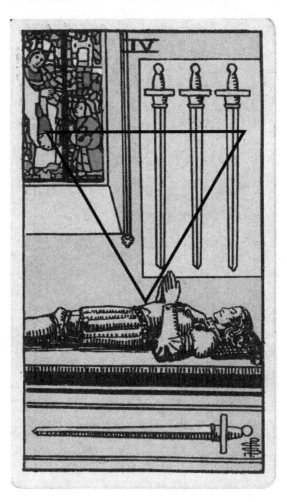

*Illus. Four of Swords Divided for One-Card Reading.*

We could use these as three spread locations:

- Window (Pax): What to filter out of your life.
- Carved Swords: What resources to draw on and keep in your life as you withdraw.
- Tomb: How to get the best recovery possible.

And so forth, down as many cards we need as we chase the fractal divination to the singular point to which every reading is always pointing.

## Desire Lines and the Poetics of Space

A tarot reading is a spatial affair as well as a temporal one. It exists as a visual metaphor, an arrangement of symbols on a usually horizontal plane. We might indicate vaguely that the temporal dimensions of the spread are "the future" and "the past", represented by cards to the left or right of the space. A card placed in the middle is often "the significant person" for whom the reading is conducted, or rather, perhaps, constructed. A card placed in the lower half of the implied spatial boundaries of the spread is often something unknown, whereas cards placed in a higher location are interpreted as representing higher things, aspirations, and goals. A card placed in some significantly spatial manner - at the top of the reading - or temporally - as the final card placed - or both - is often "the outcome", to which the central card is then beholden.

In a Grand Tableau reading of Lenormand cards, this spatial framework is even more explicit, likely because of the method deriving from the reading of coffee grounds in a cup, where location and distance are intrinsic to the reading of the symbols; a cloud at the top of the cup or below a symbol which looked like a dog was totally different than the same cloud in the dregs of the cup at the bottom or located immediately above the head of a man.

When we lay out cards, we should consider the implicit symbolism of the space between the cards - and how we move the cards once they are laid out. As we saw in *Tarosophy*, we can anchor a selected set of symbols by movement to assist a client to recall important aspects of our interpretation. We can also add to this by being aware that lifting a card higher than the others, even if only to look at it more closely, has some symbolic impact during a reading. A nervous moving of a card back and forth once down on the table might dramatically weaken our point. Using one card to flip up another card to our hand may act as a symbolic reinforcement of the relationship between those two cards - or people, should they be Court cards.

The poetics we can bring to our space, to rephrase the *Poetics of Space* (1957) by Gaston Bachelard, can be part of the art of our reading. If we lay out cards around the edge of a space first, we signify a boundary reading -

alternatively, if we lay out and read one card at a time, the client will not know how many cards, how much space, and how much detail might be about to be provided. Either option has an application, if chosen deliberately rather than used merely as a matter of preferred style or habit.

Similarly, we can look for so-called lines of desire in a spread. A desire line or path is the route made by pedestrian or animal traffic which has been repeated often enough to erode a distinct path. It often marks some short-cut or popular route amidst more formal or designated paths.[23] In a reading, we can watch either the client or ourselves in the way in which we constantly return to a significant pattern of eye or hand movement, gesture, or attention, between two or more cards, despite the overall reading. That desire line will be worth paving, making concrete by observation and utilisation, bringing it to the surface and interpreting it.

We might find ourselves saying out loud, "in this Thoth reading of fifteen cards, we have kept glancing between that troublesome Moon card and the Nine of Disks down in the left. Let us spend just a moment to mention that and speak its symbolism, particularly as we walk the three cards between them".

It is often an oracular moment to speak what we see and listen to what we find ourselves speaking. As Bachelard wrote, "Sight says too many things at the same time. Being does not see itself. Perhaps it listens to itself".[24]

---

[23] See Tom Hulme, 'What Can we Learn from Shortcuts?" at
https://www.ted.com/talks/tom_hulme_what_can_we_learn_from_shortcuts [last accessed 14th March 2021].
[24] Gaston Bachelard, *Poetics of Space* (Boston: Beacon Press, 1992), p. 215.

## The Fool Falls

Becomes
Manipulative,
Distracting the Eye,
Blind,
All surface and skin,
Strangling,
Like weeds in a forgotten garden,
Controlling,
For the sake and necessity of it,
Hypocritical,
Revealing only fear,
Caught,
In between love and the terror
Of loss.

The Fool Plummets
Becomes
A rider not the ride,
Becomes
That against which he fights,
Becomes
Blind in insight,
Becomes
Fatalistic,
Becomes
True to nothing,
Nothing at All.

The Fool Loses
By sacrificing nothing
In particular,
By transforming nothing
Worthwhile,
By Meeting his Angel
Only Half-Way,
By Surrendering to
Her Shadow.

The Fool Ruins
All that was Built
Without Spirit,

All that was Visioned
Without Truth,
All that was Dreamt
Without Light,
All the Sons and Daughters,
Twinned behind the Wall.

The Fool Discovers
In the Abyss of Forgetfulness,
Remembrance of an Angels Call,
The World Revealed,
And vows to Return.

## Shadow Work

Whilst it is beyond the scope of this present book to provide so-called shadow work, which should always be undertaken with the assistance and supervision of an experienced or trained practitioner, there are certain negative states which can be denoted by the tarot. These occur, as we would suspect, in the Court cards, using reversals:

- A Page reversed illustrates Regret.
- A Knight reversed illustrates Remorse.
- A Queen reversed illustrates Shame.
- A King reversed illustrates Guilt.

We can further denote these states applying to particular areas of life:

- Behaviour (Pentacles).
- Thoughts (Swords).
- Relationships (Cups).
- Desires (Wands).

When upright, Court cards upright show the parts of the self with opportunity for:

- Remedial action (Page).
- Acceptance (Knight).
- Self-forgiveness (Queen).
- Maturation (King).

In the area of life of their Suit, for example, the Knight of Wands shows the opportunity for work regarding acceptance of desires. We can use the sixteen Court cards as a split-deck, with reversals, to draw a card for the repressed or supressed state, and a card for the opportunity to work with that shadowed aspect and generate creativity.

# - II -

# ARCHETYPES, SYMBOLS & LANGUAGE

## The Origins of Symbolic Language

In early 2021, a discovery was made in Indonesia of a cave painting featuring a warty pig, which may well be the earliest known human example of art, dating to at least 45,500 years ago. The painting was accompanied by two handprints, which are part of the earliest writing - or prehistoric symbolism - of our most distant ancestors. In fact, recent research has proposed that during the Ice Age period, there were thirty-two common signs used by our forebearers - a number of symbols that will be immediately recognised by Kabbalists, for it is the number of paths on the Tree of Life, itself, one of the oldest symbols in ancient art.[25]

These thirty-two symbols were proposed by archaeologist Genevieve von Petzinger and have been previously associated with the entopic visions of shamanic trance.[26] In particular, seven basic symbols were associated with closed-eye states, such as spirals, zig-zags, and dots.[27] We can take the full set of symbols and discover that they not only fit onto the Tree of Life, but also illuminate correspondences to the Sephiroth, numbers and corresponding Major Arcana of the tarot.

| Kether | Chockmah | Binah | Chesed | Geburah | Tiphareth | Netzach | Hod | Yesod | Malkuth |
|---|---|---|---|---|---|---|---|---|---|
| • (1) | (2) | ▽ (3) | ▢ (4) | (5) | (6) | ○ (7) | (8) | (9) | (10) |
| Dot | Claviform | Triangle | Quadrangle | Segmented Cruciform | Asterisk | Circle | Line | Cupule | Cruciform |
| Fool | Magician | High Priestess | Empress | Emperor | Hierophant | Lovers | Chariot | Strength | Hermit |
| (11) | (12) | (13) | (14) | (15) | (16) | (17) | (18) | (19) | (20) |
| Negative Hand | Positive Hand | Y-Sign | W-Sign | Open Angle | Tectiform | Cordiform | Spanish Tectiform | Crosshatch | Flabelliform |
| Wheel | Justice | Hanged Man | Death | Temperance | Devil | Blasted Tower | Star | Moon | Sun |
| (21) | (22) | (23) | (24) | (25) | (26) | (27) | (28) | (29) | (30) |
| Spiral | Penniform | Scalariform | Reniform | Aviform | Serpentiform | Zigzag | Unciform | Half-Circle | Oval |
| Judgement | World | | | | | | | | |
| (31) | (32) | | | | | | | | |
| Finger Flutings | Pectiform | | | | | | | | |

*Illus. Ice Age Symbols.*

---

[25] By 'paths' we include the *Sephiroth*, as given by the *Sepher Yetzirah*.
[26] Genevieve von Petzinger, *The First Signs* (New York: Atria, 2016), p. 245.
[27] *Ibid*, p. 250.

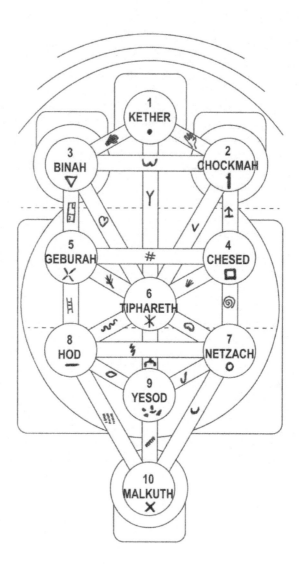

*Illus. Ice Age Symbols on Tree of Life.*

In effect, this provides us the most primitive and original set of tarot symbolism, if we were to consider that the pattern of our appreciation of the universe has remained consistently wired in our brains since we began to evolve consciousness and language. The symbols in themselves have no agreed meaning or interpretation, given the distance of time and the general lack of context of their usage or possible intent.[28] I have presented my own interpretations according to generic symbolism, etymology, and in terms of their correspondence to the Tree of Life.

The thirty-two identified signs have no intrinsic order, as they represent a collation of signs from many different areas and are not in themselves a formulated language. I have arranged them according to their best (and surprisingly straightforward) correspondences to the Tree of Life.

## The Sephiroth

1. The Dot (Kether).

This most basic of symbols or makings represents the point of Kether in which all is created. It is the simplicity of existence.

Interpretation: In an oracle, it could be interpreted as the "obvious point" or simple truth of a matter. It could also mean "to simplify" or do one thing, not many.

2. The Claviform (Chockmah).

This "club-shaped" symbol is the first extension of the universe into a simple line, from the point of Kether. The word claviform is formed from the word for 'club', which in turn has its earliest origin in the meaning of "to break". It is the first breaking asunder of the universe into differentiation and separation.

Interpretation: Striking to break something apart, making a difference, forming a new boundary. Reaching out.

3. The Triangle (Binah).

The triangle is a straight-forward symbol for Binah, the third of the Sephiroth, and the according symbolism such as the City of the Pyramids. It is the "one becomes two becomes three".

Interpretation: Triangulation, first structure, strength in numbers, pulling together to get to the point, three, not two or one. Establishing your base before extending yourself further.

---

[28] To quote one of my favourite sentences on Wikipedia recently, "The corpus of Paleolithic flutings is too complex to fit into a single meaning paradigm". https://en.wikipedia.org/wiki/Finger_fluting#Interpretations [last accessed 10th March 2021].

## 4. The Quadrangle (Chesed).

The basic shapes, becoming eventually seen as the platonic solids, are already present in this earliest of human communication or expression. The Square corresponds with the fourth of the Sephiroth, Chesed. In making these correspondences, we can further bridge to other systems, such as astrology, in this case, Chesed - and the Square - corresponding to Jupiter.

Interpretation: Structure, defence, expansion. Building, organisation, making a clear boundary.

## 5. The Segmented Cruciform (Geburah).

Similar to the Pentagram, the segmented cruciform illustrates the sorting and judging aspects of Geburah, meaning 'severity'.

Interpretation: Breaking apart to put back together, sorting out your issues, harsh times, a necessary evil. Discipline.

## 6. The Asterisk (Tiphareth).

In the centre of the Tree of Life, Tiphareth is the beauty of dynamic equilibrium, suitably illustrated by the symmetry of the asterisk. The word 'asterisk' means 'little star', and is often six-pointed, fitting the position of Tiphareth as the 'son' of the upper Sephiroth.

Interpretation: Active balancing, keeping in the centre, recognising your part in things. Harmony, diplomacy, smoothing things out, inclusivity.

## 7. The Circle (Netzach).

The nature symbolism of Netzach and its connection to the emotional world are here shown by the circle, in which habits are formed. The circle sits below the spiral of the Wheel and the half-circle of the Moon below it. As with the correspondence to Venus, which is the only astrological sigil to overlay the entire Tree of Life, the circle is an all-inclusive symbol.

Interpretations: Circular patterns, being caught in a loop, needing to break out. Habits, or more positively, setting a regular schedule.

## 8. The Line (Hod).

The claviform of Chockmah, reflected down and across the Tree of Life in a lower arc, now becomes the straight line of Hod, the Sephirah of logic and the mind. It is the simple truth of the mind, and the linear nature of thought.

Interpretation: Requiring thought, straight line thinking. Simplicity, bringing everything down to the base line. Clarity, straightforward action.

Keeping on the way you are going.

9. The Cupule (Yesod).

These half-dome depressions are cup-like, hence called cupule, which also references the base of an acorn. In terms of Yesod, this is the foundation of the Tree of Life, where the influences of all the other Sephiroth are gathered prior to connection with Malkuth. Thus, there are many, as differentiation is now present in the system, as illustrated by the "house of many mirrors" metaphor for Yesod.

Interpretation: Different ways of seeing the same thing, different opinions, a gathering together, forming a support network, ensuring an agreement. Providing a holding space.

10. The Cruciform (Malkuth).

The Cross is the material nature of Malkuth, and is also the meaning of the Hebrew letter, *Tau*, which corresponds to the World card and the path between Yesod and Malkuth. We will also see this identical correspondence of Ice Age symbols to the Hebrew letters in the Star card on the paths.

Interpretation: Base matter, absolute materiality, lack of spiritual insight, money, time, struggle, suffering, sacrifice.

## The Minor Arcana

In these signs, we can make a simple association based on shape and number to the ten Sephiroth, 'numerical emanations' of the Tree of Life. In western esotericism, these correspond to the Minor Arcana, in numerical order. The Suits of the Minor Arcana correspond to the four elements or four worlds of Kabbalah, giving forty combinations.

We could have four *Cupules*, then, with the *Cupule of Earth* (Nine of Pentacles), the *Cupule of Air* (Nine of Swords), the *Cupule of Water* (Nine of Cups) and the *Cupule of Fire* (Nine of Wands). The *Dot of Fire* (Ace of Wands) would be the first and highest emanation of the cards and the *Cruciform of Earth* the lowest, being the Ten of Pentacles and the Malkuth of Assiah.

## Court Cards

To create the Court cards, we can assign the negative hand to the Page, the positive hand to the Knight, and the sign of the Oval (as the Empress) to the Queen and the sign of the Open Angle (as the Emperor) to the King. The reader is encouraged to allocate alternative signs of their own preference and ingenium.

We then place these symbols next to their elemental representations to each Suit, either pictorially or through their alchemical symbolism:

- Earth: Circle (stone) or flat line (surface), or bisected triangle, point-down.
- Air: Cloud or dots, or bisected triangle, point-up.
- Water: Waves or ripples, or triangle, point-down.
- Fire: Flames or sparks, or triangle, point-up.

Thus, the Queen of Air (Swords) would be an oval and a cloud, whilst the Knight of Wands would be a positive hand and flames, or a positive hand with an upright triangle.

## The Major Arcana and the Twenty-Two Paths

11. The Negative Hand (Fool).

As the most basic symbol of the self, a hand-print may have been used as a form of signature or identification. The Negative Hand symbol was likely created by placing the hand on the surface of the rock and blowing ochre dye from the mouth so that the negative imprint was left when the hand was removed. This corresponds neatly with the Fool in tarot symbolism, particularly as the last stage of the spiritual ascent when the identity is resolved into unification with the divine. The act of blowing reminds us of the identification of the fool with *folle*, air-head, or madman, from the Latin, *follis*, 'bellows'.

Interpretation: Leaving something, being absent, removing yourself from a situation. Emptiness, a simple "no" or "nothing" as the answer.

12. The Positive Hand (Magician).

As the Fool is the negative hand, so the Magician is the positive hand. The hand that enacts the Will, the hand that points above or below. The hand that is positive action or hides a trick.

Interpretation: Doing something, taking full responsibility, it is entirely in your hands, willpower, a simple "do" or "yes" answer.

13. Y-Sign (High Priestess).

The Y-Sign can be seen as a sexual symbol or as an aspect of the trinity, both of which can be seen in the virginal aspect of the High Priestess as the image of Mary. It could also be taken as a symbol of intuition, where ideas from 'above' are funnelled into a single thought 'below'.

Interpretation: Intuition, trusting yourself, the feminine, carefully bringing your thoughts and feelings together, taking time.

14. W-Sign (Empress).

The Empress is the gateway of creation, and the W-symbol can be taken figurately as the breasts or buttocks, as the Y-symbol is to the Yoni. This is then a symbol of the maternal, mothering aspect, or physical nature of the world.

Interpretation: Nurturing, mothering, supporting. Take a support role.

15. Open Angle (Emperor).

The open angle can be taken as the arrow-head like force of the Emperor or the track or horns of Aries, the ram, to which this card corresponds in the Zodiac.

Interpretation: Energy, power, focus, zooming in, acting swiftly without thought, putting all your energies in one place to one goal.

16. Tectiform (Hierophant).

This symbol is shaped like a roof or rudimentary hut or building, and hence symbolises the building of beliefs, religion, churches, and society. These can be protective structure or the prison of enslavement, whether of belief or rule.

Interpretation: Beliefs and values, social conduct, going with everyone else, conforming. Sometimes the trap of believing in something over actual reality.

17. Cordiform (Lovers).

The heart symbol is an obvious choice for the Lovers card and this corresponding path on the Tree of Life. It symbolises feelings, love, the warmth of connection.

Interpretation: Relationship, connection, love, trusting your own feelings in a matter.

18. Spanish Tectiform (Chariot).

This symbol is unique to the caves of Spain and may be either a variant of the tectiform symbol, so a form of hut or dwelling, or a depiction of a canoe or similar vessel. In this context we take it as a means of transportation, and the 'canopy' of the Chariot.

Interpretation: Movement, transport, leaving one place or situation and going to another, support will be found (or given) during a transitional period.

19. Crosshatch (Strength).

The weaving together of lines to make a stronger pattern is ideal as a symbol of Strength. It shows the power of repeating something that works, building on a structure, and consistency.

Interpretation: Sticking to what works, repetition, weaving together people or events to make a better position, situation, or pattern.

20. Flabelliform (Hermit).

This symbol was one of the three remaining symbols after the most obvious symbols were allocated between the Ice Age symbols and the thirty-two paths and corresponding tarot cards. Similarly, the Hermit, Lovers and Chariot remained on the other side of the equation. As the cordiform was found to represent a heart, making correspondence to the Lovers, that left the Spanish Tectiform and the Flabelliform (a fan symbol) to allocate - as the Flabelliform was originally assigned to the Lovers. Once the Spanish Tectiform was discerned to be a mode of transportation (in some interpretations) it was straightforward to allocate that to the Chariot.

The flabelliform, or symbol of a fan, was thus the de-facto correspondence to the Hermit. It can be seen as a means to hide oneself, as well as advertise one's status, heavily symbolic in this regard in Japan, amongst other countries. When we consider the Hermit has removed himself, yet it still pictured at the top of a mountain holding a bright light, we can see how the lantern functions in the same symbolic manner as a fan; it both conceals the person yet at the same time reveals their status and availability in some manner.

Interpretation: Step back but remain visible. Patience, awaiting others, leave a sign that they can follow. Invitations. Not revealing too much.

21. Spiral (Wheel).

The spiral is an ideal correspondence to the Wheel in motion and is symbolic of the swirling change that turns the square of Chesed into the circle of Netzach. It is literally the movement of the stars and all things and one of the most fundamental patterns of existence.

Interpretation: Change, turning everything around tightly, sweeping up and doing something differently in the space, movement, initiation, going somewhere new.

22. Penniform (Justice).

This feather-shaped symbol represents the feather of Maat, or Justice, and is an already-associated symbol of Justice. The feather writes the laws or fundamental patterns of existence and whilst light, must be weighed against the heart to assure truth has prevailed.

Interpretation: Lack of guilt, shame, or regret, doing what is right, honesty, transparency, lightness of touch, deftness of action. No blame, no fault.

23. Scalariform (Hanged Man).

The symbol of a ladder is one of the most interesting correspondences of this set and fell into place within the final few remaining correspondences. The symbol was not originally recognised as a ladder, so became obvious as associated with the Hanged Man upon reading the etymology of "scalariform". The Hanged Man symbolises the above made present in the below, the sacred being part of everyday life and matter. It also symbolises our ascent through initiation up the cosmic realms, degree at a time. This ascent is often symbolised by a ladder.

Interpretation: Scaling a situation up or down, reversing your point of view, getting a higher overview, or climbing out of a situation. Taking the highest path.

24. Reniform (Death).

This kidney-shaped symbol is allocated to the Death card as it functions to filter toxins and waste substances in the body and is the most visceral symbol of the set. As a symbol it represents the deep "inside" of the body and the person and is a literal organ of transformative.

Interpretation: A matter of life and death, importance of omens, filtering out negativity, removing bad influences.

25. Aviform (Temperance).

The Angel of Temperance is here represented by the shape of a bird, symbolic of flight, ascent, and higher matters. Whilst this does not reflect the totality of the Temperance card, no correspondence will ever be a total match throughout the systems being compared - otherwise, they would be the same system. In this context, the Aviform is symbolic of the connection to higher realms within each person and situation.

Interpretation: The presence of a higher meaning to the situation. Taking notice. Rising above the everyday or limited view. Gaining a wider perspective. Looking to new horizons.

26. Serpentiform (Devil).

The correspondence of the serpent symbol and the Devil is relatively straightforward, as it is to some extent with the symbol of the snake in the Lenormand deck. The snake represents danger, temptation, and hidden influence, as reflected in the interpretation.

Interpretation: Hidden danger or influence, other involved person (or people) who are not known, possible temptation. Beat about the bush to scare any hidden influences out into the open.

27. Zigzag (Blasted Tower).

The lightning-shaped zig-zag symbol reminds us of the lightning striking the tower of god on this card. It is the path between the circle of Netzach and the straight line of Hod, marking the constant movement that results from balancing these two aspects of existence. In some ways, this is a symbol of tacking in sailing; using the energy of air and water to go from side-to-side and move forwards as a result.

Interpretation: Moving through change, going from one side to another. Making a new way ahead that is not straightforward. Planning for a few more stations in the road. An immediate result or progress is not to be expected.

28. Unciform (Star).

The unciform is a hook-shape, and immediately corresponds to the Hebrew letter *Tzaddi*, fish-hook, which in turn corresponds to the Star.

Interpretation: Diving deep, hooking onto an idea or a vision, perhaps sinking bait. Getting an idea out there, seeing what happens. Simply, fishing around. Having some patience.

29. Half Circle (Moon).

The half-circle of the lunar crescent is one phase of the Moon card and can be contrasted to the Y-symbol of the High Priestess, who also has a lunar symbolism. The moon provides more of a vessel than a transmission; it is more place or state of mind that a communication. On the Tree of Life, it connects the circle and the cross of Yesod and Malkuth, partaking somewhat of both symbols.

Interpretation: Receptivity, awaiting inspiration or intuition. Divination.

30. Oval (Sun).

Although the circle might also be a convenient correspondence, the oval eye-shaped symbol is chosen as representing the "eye" of light often associated with the Sun, such as the eye of Ra in ancient Egyptian mythology. The Earth is also situated on an orbit that is far more oval than it is circular around the Sun.

Interpretation: Opening up, seeing something new. Observation is key, light. Taking time to see what is really happening before taking action or making a decision. A day or a year. Time.

31. Finger Fluting (Last Judgement).

These signs made by fingers scribbling down a wall may be meaningless, but have been assigned potential interpretations as serpents, water, or hunting marks, such as paths to gatherings of animals. They could be simple counting. In our interpretation, we see them as the divine connection from above to below, calling us on new paths in a new life. The description of these signs as fluting carries an unintended resonance to the trumpet blown by the Angel.

Interpretation: Finding your own way, following your own path or calling by making it.

32. Pectiform (World).

This comb-shaped sign may indicate a literal comb, whose basic function is to untangle. The comb is also a symbol of the feminine and magic. In the third story of *The Snow Queen* by Hans Christian Anderson, 'The Flower Garden of the Woman Skilled in Magic', a golden comb is used on the little girl, Gerda, to make her forget her previous life. In such, it might be considered as a symbol of the world in its ordering of our lives and the forgetfulness into which we might sink. In a purely stylistic manner, the line is creating smaller lines in an act of self-creation.

Interpretation: Sorting, creativity, action. Untangling a situation before it tangles further. Remembering what is most important.

The reader may be interested to create a personal hand-made tarot-deck composed of these simple signs, to divine from the earliest set of symbols ever created by humans.

Whilst it is of course impossible to ascribe specific or singular meaning to such ancient symbols, we can think of them as a dream-book from which we create our own grammar.[29]

Tarot symbols, as we take them back to this most primitive of conceptualisations, offer a language, a symbolism, a writing of sorts, but "Not a writing which simply transcribes, a stony echo of muted words, but a lithography before words: metaphonetic, non-linguistic, alogical".[30]

## Example

If we were to conduct a three-card reading using a deck created with this most ancient of symbols, we might receive Serpentiform (26) + Spanish Tectiform (18) + Zig-Zag (17). This would signify as an oracle the following message:

> *There is hidden danger in the way you are intending to go. There will, however, be support for you if you make good preparations before you start and know your intended route. It is advised that to avoid the dangers that you cannot presently see, you make more steps or stages in your plan, even if it delays it or makes it more frustrating. You must test each stage from one extreme to another and not let people know exactly where you are heading as a destination. Then the hidden dangers will not be able to wait for you in any particular place or time.*

## Archetypes

> Archetypal patterns are part of the field, flowing around us and through us, dancing their ancient dances wearing contemporary clothes. When we name them and sponsor them, we can find gifts in their presence and meet the challenges they present.
>
> - Selene Vega, 'Movement Practices for Self-Relations' in Stephen Gilligan, *Walking in Two Worlds: The Relational Self in Theory, Practice, and Community.*

---

[29] See the philosophical discourse on symbolism, meaning, writing, and dreams in Jacques Derrida, 'Freud on the Scene of Writing' in *Writing and Difference* (Chicago: The University of Chicago Press, 1978), pp. 208-9, where Derrida quotes Freud on divination; "The Egyptian priests, the first interpreters of dreams, took their rules for this species of DIVINATION, from their symbolic riddling, in which they were so deeply read: A ground of interpretation which would give the strongest credit to the Art; and equally satisfy the diviner and the Consulter: for by this time it was generally believed that their Gods have given them hieroglyphic writing". Tarot images, like dreams, have no singular *traumbuch* ('dream book') but can be said to "follow old facilitations" of symbolism and context.

[30] *Ibid*, p. 207.

When we consider archetypes, we are working with an arguable and vague concept, even in the writings of Jung himself over time. We use the word interchangeably as both "archetypes" and "archetypal images". The "fool" for example is an archetypal image of the archetype of the "fool", but it remains unclear as to how the archetype exists without any representation - perhaps as a 'tendency' or 'complex' in the unconscious or the universal unconsciousness.

In tarot, we can perhaps think of the Major Arcana as the clothes of the archetypes, whatever-they-may-be, so the Fool is the contemporary clothing of the 'Sacred Fool' archetype, which is present in different clothes in many cultures and across many times. Yet how a tarot designer depicts the Fool card is perhaps a constellation of their own relationship to an archetype; perhaps it may be closer to a trickster, or even a clown. Similarly, how we ourselves relate to the images and the archetypes they depict will have much to teach us about our own process of individuation and relationship to these illustrations.

In terms of interpretation, we can see how the Major Arcana are utterly multivalent - and perhaps in a way much broader and deeper than their Minor Arcana counterparts. The Fool alone can be interpreted as "you are free to choose", "nothing is certain", "you are heading towards the truth of the situation", "You can find balance in your work", "You must play more in the relationship", "Just create and let the world look after itself", or "It will change".

The archetype is clothed with the illustration and the interpretations are descriptions of the clothing. Profoundly, our life is also the cloth of the archetypes, and we are illustrating their patterns in every situation. It is not we who imagine the archetypes, but it is in their pattern, their presence, in which we arise. As do the cards. In the end, every tarot reading comes down to comparing pictures - the pictures on the table and the picture of our life.

## Tarot Symbols

When we consider tarot, we consider a wide gamut of concepts, such as meaning, interpretation, divination, archetypes, and symbolism. In this section we will consider symbolism, following our introduction of the most ancient primitive signs, and recommend several reference books for standard interpretation of symbols.

In one sense, a symbol is much like a tarot or Lenormand card, in that we must interpret it in context. A snake may be a symbol of masculinity, evil, another woman, temptation, a hidden danger, etc., but to someone who has several snakes as pets it may have a very individual meaning. To a student of the bible, the snake may be a very loaded symbol, as it will be to someone who suffers from Ophidiophobia. To one practitioner of shamanism, it may very well be their guide. A snake may be genuinely friendly and supportive in one person's dream and extremely threatening in another person's dream, in contrast to either of their conscious reactions to the reptile.

What exactly is a symbol? The word 'symbol' itself derives from the Greek, σύμβολον, *symbolon*, meaning literally "to throw together". It comes from the original practice of breaking a coin or token into two parts, which each part would together represent an agreement or token of contract. Thus, a symbol stands for something else, it allows us to compare or contrast one thing to some other veracity or external authenticity. A symbol is basically something that points to something else, to which it has some relationship.

A symbol as it is commonly used can stand for a concept, object, or relationship. A heart stands for love, but also could be the label on a jar in a mortuary - context is, as ever, all important. A black heart with three swords in it could stand for a troubled relationship. An "equals" sign of two short straight lines atop each other of equal length could stand for an equal relationship but is more likely to be found expressing a mathematical relationship.

A single tarot card image is usually a collation of symbols, creating a complex metaphor; each symbol may change the overall interpretation of the card, or only one symbol might be selected for the overall reading.[31] If we described a card as a man rowing a boat in which are stood six swords, thrust into the boat, which also carries two hooded figures, one of which looks like a woman and the other a child, we have a wealth of symbolism at our fingertips.

The success of a deck, at least in terms of being a tool for divination and not just on artistic merits, will depend on the consistency of its symbolism and the multivalency of those symbols. The structure of tarot appears to be

---

[31] See the concept of 'pinpointing' and 'bridging' in Tali Goodwin & Marcus Katz, *Practical Tarot Techniques* (Woodbury: Llewellyn Publications, 2019), pp. 4-9.

already optimised, so varying a deck by adding a Suit or 'bonus cards' will have some - but minimal - impact on its utility. The Waite-Smith design remains dominant due to both these characteristics; the consistency to the Golden Dawn codification of correspondences in Book T and the multivalency of Shakespearean and theatrical sources, already recognised as universal narratives. If Pamela Colman Smith had been a more consistent student and artist and shared Waite's knowledge of higher-grade materials, the deck would have been even tighter. Waite's second application of symbolism to the deck in the Waite-Trinick Tarot, ten years later, is more abstract and requires deep knowledge of the design for any reference to its images.[32]

However, there will come a time when the dominant designs and even the basic symbols will shift. Symbols are also time-bound as much as they are cultural; Heinrich Zimmer wrote, "Symbols hold the mind to truth but are not themselves the truth, hence it is delusory to borrow them. Each civilisation, every age, must bring forth its own".[33]

Consider how symbols might not only be time-bound but might also have to be constructed to communicate a message for a timeless period. This is the task faced by the nuclear waste industry who have long been working on methods by which a buried nuclear waste dump might carry warnings that could still be understood in ten thousand years.[34] The snappily-named *Human Interference Task Force* have considered the levels of meaning that are required to be communicated and how a message may be preserved longer than any human construction has survived to this time.

Even if tarot, as some propose, is said to communicate a specific hidden teaching, it has only existed for a few hundred years, and certainly not yet tens of thousands of years. A field of thorn-like granite structures with pictures of exploding nuclear bombs carved into each structure might stop farming and warn present-day people away from an area, but would that merely symbolise an ancient shrine to be excavated to our far-future population? One idea proposed was to form an *atomic priesthood*, a sect modelled on the Catholic Church who would preserve the gospel of radiation danger for timeless generations.[35]

I would recommend the following reference books as guides to traditional

---

[32] See Tali Goodwin & Marcus Katz, *Abiding in the Sanctuary* (Keswick: Forge Press, 2011).

[33] Heinrich Zimmer, edited by Joseph Campbell, *Philosophies of India 9* (Princeton: Princeton Univ. Press, 1969), pp. 1–2.

[34] See the documentary *Into Eternity* (dir. Michael Madsen, 2010).

[35] https://en.wikipedia.org/wiki/Long-time_nuclear_waste_warning_messages [last accessed 11th March, 2021] and also refer to the classic science-fiction novel by Walter M. Miller, Jr., *A Canticle for Leibowitz* (1959). This astonishing novel deals with vast spans of time and the preservation of knowledge through blueprints and religious orders, amongst other themes.

interpretations of symbols, whether they be for dreams, cards, or visions. I have placed them in order of personal recommendation as each will build on the previous title and obviously no book will be complete.

**Symbolism Reading List**

- Juan Eduardo Cirlot, *A Dictionary of Symbols* (New York: New York Review Books, 2018).

- Jean Chevalier & Others, *The Penguin Dictionary of Symbols* (Penguin Books, 1997).

- Hans Biedermann, *Dictionary of Symbolism* (Plume, 1994).

- Jean C. Cooper, *An Illustrated Encyclopaedia of Traditional Symbols* (Thames & Hudson, 1987).

- Adele Nozedar, *The Element Encyclopaedia of Secret Signs and Symbols: The Ultimate A-Z Guide from Alchemy to the Zodiac* (Harper Collins, 2009).

- Jack Tressider, *Watkins Dictionary of Symbols* (Watkins, 2008).

# - III -

# THE 21 PRINCIPLES OF TAROT

## THE 21 PRINCIPLES OF TAROT

Whilst there are numerous ways of looking at tarot and its practices, over the years several significant principles seem to arise from the approach of Tarosophy. When these were formulated, they corresponded – as might be expected – to the archetypal sequence of the Major Arcana. These principles were shared and discussed amongst a small group of students and eventually settled in the following statements:

0. Aim in All Things to Restore the Spiritual Dignity of Tarot.
I. Remember that Tarot Starts and Ends from Within.
II. There is No Such Thing as an Accidental Oracle.
III. Tarot is a Connection to Meaning.
IV. All Readings are for Yourself as they are for Others.
V. The Oracular Moment is Sacrosanct.
VI. Tarot is the Loss of Forgetfulness and the Beginning of Choice.
VII. Be Confident and Considerate in All Readings.
VIII. Tarot is Recognising Relationship.
IX. Tarot is the Learning of a Lifetime.
X. Always Continue to Discover Mystery.
XI. Apply the Lessons of Tarot in Every Day.
XII. Seek to Find the Answer that is There.
XIII. Learn to Hear the Real Question.
XIV. You Do Not Need to Know Everything.
XV. Every Reading is as Important as Every Other Reading.
XVI. Prepare to Face Ten Thousand Readings.
XVII. Spreads are for Beginners. Later, One Reads Only the Cards.
XVIII. Learn the Meanings with Precision, Reading is another Matter.
XIX. See the Spaces Between the Cards.
XX. Be Serious in your Study but Inventive in your Practice.
XXI. Tarot is to Engage Life, Not Escape It.

We can then further apply these principles to specific practices, examples, and tips, as Tarosophy is an entirely practical approach to divination. The principles which arise from practice and reflection then give rise to further practices. We can also see that these practices are cumulative and as they follow the order of Major Arcana, provide an entire method of teaching tarot from an absolute beginner level to relatively advanced within twenty-one lessons. This teaching was worked online with a large group of students in China, who were extremely engaged in the process, and the practices proved highly effective. It provides a new method of teaching Tarosophy where the core principles and practices are bound together in the delivery of the teaching.

In the following part of this section on the Tarot Principles, we will review each principle and provide an extended commentary. We will also present the associated practice and teaching of each principle as providing a new curriculum of Tarosophy.

This is an inbuilt course which can be taken for daily practice, meaning that it can be conducted in twenty-one days, i.e., about three weeks, and the practices have been written with this in mind, so refer directly to the student and refer to the daily practice if the reader is following it.

This approach of teaching can also provide an experienced, intermediate, or advanced reader with a means of reviewing their own experience and a reset to the Tarosophy approach, which can be integrated within their own style of divination. It can also be conducted prior to following the "Reading the Majors" syllabus later in this book, which is a further thirty-two day course if conducted daily.

## - I -

### REMEMBER THAT TAROT STARTS AND ENDS FROM WITHIN.

The Tarot is a Tool.

It provides a means for divination and the oracular state.

Every person who reads Tarot will have their own experience and knowledge.

So, every person will eventually find their own voice.

Remember then, from the very beginning, that the tarot is the key to your state, your voice, your expression.

This will never be any different, from the beginning to the end.

### Practice

For each card, commencing with the Majors, Minors and then the Courts, simply look at the image and write three single sentences (or one combined) to indicate how that card might picture or be interpreted as:

*A*
Challenge
Resource
& Lesson

Write whatever comes to your mind, even as an absolute beginner - use the tips below if something does not come immediately or easily to you at the beginning. These three aspects of a card are modelled from their use in real tarot readings as readers structure a story or narrative from the cards.

### Example

The 3 of Cups is the *challenge* of meeting new people, the *resource* of friendships and a *lesson* that being open to new experiences brings rewards.

*Illus. The Three of Cups as Challenge, Resource and Lesson.*

## TIPS

If an idea does not immediately spring to mind, move onto the next card.

To consider the *challenge*, imagine how the image of the card would be an obstacle in a hero's journey.

To consider the *resource*, imagine you could plug yourself into the card and draw energy from it - what sort of positive energy would it give you?

To consider the *lesson*, imagine if the card was an illustration in the back of a book for the final chapter, which gave the lesson of the whole story. What would be the sentence or cliché?

- II -

THERE IS NO SUCH THING AS AN ACCIDENTAL ORACLE.


The Tarot is a Connection and a Communication.

It provides us a glimpse of a living mystery.

Everything is oracular when we are in connection with our universe
through our own unique experience & knowledge.

So, every event is a communication.

Remember then, from the very beginning, that a tarot reading is one
glimpse - in that very moment - of an infinite number of connections.

This will never be any different, from the beginning to the end.

### Practice

There are 1.2 Trillion possible combinations of seventy-eight Cards in ten
Positions of the Celtic Cross.

To put that in perspective, if you worked through one unique combination
of the Celtic Cross every second without repeating yourself, it would take
approximately 32,000 years to lay all possible combinations out.

Think about that.

It is likely when we perform a Celtic Cross 10-card reading with 78 cards,
not one human being - ever - will come across that exact spread of 10 cards.
Not ever.

We have only had Tarot on the planet for about 300 years, and if we
imagine since then, even if 1,000 readers every day are laying out at least one
Celtic Cross, and none have been the same so far, that's only 109 million
combinations – 109,000 days with 1,000 spreads a day.
That is only .009% of the total number of combinations.

Your Selection and layout of cards is most probably an utterly unique
moment in the universe. Really.

You (and your client) may be the only human being to ever see that particular combination of cards when you lay out a 10-card (or more) reading.

So …

Today, we do one simple task – before we even get down to 'interpreting' or 'reading'.

Shuffle. Take ten cards from your deck.

Lay them out in any way you like, Celtic Cross or in a line, a cross, a triangle – anything.

Just spend today contemplating the uniqueness of your cards.

You do not have to "read" the cards, look at them particularly (unless you want to - they may have a message) - just lay them out.

We may come back to these cards over the next three weeks, so just in case, make a note of them or take a photo.

However, whilst you think about this – do one more thing – see if you can apply that realisation of uniqueness to as much as possible in your life today.

You may wonder at your uniqueness. At the combinations. At the singleness of each moment. And perhaps, you may become aware of connections.

And even, a communication.

## TIPS

Be aware all day of obvious things – a found item, a chance encounter, an overheard word, a weird triviality, a line from a song, a radio, a gift, a meme

…

## - III -

### Tarot is a Connection to Meaning.

The Tarot is a Blank Bible.

It provides an illustrated interpretation of all experience.

Every reading is connected to every event.

So, we can use tarot as a reminder of our own connection.

Remember then, from the very beginning, that the tarot is telling you something just by its existence in the world.

This will never be any different, from the beginning to the end.

### Practice

We return to our simple practice today.

Shuffle your deck, thinking of the word "connection".

When you feel ready, select out three cards.

Lay them out face down in a line, left to right.

Do not look at the cards.

We take these three cards as an illustration of our connection to the world.

Turn over the first card, saying … "My challenge in connecting to the world is …"

Interpret this card as a challenge.

Turn over the second card, saying … "However, I have the resource of …"

Interpret this card as a resource.

You can also say "This card shows me what I can draw upon and it is telling me I can draw upon …"

Turn over the third card, saying … "And when I do so, I will learn the lesson of …"

Interpret this card as a lesson.

Say whatever comes to your mind, even as an absolute beginner - use the tips below if something doesn't come immediately or easily to you at the beginning.

## Example

"My challenge with connecting to the world is … in trying to contain my emotions".

[I looked at the fish in the cup on the Page of Cups]

"However, I have the resource of … being willing to change when it takes me forwards".

[I see the Wand held by the Knight of Wands, who appears more mature than the Page of Cups and prepared to look to where he is going]

"And when I do so, I will learn the lesson of … Magic … which is being who I am, where I am, when I am, connected to the simple truth".

[I am looking at the Magician card, and those words came to me]

## TIPS

If words do not immediately spring to mind, say the sentence out loud. Imagine you can hear an imagined wise tarot reader in your own head or as if you were watching them read the cards on a TV show – what might they say?

It is OK if you change the words of the suggested sentences slightly, although consider why you have done so and what it offers you instead of the suggested words.

If you draw a complete blank, go back to the first Principle, and take time looking at other cards with the three key themes.
Then return to look at your reading.

These principles can be returned to many times, as they are designed so that you will always see something new in them each time.

## - IV -

## ALL READINGS ARE FOR YOURSELF AS THEY ARE FOR OTHERS.

The Tarot is a Means of Recognising Your Own State.

It provides a guide towards a more consistent, comprehensive, and congruent state.

Every card and combination is an image of your own existence in the world.

So, we can use tarot to see into our own life as we see into others – and our relationship to their life at that moment.

Remember then, from the very beginning, that the tarot is a powerful machine to engineer your life as much as it can change another's.

This will never be any different, from the beginning to the end.

### Practice

We continue with our simple practice today.

Imagine that you are reading for someone else – an imagined person we will call Alex.

Alternatively, find someone in your life with whom you can practice and has no particular expectations of your reading.

*If you are reading for a real person, ask their permission and share the reading with them.*

Shuffle your deck, thinking of the other person.

When you feel ready, select out three cards.

Lay them out face up in a line, left to right.

We take these three cards as a reading for the other person.

Look at the first card, saying … "Your challenge is …"

Interpret this card as a challenge for the other person.

Look at the second card, saying ... "However, you have the resource of ..."

Interpret this card as a resource which may not have been considered by the other person.

You can also say "This card shows you what you can draw upon and it is telling me that you can draw upon ..."

Look at the third card, saying ... "And when you do so, you will have the outcome of / avoid ..."

Interpret this card as an *Outcome* or *Outcome which will be avoided* depending on the card.

Say whatever comes to your mind, even as an absolute beginner - use the tips below if something does not come immediately or easily to you at the beginning.

Do not be concerned if you are unsure as to the meaning of each card – we will return to 'meaning' in the next lesson.

For now, get used to the idea and speaking as if you were reading for someone else, using the same approach that you have already practiced – nothing more.

In our next lesson, we will go around the cards in another way, continually deepening our readings; and so far, we are neither relying just on intuition, guesswork or learning static meanings – we are doing a bit of everything.

In fact, we are doing something totally different.

## Example

*Illus. Knight of Pentacles + Hermit + Ace of Swords.*

Cards: Knight of Pentacles + Hermit + Ace of Swords.

"Your challenge is to throw your seeds into fertile ground – which to me means that you have a challenge making money".

"However, you have the resources of a hermit – you know that you are on your own path and can give illumination to others".

"When you continue to stick to your own path and insights, you will have the outcome which is the sharp sword of clarity and then the bees will make honey from the roses".

"I take this to mean that your clear thinking will make you money – because you have stuck to your own path and not followed others".

## TIPS

Much the same as the previous lesson and …

If you are unsure whether the third card is an outcome or an outcome which will be avoided by meeting the challenge with the resources, then consider how the card looks compared to the other two cards.

If it looks more 'negative' then it is likely an outcome which will be otherwise avoided.

If it looks 'positive' we assume it is an outcome that will be attained by meeting the challenge in the manner suggested by the second (resource) card.

We say this because all readings are generated towards a positive outcome.

## Recording Your Reading

To record your tarot readings, you are encouraged to adopt a common key, as follows (from *Tarosophy*).

Minor cards: Label as the number and suit. For example; 7P, 3C is Seven of Pentacles, Three of Cups. You can label Aces as 1 or A, so 1C or AC would be Ace of Cups.

Major cards: Label as their Latin numerals. For example; III is The Empress, XVIII is The Moon.

Court cards: Label as abbreviation of type and suit, with Kn for Knight and K for King, to avoid confusion. For example; KnS is Knight of Swords.

Thus, ten cards in a Celtic Cross spread, in order, might be written as: AP, 4C, KnW, IV, 7P, 9P, QC, XVI, 5S, 4C.

So long as you are consistent in your layout and order, this is enough to record the reading with any commentary you wish to place upon it. Our example reading today would be recorded as KnP/IX/AS.

## Intermediate/Advanced Exercise

*In this fourth principle, we start to add optional exercises for those who wish to extend their practice.*

Consider how knowing this reading affects the way you think about the other person and their situation.

After you have read the cards as if for another person, consider and make a note of any situation in your own life where this reading would have applied to you.

- V -

THE ORACULAR MOMENT IS SACROSANCT.

The Tarot is a way in which truth speaks to power.

It provides a truth that is outside of oneself and in relationship to the real world.

Every symbol in the cards is a possibility of connecting to the sacred. So, we can use tarot as a divine system – a true divination.

Remember then, from the very beginning, that the tarot is neither church nor temple, priest nor priestess, but the moment in which we ourselves can hear truth.

This will never be any different, from the beginning to the end.

## Extended Commentary

*When we say that tarot is a way in which truth speaks to power, we mean primarily that it offers itself as a vehicle in which our own inner truth – the very nature of our relationship to the divine – can speak to the power of our own psyche. It is our psyche which is generated from this inner relationship and by means of the various processes of ego maintained in a state of necessary separation. The Tarot – like a living dream – like a ritual trance – like a vision or breakthrough following trauma – is a key which opens the portal of truth by its very existence.*

## Practice

We extend our method of interpretation today and add a new practice; that of ritual. We can have a day off if we want from reading the cards – we never want to force ourselves or make it difficult to read.

Now, by ritual we do not mean a complex ceremony but merely a simple practice, one which separates out the oracular moment.

This is not to say that every tarot card reading must be conducted in high rites or solemnity – quite the opposite. When we recognise the oracular moment is revealed in every moment, a light-hearted draw of a cereal box from a shelf can provide a meaningful message from the deities.

I most often recite this verse when I am shuffling my deck:

*In the divine name LAO, I invoke thee, thou Great Angel HRU, who art set over the operations of this Secret Wisdom. Lay thine hand invisibly on these consecrated cards of art, that thereby I may obtain true knowledge of hidden things, to the glory of the ineffable Name. Amen.*

It is from the Order of the Golden Dawn and the Angel HRU is also invoked in a particular piece during the consecration of the Vault of the Adepti. I see this Angel as particularly appropriate to Tarot and Divination because it is also called upon to assist our "spiritual perception" and rise beyond our "lower selfhood" into a state of divine union.

However, you can utilise any verse; even something as simple as "I shuffle these cards one, two, three/secret things they will tell to me".

Choose or create a short verse that you can remember and recite it several times when next shuffling your deck.

This may seem an easy exercise today, but consider this – firstly, you may want to take today to also practice another three-card reading – and secondly, in constructing a verse you are having to state how YOU see the cards working, what you feel they are for, how they work, and what you want to achieve.

Your verse is a sacred statement. It separates out your reading and your state into something different than the everyday.

## TIPS

Your verse will never be set in stone. It is just for now. You can change it as you make progress, and it reflects your deeper learning.

Consider it as a 'magical name' in a sense, that it represents your understanding of your current relationship to the divine in a single sentence or so.

Even the most mundane and obvious sentence or two can become an invocation:

"I shuffle these cards and connect to the divine/In doing so they will speak beyond time".

## Intermediate/Advanced Exercise

Lay out a three-card reading as previous lessons.

Look at the colours.

Look at the shapes and patterns.

Close your eyes.

Allow a sound to be generated for each card.

You can keep opening your eyes until you have the sounds.

Notice how they compare and contrast with each other – do they go up in volume, are they all quite different, do they smooth out or get more jagged?

Now run them all together in a sequence, one after another – each sound – making them go around faster and faster in your mind - until they begin to blur into one final sound or noise.

What does the final sound tell you?

What flow or story comes from the three individual sounds?

Tomorrow we return to card interpretation in much more detail.

## - VI -

TAROT IS THE LOSS OF FORGETFULNESS AND THE BEGINNING OF CHOICE.

The Tarot is a memorial of the soul.

It reminds us of both separation and unity through each illustration.

Every shuffle – in the very act - tells us that there is change and choice. So, the cards tell us to remember ourselves.

Remember then, from the very beginning, that whilst the question most asked is about relationship, the answer to every question is only always about relationship.

This will never be any different, from the beginning to the end.

### Extended Commentary

*The tarot should not be used to wallpaper our prison cell but as a map of escape. And when we say escape, we do not mean from life but rather escape from our forgetfulness. We are all always already connected to everything – we do not need to learn this, but rather learn to forget our loss of memory. Tarot provides us, from the very first reading to the very last, a keepsake of this truth.*

### Practice

We return today to the means by which we interpret tarot. Every card has what we call a "strange attractor" but is also "multivalent".

In simple terms, every card can mean anything, but each card tends towards one meaning rather than any other.

That is to say, the Three of Swords could possibly, in certain circumstances, in a reading, mean "love", "bliss", "a helicopter" or "smug satisfaction" (a keyword associated usually with the Nine of Cups) but it will tend to mean "separation", "sorrow", "an emotional cutting of attachment", etc.

The cards work because they can be interpreted in any way for any situation – the symbols are 'multivalent', having many possible meanings. But they also work because they each have specific meanings that they tend towards – their 'strange attractors', which they never meet so are never 'fixed' to that meaning.

If every time the Three of Swords came up you had to say, "you are heartbroken", or "you have been heartbroken" or "you will be heartbroken" and nothing else, we would be very stuck with our tarot.

It is just the way in which we see the world that has resulted in a stabilisation of a system with exactly seventy-eight elements in it divided into four sets of ten, four sets of four and a set of twenty-two.

It is seventy-eight because of the same reason that seventy-eight is the revolutions per minute (rpm) on old vinyl records – both result from the existing ratios of the entire universe as we interact with it.

The exercise for today is to take three cards from your deck – any three cards. No question, no reading, just take three cards out.

Look at the first one and interpret it as meaning "a type of greed".

Look at the second one and interpret it as "being something to do with sport".

Look at the third one and interpret it as "an upset child".

When you have an idea as to how you might word these interpretations, shuffle those three cards around and do the same exercise.

If you get the same card for the same interpretation, do it again, either consolidating your first thought or coming up with another angle.

## EXAMPLE

Cards: Ace of Pentacles + Nine of Swords + Fool.

*Illus. Ace of Pentacles, Nine of Swords & Fool.*

"The type of greed in the Ace of Pentacles is that of grasping the resources and seed of something, like owning the idea and not giving it to anyone else".

"The Nine of Swords pictures an athlete who has been injured and is facing despair that they cannot continue".

"The Fool is an upset child because he is going to throw himself to the ground to get attention".

[Interesting, I never saw the Fool as a card of "attention seeking" before.]

If I then shuffled them around and got the Nine of Swords as "an upset child", I might say "The Nine of Swords is an upset child who is refusing to go to sleep".

In this way, like weight-training, you will exercise an essential skill whilst also unconsciously installing the principle; that the cards are multivalent.

In Tarosophy, we would never expect a student to ask, "Which card means an unfaithful person?" We would expect our readers to be able to interpret every card in terms of aspects of "unfaithful person".

And yes – this way of teaching tarot is back-to-front to how you might have thought you would learn or have learnt in the past.

But each exercise is specifically designed to take your natural and existing skills (i.e., to interpret a picture as a symbol) and exercise them into essential practices before we add the "methods".

Then, you will already be ready for the method before you even know it.

"Skill up first!"

**TIPS**

Use your Verse whilst shuffling the cards.

Do not force anything, and even if your first thoughts seem a bit weird or not quite fitting, go with them until the next time round.

There is no singular answer to any of these questions or cards, but feel free to ask on our Facebook group for thoughts.[36]

**Make a note of the three cards as we will return to them later.**

### Intermediate/Advanced Exercise

Go back to the three cards you used in the exercise yesterday.

Perform the same exercise with those three cards.

If you want to exercise this skill further, take the Major Arcana and interpret each as an aspect of "you should *not start* the project".

Then go back and read each Major Arcana as a reason to *definitely start* the project.

---

[36] Search for 'tarot professionals' group on Facebook, or use this URL: https://www.facebook.com/groups/tarotprofessionals.

## - VII -

### BE CONFIDENT AND CONSIDERATE IN ALL READINGS.

The Tarot is both a map of our journey and the compass for its navigation.

It illustrates the characters, situations and patterns that arise through creation.

One card can change everything. Many Readings can be ignored.

So, the cards can be our constant companion on the Way.

Remember then, from the very beginning, to read the cards. Read them as well as you can, mindful of the moment and all moments.

This will never be any different, from the beginning to the end.

### Extended Commentary

*The act of reading tarot cards is a practice. As with any practice, it can come naturally, be taught and learnt, be improved and changed over time. Tarot is its own teaching and each reading teaches us more about reading as surely as it teaches something about life. As the Oracular Moment is Sacrosanct, so we cannot determine the impact of any particular reading. We should aim to be as comprehensive, consistent, and congruent as possible. We should not omit anything, be true to the cards and apply them to the situation as fully as we can. This means that we must therefore consider clearly how we deliver such information – to ourselves and to others. We do not second-guess the cards, but we can be thoughtful about our communication.*

### Practice

We turn today to how we read for others as well as ourselves. However, in the way of these Principles, we are also going to install a few ideas during the practice.

Ask the cards, "What is the most difficult but useful thing you can tell me at this time?"

Shuffle your Deck. Say your Verse.

Lay out three cards in the full knowledge that it may be difficult for you to hear the advice that the cards can offer you.

Allow the cards to sit with you all day. Do not try and read them deeply.

Listen to any first impressions or feelings but do not consider them to be the absolute answer. Spend time considering them. Do not rush. This is not a competition or a race. There is no correct answer, nor is the answer particularly important.

The important thing is to hold the emptiness and allow the cards to provide their answer within it.

Do not seek to *read* the cards – allow *them* to speak to you as you go about your way.

At the end of the day, return to your cards. If you have no answer, no problem. You have successfully completed the exercise by allowing the cards their time.

If you have an answer, no problem. Allow it to sit with you and decide what action you might take because of hearing a difficult but useful suggestion from your companion.

## TIPS

Having laid out the cards, walk away from them several times and come back to them. This is an exercise.

Turn them back face-down and turn them back up again.

Look at them one at a time and in pairs.

### Intermediate/Advanced Exercise

Repeat the same exercise in the same way but with a different question:

"What is the most difficult yet useful thing you can tell me about my relationship to … [choose a person or situation, or "money" etc.]?"

## - VIII -

### TAROT IS RECOGNISING RELATIONSHIP.

The Tarot is read through relationship between symbols and cards in the context of the situation.

It provides us metaphors which can be applied to both pulling apart a challenge and putting together resources for a solution.

Our own minds are pattern-makers as much as they are pattern-breakers.

So, a reading is a re-thinking of our relationship with the way in which we see the world and changes the way in which it is arising.

Remember then, from the very beginning, that you are engaging with the cards in relationship to the very highest and lowest principles no matter what is communicated.

This will never be any different, from the beginning to the end.

### Extended Commentary

*Taking time to read tarot is a form of meditation or contemplation. It is a form of mindfulness. It is a form of remembering our own presence and place in the universe. It connects to our deepest story and offers a recognition of our own relationship to the past and future. A reading places us, no matter how briefly, at the centre of our universe, present and correct. That we can see life through symbols and the metaphors of each card is a miracle in itself. It implies that life itself is a miracle, full of invisible connections that bind the universe together.*

### Practice

As we have now established several fundamental principles in our approach to tarot, we can start to look at meanings and interpretation.

It is important to understand first that the cards are multivalent and open to any interpretation before we even begin to look at 'meanings'.

The answer to "what does this card mean?" to any reader trained in Tarosophy is simply, "Possibly Everything".

We should quickly look at a few technical definitions as they apply to our approach; 'symbol', 'metaphor', 'meaning' and 'interpretation'.

*You can skip over this following semi-semantic analysis and discussion if you just want to get practising – but please do come back to it at some point.*

As far as this lesson needs it, a SYMBOL is found where we choose any part of a card and relate it to something else.

Examples: The figures falling from this tower are your old plans failing; the blue sky behind the Knight is your clarity in the future; the Crown is a symbol of Kether on the Tree of Life; the child is you, giving yourself the gift, which is excitement.

Sometimes a symbol points to another symbol, which in turn points to something in the situation. This is usually through *correspondence*; "the crown symbolises Kether on the Tree of Life which represents the highest ambition of the project".

A METAPHOR (in its simplest terms) is a collection of symbols which makes a story – which in turn, can also relate to the question or situation.

Example: turning seven symbols from the Five of Cups into a metaphor for a single emotion; The man in a dark robe, bowed down in contemplation, behind which are a particular number of cups, which are spilt, and there is a bridge, over a river, with a building on the other side of it ... is a picture of your disappointment.

A MEANING is a complex issue, but for the sake of our purpose, it is a reference to something abstract or real that applies to the situation.

Examples: This card *means* that the problem will be over swiftly; this symbol *means* you will not succeed if you continue to work alone; this reading *means* that you will be happy with your new relationship.

A card does not really 'mean' anything until we make a correspondence to the situation from the symbols and metaphors that are illustrated by the cards.

An INTERPRETATION is the activity or process of bridging the SYMBOLS and METAPHORS by giving them a MEANING in relationship to a situation.

Example: "I *interpret* this card, particularly due to the *symbol* of the toppling crown, and the overall *metaphor* of a collapsing tower from which people are ejected, as *meaning* (in this case, for your *situation*) that you will not succeed if you continue to work alone".

This is still all about relationship – relating symbols, relating cards to the world, relating our interpretation to situations.

Pick a card.

Look at it and think about – or write down - as many individual symbols as you can find.

Place a few of those symbols together as a metaphor and think about – or write down – what that might mean when applied to the world.

Take another card.

Do the same thing – recognise symbols and metaphors – apply them to a situation.

Now take any symbol or metaphor from one card and pair it with any symbol or metaphor on the other card.

What interpretation comes to mind when you try and sense meaning in the relationship of this pair of symbols or metaphors?

If it helps, consider it in the context of the question which is asked three times out of every five questions; "What can you tell me about my relationship?"

## EXAMPLE

### The Hanged Man

I see a figure hanging upside-down, an ancient Egyptian Ankh symbol, two flying fishes, and a whale under the sea.[37]

I also see a dragonfly.

---

[37] In this example, I used the Jolanda Tarot to provide a different range of symbols than the Waite-Smith Tarot.

Looking further I might see symbols in the cross of the tree, the eternity symbol of the rope, the leaves of the tree are green, and the figure wears red – colours and shapes, numbers and patterns are also symbols.

I interpret the figure as getting things the wrong way around and being stuck with a misunderstanding. I interpret the Whale as a big issue under the surface of the situation. The flying fish seem to be talking into the ears of the figure, so I interpret these as different pieces of advice from other people.

The whole metaphor of the Hanged Man I take as being stuck in a situation which whilst not negative, is deliberately ignoring advice or issues.

## Seven of Coins

A dog with his mouth open looks up at a rose bush. The background is with a lake and mountains. The plant has birds on coins as flowers and the rose blooms with a female face who sheds a single tear. The rose is thorny. The birds seem to be happy.

I take the symbol of the dog as a faithful companion. The rose is a symbol of love but also here is yellow and flowering with many different birds.

## Nine of Cups

A young woman reaches out to catch a falling star. A fountain is pouring water into eight cups from one large central cup. A crescent moon and stars are in the sky. The ground is cobbled with stones and mountains are in the distance.

I take the symbol of catching a falling star to mean that dreams are within reach. The fountain is a positive symbol because it is endlessly filling the cups. The cups are symbols of emotions, so are being fulfilled.

The whole metaphor is one of happiness, having good emotional satisfaction within reach.

## Six of Swords

A naked witch with a large hat rides a broomstick quickly across a background which is six swords. They have butterfly-handles. The butterflies appear to have eyes on their wings.

Four roses make a garland above the scene.

The symbol of the witch means to me that there is a rapid and natural progress being made in the situation. The swords are symbols of thought and have been placed in the background.

I take this as a metaphor for doing what comes naturally, going with the flow and not being caught up in logic or arguments.

### Nine of Cups + Six of Swords

I take the *shooting star* from the Nine of Cups and the *flying witch* from the Six of Swords. Together they both represent natural forces and very fast movement. I interpret them together as meaning "allowing things to happen in their own time, keeping a watchful eye, and welcoming what happens naturally will bring about fast progress".

I might further add a *commentary* on my *interpretation*, which is "... so do not force things, do not rush and do not make things more complicated".

### TIPS

Look up symbols in a good symbol dictionary or dream interpretation book; all symbols have common sources, usually based on the *attributes* of the objects.

The Sun is light and gives life to things, these are its natural attributes. So, we further attribute "positivity" and "growth" to it.

Another *attribute* is that it is at the centre of the solar system, so it becomes a *symbol* of the self, at the centre of our system of personality.

### Intermediate/Advanced Exercise

Intermediate or Advanced Readers will recognise this method as a variation on "pinpointing and bridging" which we developed for beginners and use in several books and our tarot training.

An intermediate/advanced exercise would be to lay out four cards in a square, and practice pairing symbols between each of the two pairs them, then pairing the two resulting interpretations to result in one overall interpretation.

## - IX -

## TAROT IS THE LEARNING OF A LIFETIME.

Tarot is responsive to change throughout our lifetime.

The questions asked of the most ancient oracles are the questions that are asked now and will be asked in a thousand years.

Tarot becomes part of the way we view life and the way we live it. So, we learn what life reveals in every card.

Remember then, from the very beginning, to discern the biggest picture and the smallest detail.

This will never be any different, from the beginning to the end.

### Extended Commentary

*This principle applies at every stage of learning tarot, from the beginner, to the experienced professional, to the enthusiastic with many years of passion. We should allow tarot to encourage our insight into the patterns that play out over a whole lifetime as much as we try and see detail in every symbol. In the asking of questions from ourselves and others, we begin to become aware of the similarity of behaviour and response despite the diversity of circumstance. If we continue to read tarot over decades, studying the distant past and proposing new futures, we are changed by it and our life is changed by it. In turn, this makes us a better reader, able to see beyond the present moment and into the bigger question.*

### Practice

One of the things we hear many tarot readers say after ten or twenty years – even thirty years or more – is that they still always have something more to learn about tarot.

So, whilst we can teach someone to read tarot in three minutes, or ten minutes, if we have time, it is like chess – the rules are simple, but the play is endlessly complex.

Today, take out the Hermit card from your deck.

The Hermit can represent Solitude.

Notice today the moments that you are by yourself.

Notice today the moments you are in company – of any sort.

Notice today when you feel alone even if you are with other people.

Notice today when you feel like you want to be alone or in company.

Notice today when you see someone else who is alone.

Notice today when you see a person in a crowd.

Learn to see the Tarot in your lifetime, learning every moment.

## EXAMPLE

I am presently writing by myself. I look out the window and see someone crossing a road, by themselves. Tonight, I will go to a Karate class and be with other people, but I will have to face my own individual limits and successes in training.

## TIPS

Be aware of the exercise as often as you can through the day.

However, if you forget, gently bring yourself back to it.

It is better to notice one thing properly than many things improperly.

### Intermediate/Advanced Exercise

Extend the practice to solitary items, objects, or even abstractions.

Consider a "single thought".

Consider how a tarot deck is a collection of seventy-eight cards, not just the Hermit.

Consider how you choose one apple from a box of many apples.

Consider how one word might change a life or shine a light on one particular thing previously lost in a confusion of many things.

Consider that a particular moment is unique amongst all moments.

Be the Hermit today in everything and see what you learn in living life through tarot.

## - X -

## ALWAYS CONTINUE TO DISCOVER MYSTERY.

Tarot is a Token of Mystery.

The cards are a play of fate, fortune, and destiny.

Tarot allows us to read our fate and turn it into our destiny.

So, we learn to incorporate and utilise whatever is happening in the moment.

Remember then, from the very beginning, to understand that every reading is the centre of a revolution.

This will never be any different, from the beginning to the end.

### Extended Commentary

*The 21 principles are given as core approaches to Tarot which provide a firm basis for individual study and practice. There is no end to the mystery of Tarot as it plays out in every life, and this 10th Principle can be taken with the 9th and 11th Principle for deeper contemplation. The student of the Principles may benefit from comparing different principles, taking them together in pairs and triads, etc.*

### Practice

Today, we will look at the Major Arcana. These are the big patterns that play out in our lifetime.

Sometimes they are so obvious that we might miss them, and they remain a mystery hidden in plain sight.

An example is that the twenty-one Principles of Tarot (and the Zero principle) are based on the Major Arcana.

Yesterday, for example, was the Principle of the Hermit (IX), "Tarot is the Learning of a Lifetime". Today is the Principle of the Wheel (X), "Always Continue to Discover Mystery".

If you start at the first Principle, corresponding to the Magician, you will now see how the Major Arcana themselves have given us these Principles.

A Mystery, in Plain Sight.

The Fool is the Overall Mystery so does not have a numbered Principle, but we will share that Principle when we get to the World, the 21st Principle.

So, today, we will look not only at the Principle but the Wheel card itself.

In the series of twenty-two cards, the Wheel is card ten, sort of half-way through the sequence – if we take the Fool out as an "unnumbered" or "zero" card.

The Wheel shows how patterns tend to go around in a circle.

Either side of the Wheel (10) we have the Hermit (9) which is ourselves on the road of life and Justice (11), the scales of balance.

The exercise today is to use the Major Arcana to uncover a pattern in our lives.

We tend to teach that due to their nature, the Major Arcana are quite obvious cards to interpret; by definition, we all mostly know what the "Devil" is, or what a "Lightning-Struck Tower" might signify.

Take out the twenty-two Major Arcana – the cards including the Fool and numbered, usually in Latin numerals, from I to XXI.

Shuffle them whilst thinking about your life and all its ups and downs.

Turn the deck of twenty-two cards face-up and carefully look through them until you find the Wheel.

Take out the Wheel and the two cards either side of it.

**Hint**: If the Wheel is at the top or bottom of the deck, take the card below/above it and the card at the other end of the deck.

Take a look at the two cards.

What might they tell you about the way in which you are stuck to a pattern?

What is that pattern?

Leave these cards out, as tomorrow we will look at them using the Minor Arcana.

If you want more keywords, please consult *Tarot Flip*, the book I personally use most when reading for myself.

It is the smallest book we have written, but the most powerful as it condenses thousands of real readings to work out what the cards usually signify in actual readings in real life.

It is the first book to take a massive survey of actual readings as the source of keywords, rather than make them up or copy them from other sources.

## EXAMPLE

The High Priestess and the Moon, either side of the Wheel.

*Illus. The High Priestess, The Wheel & The Moon.*

I first see that both cards have two pillars or two towers. The High Priestess can be most simply read as "Mystery" and the Moon as "Fear".

There is a pattern here of "fearing secrets" and both cards are aspects of the feminine.

In fact, the correspondence of the High Priestess is the Moon.

This is a personal and powerful lesson to see in the cards and it is generated by just three cards.

You may wish to practice and introduce it for your own clients if you read for other people.[38]

## TIPS

Consider how the Major Arcana arise in life. The Fool arises in every situation where you need to step into the unknown. This can happen from considering a job offer in another country to selecting a new cereal in the grocery store.

Big and Small. The Pattern is still the Same.

Consider the "spiral". How many times do we see that pattern? In a bathtub to a galaxy, in the way a roulette ball goes to the way we go around a problem until we face it.

Big and Small. The Pattern is still the Same.

## Intermediate/Advanced Exercise

Having received the two cards either side of the Wheel, look out for them in your life today as you did for the Hermit.

---

[38] See Marcus Katz, *Secrets of the Thoth Tarot Vol.I* (Keswick: Forge Press, 2018) for the core meanings of the Thoth Major Arcana based on Crowley's own life, work and Magick.

## - XI -

### APPLY THE LESSONS OF TAROT IN EVERY DAY.

Tarot is an application of wisdom in life.

Our readings allow us to look through the World.

Tarot shows us that every day is a challenge, a resource, a lesson.

So, we seek wisdom not only in the tarot but in life.

Remember then, from the very beginning, to see the way of wisdom in the cards.

This will never be any different, from the beginning to the end.

### Extended Commentary

*The Living Wisdom of Tarot, 'Tarosophy', is a set of principles and approaches to the methods of cartomancy. It takes the act of divination into everyday life and uses tarot as a language. As a result, we learn to see life as an active illustration of our connection to the divine. We learn to learn from life. Every day becomes an opportunity to make progress to a deeper sense of reality, a deeper presence.*

### Practice

In this exercise, we take the stuck and cyclic pattern we discerned yesterday and use it as a question back to the Minor Arcana.

Select out the forty Minor Arcana of the Deck.

Consider your two Major Arcana from the previous Wheel exercise and the way these illustrated a pattern in which you are stuck.

Ask the cards as you shuffle, "what one thing can I do today that will be a lesson in making progress from this presently stuck pattern?"

Or you can word it as you wish, such as "What can I do to escape this Wheel?"

Ensure that it is a "doing" question. The Minor Arcana are events and situations, relationships, and dynamics – they are things that happen or actions you take.

Select out one card.

Lay it face-up and take it as the first answer. What is it that is pictured for you to do?

Then allow another question to arise as you look at this card and consider its suggestion.

You may ask for more clarity, or warning, or a further "how exactly?"

Select a point on the card which symbolises your next question or strikes you as needing more explanation.

Imagine you are talking it over with a friend. Nothing heavy, just a conversation about something to do today.

Shuffle and take another card.

Lay it out on the first card, placing the corner on the part of the first card which you chose as representing your next question.

You can stop at this point or keep selecting cards, engaging in a live conversation with your Minor Arcana.

Do not forget that you are still working from the first question – "What can I do today …?"

When you have an answer with which you are happy and can do today, pack up your cards and go do it.

It may be, that whilst doing it or after, you realise something new about that revolving stuck pattern of the past – and how you can move on from it.

Perhaps it had something still to challenge you with, so you could grow.

Perhaps it hid a powerful resource when you look at it differently.

Perhaps it is now an important lesson as you see it in your past.

The Scales of Justice balance themselves in the everyday everything.

## EXAMPLE

Considering my cards yesterday, the High Priestess and the Moon, either side of the Wheel, I shuffle the forty Minor Arcana.

The first card I draw is the Five of Cups.

*Illus. Five of Cups.*

Briefly, this card says to me that "You should spend today thinking back to emotional losses to move on from the cyclic pattern".

I then look at the big black cloak on the illustration and feel how heavy it is.

So, I ask, "Is there any activity I can do whilst I do this thinking today?"

I draw the Ten of Pentacles.

*Illus. Ten of Pentacles.*

This card suggests I stay at home, perhaps talk to my family.

I see the small child holding the dog, and think, "OK, is there anything I should do for myself as well as talk to my family today?"

I draw the Ace of Pentacles.

*Illus. Ace of Pentacles.*

Ah. Spend some money. Not something I would have considered doing today.

I look at the open gate and ask, "On what should I spend some money today?"

I draw the Nine of Cups.

*Illus. Nine of Cups.*

Something nice to drink and perhaps something nice to eat with it. As a treat.

I can then carry on, but for now I have some things to do today. It already feels like a good thing to do – spend time talking to family, and not something I had planned to do today.

What will your cards suggest for you in response to your stuck pattern?

## TIPS

Allow the pictures to do the talking and keep it very simple.

Take the cards literally and then work from that.

Imagine them as a friend who knows a bit about you but doesn't really have a lot of time just now to talk to you other than offer something obvious.

### Intermediate/Advanced Exercise

Consider that you can do this reading method for any situation – select a Major Arcana card for the issue and do a two-card reading as yesterday in order to illustrate the situation. Then do a Minor Arcana reading as today in order to plot your way out of the situation.

Examples might include using the Blasted Tower to ask, "How can I regain perspective after a shock?", or the Emperor for "What issues are causing me to feel powerless?"

This method not only gives you the answer, but something to do about it.

## - XII -

### Seek to Find the Answer that is There.

Tarot is both the Answer and the Question.

In the cards we can enter a dialogue with the deepest patterns of our life.

Tarot allows us to gain a new perspective, as if from another source.

So, we should consider that the Universe is a process of Enquiry.

Remember then, from the very beginning, to ask the question.

This will never be any different, from the beginning to the end.

### Extended Commentary

*The graduation of initiation is signposted by the questions which remain to be asked – and answered. That which is asked is a marker of value, perspective, and identity, whilst also signifying present attachment. A tarot reading (or other divination) may be utilised to undo attachment, release identity, shift perspective and change value through action. We should aspire that anything less is a waste of an opportunity in a reading.*

### Practice

In this lesson, I provide a set of keywords and phrases to assist readers in the second half of this course, taken from our free Beginners Guide written under the pen-name Andrea Green.

The full booklet, *Tarot Keys*, containing these keywords and nine spreads to use as a beginner is available on the *My Tarot Card Meanings* site, along with a free course you can take which is delivered to you every day.[39]

As we have seen in the first half of these lessons, our aim is to be able to read any card in most any way – so these keywords are to be considered comparisons to any other meanings you ascribe to the cards, not as fixed meanings.

---

[39] My Tarot Card Meanings site at www.mytarotcardmeanings.com [last accessed 22nd April 2021].

## The Major Arcana

0.  Fool: Freedom, Inspiration, Risk, Adventure, Innocence.
1.  Magician: Success, Skill, Trickery.
2.  High Priestess: Intuition, subtle change, divine law.
3.  Empress: Harvest, natural growth, pregnancy.
4.  Emperor: Power, control, dominance, energy.
5.  Hierophant: Professional, advice, wisdom, revelation.
6.  The Lovers: Love, relationship, choice.
7.  The Chariot: Driving, ambition, control, force.
8.  Strength: Management, maintenance, equal relationship.
9.  The Hermit: Single person, loneliness, perspective, inspiration.
10. The Wheel: Luck, chance, cycles, habits, patterns, ups and downs.
11. Justice: Balance, Fairness, Right, Deserving, Rule.
12. The Hanged Man: Reversal, betrayal, lack of dignity.
13. Death: Transformation, change, moving to a new phase.
14. Temperance: Watering down, peace, diplomacy, mixing.
15. The Devil: Ignorance, attachment, secrets, darkness.
16. The Blasted Tower: Shock, sudden change, surprise, clearing away.
17. The Star: Vision, hope, guidance, seeking a direction, following.
18. The Moon: Changes, dreams, fear (unnecessary).
19. The Sun: Light, energy, power, growth, radiance.
20. The Last Judgement: Decisions, a calling, invitation, new life.
21. The World: Time, coming together, resolution, closing one door.

## The Minor Arcana

### The Suit of Pentacles

The Pentacles, disks or coins suit are all about the material things in life, be it money, resources or your time. They show us all the different stages of financial issues, from investing (Ace of Pentacles), saving (Four of Pentacles), through poverty (Five of Pentacles) to retirement (Ten of Pentacles).

- The Ace of Pentacles: Investment, Seed.
- The Two of Pentacles: Juggling, uncertainty.
- The Three of Pentacles: New skill, assessment, learning.
- The Four of Pentacles: Saving, holding, possessing.
- The Five of Pentacles: Holding back income, dispossession, poverty.
- The Six of Pentacles: Charity, give and take, work/life balance.
- The Seven of Pentacles: Review, assessment, taking stock.
- The Eight of Pentacles: Work for its own sake, constant labour, skill.

- The Nine of Pentacles: Things being good, but suffocating.
- The Ten of Pentacles: Stability, financial settlement, family.
- The Page of Pentacles: Contemplating a new project, planning.
- The Knight of Pentacles: Solid work, consistency, trust, steady action.
- The Queen of Pentacles: Nurturing, rewarding, holding.
- The King of Pentacles: Riches, Wealth, Reward.

## The Suit of Cups

The Suit of Cups are the dreamy, emotional aspects of our life, and all to do with relationships. All the cards show relationships, and lessons, but the Cups are specific; so, we have the partnership of the Two of Cups all the way to the happy family of the Ten of Cups.

- The Ace of Cups: Overflowing, abounding, joy, delight.
- The Two of Cups: Equality, partnership, meeting of hearts and vision.
- The Three of Cups: Celebration, party, support of friends.
- The Four of Cups: Missing a trick, being stubborn.
- The Five of Cups: Sorrow, loss, disappointment.
- The Six of Cups: Gifts, freely given, childhood, nostalgia.
- The Seven of Cups: Getting distracted.
- The Eight of Cups: Moving away from a long, outworn situation.
- The Nine of Cups: Smugness, satisfaction, accomplishment, showing off.
- The Ten of Cups: Family, Deserving, Reward, contentment.
- The Page of Cups: Novelty, surprise, creativity.
- The Knight of Cups: Vision, questing, on a mission.
- The Queen of Cups: Deep emotional understanding, contemplation.
- The King of Cups: Hidden depths, connection, wisdom.

## The Suit of Wands

With Wands, we look at our lifestyle; our ambitions and decisions in the world. They are like the walking staff that supports us in our journey in life, they show us our beliefs and intentions, that guide us in our behaviour. So, they are connected to the other suits, as they provide the foundations of all our thoughts (Swords), feelings (Cups) and actions (Pentacles).

- The Ace of Wands: Power, control, energy, will, direction, explosion!
- The Two of Wands: Planning, comparison, strategy.
- The Three of Wands: Setting things in motion, going ahead.
- The Four of Wands: Invitation, friendship, mutual benefit.
- The Five of Wands: Confusion, argument, re-arrangement.
- The Six of Wands: Success, but beware of pride, leadership.
- The Seven of Wands: Standing your ground, fighting off others.
- The Eight of Wands: Swiftness, movement, travel, news.
- The Nine of Wands: Holding fast, ignoring other opinions.
- The Ten of Wands: Overburden, responsibilities, overload.
- The Page of Wands: Journeying, adventure, following a calling.
- The Knight of Wands: Activist, doer, fiery passion.
- The Queen of Wands: Wisdom, experience, confidence.
- The King of Wands: Dignity, honour, living to one's word.

### The Suit of Swords

The Swords are the Suit of the Mind, all our thoughts and plans. As a result, they show us our worries, our concerns, and matters of knowledge and education.

- The Ace of Swords: Decision, cutting, black and white.
- The Two of Swords: Denial, holding off, avoidance.
- The Three of Swords: Separation, judgement, sorrow.
- The Four of Swords: Rest, respite, recuperation, removal.
- The Five of Swords: Putting arguments aside, regrets.
- The Six of Swords: Movement, assistance, travel.
- The Seven of Swords: Treachery, sneaking, underhand action.
- The Eight of Swords: Holding yourself back, an old habit of thought.
- The Nine of Swords: Pity, grief, sorrow, and worries. Not thinking through.
- The Ten of Swords: Pinning something down, everything out in the open.
- The Page of Swords: Watch and wait, spying the land before action.
- The Knight of Swords: Rushing ahead, entering the discussion.
- The Queen of Swords: Calm but swift action, decisiveness.
- The King of Swords: Wisdom of experience, applied to fair decisions.

In this exercise, shuffle the entire deck to ask a question – make the question a noticeably clear one and one which requires some action.

It does not matter if it is a very minor question, the most important thing is that it is a simple question that can be clearly stated.

## Example

What can I best do this weekend to most successfully finish [a specific thing]?

Shuffle and lay out five cards in a cross as illustrated.

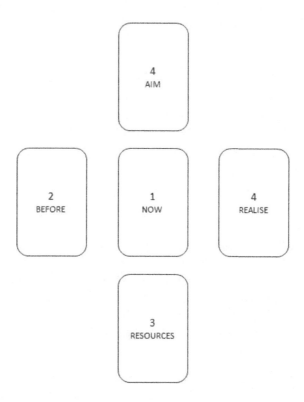

*Illus. Simple Cross Spread.*

Now read the cards individually as below, using your own or the suggested sentences.

Rather than give "positional meanings", in Tarosophy we give "suggested sentences" as every reader will be *saying* their interpretations, whether to themselves or other people.

Do not force the sentences together.

Take each one at a time, independently of the others.

1. The Centre card "In this centre card is pictured my current situation with [specific thing] and it seems to tell me that the most important/interesting/new/obvious thing about what is happening is …"

2. The Left card "The situation has developed because of what has happened before, which is … [read the left card or use the keywords]"

3. The Bottom card "I have the resources to draw upon to [subject of question, i.e., finish the specific thing] by following the advice of this card, which suggests …"

4. The Top card "In drawing on those resources, mindful of the past, and in the current situation, I should aim for … [read card as something that will be obvious when achieved]".

5. The Right card "And if I do so, I will realise that … [read card as a lesson, or perhaps a further challenge we can meet, or a resource that you can find for yourself in this situation].

Remember, take each card and each sentence one at a time.

**EXAMPLE**

I have mainly stuck to the keywords as given in this lesson and a little bit of additional interpretation of the specific illustrations and symbols in the cards, which I used in this case from the Jolanda Tarot.

1. Seven of Wands: In this centre card is pictured my current situation about the project and it seems to tell me that the most important thing about what is happening is that I feel as if I am fighting off a lot of unknowns – or perhaps I am attracting attention from dangerous animals? I have a light and a club, but am I ready?

2. Three of Wands: The situation has developed because of what has happened before, which is that things were set in motion. Perhaps it was originally done in a light-hearted, almost naïve, fashion? This is in the past.

3. King of Cups: I have the resources to draw upon, to be successful in the project, by following the advice of this card, which suggests drawing on my inner depths and wisdom – i.e., experience. This is rather than any other factors, I should stress my experience rather than anything else.

4. [Comparing cards 2 & 3 really says "it is time to grow up about it"]

5. Devil (XV): In drawing on my experience, mindful that I need to be more serious, and in the current situation where I feel overwhelmed, I should aim for dispelling ignorance, banishing shadows, and putting everything utterly out in the open. Be a devil for good!

6. High Priestess (II): And if I do so, I will realise that things have changed over time, and that there is a spiritual progress already in motion that will be fulfilled in this project.

I can then spend time comparing and contrasting the cards, particularly positions 2 & 5 and 3 & 4. I may smooth over the sentences too and weave them more together as whole.

## TIPS

Use everything you have learnt already.

Feel free to go back and look at any previous principle or all of them.

Have several goes at it if you want.

Take all the time you want.

Word it however you want.

Allow things to not make immediate sense.

Seek only to find the answer that is there.

## Intermediate/Advanced Exercise

Look at the card that remains on the bottom of the pile once you have laid out the five cards.

Take this as an illustration of what is really going on underneath the whole situation – the real answer to the whole question.

How does it work with the five cards – is it confirmatory or conflicting?

## Example

Base Card – Five of Cups: This situation has put me in touch with something powerful in the past which was disappointing. I do not need to take that into the new situation other than as a challenge to enjoy myself in comparison to the past.

## - XIII -

## LEARN TO HEAR THE REAL QUESTION.

Tarot is a matter of life and death.

In a reading we can discern more questions from every card.

Tarot opens the gates to universal truths transcendent of space and time.

So, we should honour the question.

Remember then, from the very beginning, to listen and listen again.

This will never be any different, from the beginning to the end.

### Extended Commentary

*The 12th Principle and 13th Principle are coupled together, reminding us to ask the question and seek the answer. To listen to - and to speak - the truth of the matter. It appears obvious that we should ask a question and divine the answer, however, in this very process are the real questions; How does the Universe work to allow this? Why am I doing this? What does this tell me about the Universe? The real question under every question is "Am I Real?" but even this too changes from level to level of the spiritual journey. The enquiry undergoes transformation as we die to our old selves in each question – and each answer.*

### Practice

When we conduct a reading, we can also use the cards in many ways to explore the original question. This is the case even if the question is "Can you do me a reading?" or "What is it I most need to know at this time?"

An important way is to turn the question into a spread using 'Clean Language' – a form of therapy developed from the work of the late David Grove.

The concept of Clean Language in Tarot was first introduced in *Tarosophy* (2011) and this specific method first published in *Tarot Face to Face* (2012), now republished as *Practical Tarot Techniques*.

When someone expresses their question, it usually has an emotional content, and this can be turned into a *metaphor* – then a spread - by a specialized but straight-forward series of clean questions.

It takes less than a minute or two, and then you have a precise metaphor of the question against which to design your spread – right there and then on the table.

This provides a powerful reading for the client because it uses their own model.

The sequence of questions is as follows, with the essential sequence highlighted in bold:

Querent: My question is X [including some emotional content, such as "and I'm concerned that I may not make the right choice"]

Reader: ... so, *I'm concerned* [saying it exactly like the client]. **Where is** your concern?

Querent: In my stomach [or Querent will gesture unconsciously even if they say "I don't really know"]

Reader: ... in your stomach. **Is it outside or inside**? [you will likely already know from the way the client has moved or gestured, etc.]

Querent: Inside, in the pit of my stomach.

Reader: ... inside, in the pit of my stomach [always repeat what client has said exactly]. I'm wondering how you'd best **describe the size** of that? [not 'describe it' but 'how best would you describe ...']

Querent: Well, it's hard to say, it feels tight and small.

Reader: Tight and small, and **what shape** is it?

Querent: I guess it's about the size of... [makes a gesture like a small ball].

Reader: ... And so it's the size of [makes same gesture] **And that's like what?**

Querent: It's like a clenched-up fist, that's what.

Now we have a metaphor, the "clenched-up fist".

We simply use this as a spread, saying something like, "let's use that as a spread – suppose I lay out five cards to represent the five fingers on your hand. These will tell us what is holding the anxiety in a fist in your stomach.

Then I will lay out five cards on top of those cards to show you how you can release that anxiety and make the right decision. In fact, I will place one card down after that, in the palm of your hand – because you hold the answer in your own hand".

These readings will likely replace any given 'spread' as you get practiced with them, because they are so powerful and speak to the client's deepest representation of their question.

To recap, the questions are, in this sequence:

WHERE IS … [abstract emotion or concept]?

IS IT INSIDE OR OUTSIDE?

WHAT IS THE SIZE?

WHAT SHAPE IS IT?

[Optionally, also, what colour is it?]

AND THAT'S LIKE WHAT?

You will see that the specific order gives the client no way out of ignoring or not answering the next question. If you have a feeling, it must be somewhere. If it is somewhere, it must be inside or outside. If it is inside or outside, it must have a size. If it has a size, it must have a shape. If it has shape, it must be like something else – which is the symbol or metaphor for the original feeling.

## TIPS

You can frame the questions in any particular way, following the Querent's own language. The faster you do it, and the more you pay attention to their whole communication, including non-verbal gestures, the more noticeable it will be that the question suggests its own spread in response.

## Beginner Method

The method given with this principle might be considered intermediate/advanced – if you would like to apply the principle as an absolute beginner, start with this alternative method.

When pointing out any symbol in a card, say it out loud and ask the client – or yourself – "…and that's like what?"

It will help you (if it fits your particular style of reading) discover more, with the client, of their actual situation and question.

## Example

Reader: "So, the Trumpet in the card … and that's like what?"

Client: "Ah, I guess it's like an alarm clock".

Reader: "And what do we think it is waking you up to?"

## - XIV-

## YOU DO NOT NEED TO KNOW EVERYTHING.

Tarot is an imitation of life in as much as life is an imitation of reality. In a reading we can see the map laid out, but it will always be incomplete.

Tarot allows us to make a map of the map.

So, we might wonder from every reading, what new land has been revealed.

Remember then, from the very beginning, to look as far as you can, knowing that you cannot see everything.

This will never be any different, from the beginning to the end.

### Extended Commentary

*There is always something new to learn in that the universe is a process of radical enquiry. The landscape of the soul is revealed in relationship to reality through the illustrations of the tarot. It neither predicts nor prescribes, it is only a presumption. At the very least, the cards offer us a constraint, a check and a challenge. They may highlight the resources and signpost us to the lessons. But it is up to us to travel, to do, to act, to go. There is a reason there are twenty-one principles and not twenty-two; sort of.*

### Practice

Today we have several simple practices which are recommended to be done quickly and in sequence, without too much preparation.

As we do not need to know everything, and some things will always be tempered by our ability and experience, we can simply practice for fun.

### Exercise 1

Shuffle Your Deck, thinking, "Tell me something funny".

Select a card. Look at it, note it, perhaps consider what it is saying.

Return it to the deck and carry out exercise 2.

## Exercise 2

Shuffle your Deck, passing it from one hand to the other like a flow of water.

Think, "What is best and what is worst right now?"

Take two cards, top and bottom and look at them.

Note them.

Perhaps consider whether they answer the question immediately.

Compare whether they are Court Cards, Minors or Majors, and if that tells you anything else immediately.

Return the two cards to the deck and carry out exercise 3.

## Exercise 3

Shuffle your Deck, passing it from hand to hand.

Think, 'What is a Question I have not Asked and What is the Answer'?

Select the top card from the deck and consider it as a question.

Is it one you had not thought to ask?

Turn the deck upside-down and look at the bottom card.

Consider it the answer.

Does it answer the unthought question?

## Exercise 4

Shuffle your Deck, considering that we sometimes have two conflicting parts of ourselves.

Turn the cards over one at a time until you have a Court Card.

Lay out the Court Card and continue turning the pile until you have a second Court Card.

Lay the two Court Cards side by side.

Look at them during the day.

At night, consider both of them before you go to sleep.

Perhaps consider them in a relationship. What would that be like?

Record any dreams in the morning or your general feeling when you look at the two cards in the fresh light of the morning.

Notice any changes in your own attitude or behaviour – no matter how apparently insignificant or obvious – during the day.

Also notice any strange occurrences.

## TIPS

Perform these exercises as a flow and as play, whilst remaining aware they can be powerful and significant.

### Intermediate/Advanced Exercise

Continue to shuffle.

Think, "Tell me a New Exercise that I could do with the Tarot".

Draw 2 Cards and spend time developing a whole new way of working with your cards from the suggestion of the two cards.

You can draw a third card if required for further inspiration.

This method produced the Fourth Exercise.

## - XV -

## EVERY READING IS AS IMPORTANT AS EVERY OTHER READING.

Tarot is the story of everyone as told by someone.

It is also the story of someone told by everyone.

A Tarot reading can be the most important thing that someone ever ignores.

So, we might never know (as with everything) the full consequence of our cards.

Remember then, from the very beginning, to treat every reading with respect.

This will never be any different, from the beginning to the end.

### Extended Commentary

*The first reading that ever tells you something should stop you ever reading again until you have come to terms with the consequence of the working of tarot. If it works, then what does it tell you about yourself, the universe, time, space, and the relationship of these things? What does it suggest as to the notion of purpose, of free will, of fate, fortune and destiny? How does it work to reflect all possibilities in one deck? Every reading engages in this fundamental act of enquiry; what is possible? And, most importantly above all considerations, every reading is the possibility for initiation.*

### Practice

In this exercise, we look at the final set of cards in a deck, the Court Cards.

There are many ways of working with Court cards, which we have cover in our books.

In these Principles, we will return to the key concepts introduced in *Secrets of the Waite-Smith Tarot* with additional material.

## RANK

Page: Unformed (make a start of …)
Knight: Directed (make a movement towards …)
Queen: Experienced (recognise the experience of …)
King: Established (work with the establishment of …)

## SUIT

Pentacles: Resources (finances, time, health, family)
Swords: Thoughts (education, learning, mind, logic, speaking, communication)
Cups: Emotions (feelings, intuition, depth, unconscious, unspoken)
Wands: Ambitions (will, direction, spirituality, lifestyle)

To practice with the Courts, select out the sixteen Court cards into a separate deck.

Shuffle whilst thinking "What do I need to know today about relationships and people?"

Select one card.

Look up the key concepts by Rank + Suit.

Make a sentence as an answer to your question, modifying the words and grammar if necessary.

Then – and most importantly, extend your *interpretation* with *commentary*, by saying "Today I will …" and decide on one particular action or attitude that you will take today.

## EXAMPLE

*Queen of Cups*

(I) Recognise the Experience of (that which is) Unspoken.
Today I will, at least once, speak something that has remained unspoken.

## TIPS

Ensure that the action is something that you can do and has an observable action or impact. Rather than "I will be happier" state "I will watch at least one comedy video" or "make one person smile".

Visualise the card when you take the action.

### Intermediate Exercise

At the end of the day, consider not only how the card related to your action but also the results and consequences of that action, particularly if it involved another person or people.

How would you see them in terms of court cards?

### Advanced Exercise

Consider that this 15th Principle corresponds to the Devil (XV) card of the Major Arcana. What does the Devil mean in the context of personality and people?

How might this exercise reveal something about the 'shadow', an *attribute* of the Devil?

## - XVI -

### PREPARE TO FACE TEN THOUSAND READINGS.

Tarot is a dynamic engagement with every situation in time.

When we read for others or ourselves, we re-align ourselves to the present moment.

Tarot teaches us that time is the moving likeness of eternity.

Time is a Tower that is endlessly building and collapsing.

Remember then, from the very beginning, that every reading, time and again, is a reminder that you are present.

This will never be any different, from the beginning to the end.

### Extended Commentary

*The secret of tarot is time. All our creation is bound by the process of time and a reminder that we transcend it in every moment. The mystical teaching of tarot can be discovered in every reading, even if we have to conduct ten thousand readings to see the truth of the matter. At some point, we will know that every reading is one reading, endlessly infinite and constantly unified in change. This realisation is like the lightning that strikes the place of the divine and releases us from our illusion.*

### Practice

Shuffle Your Whole Deck.

Consider any situation for which you would like clarity.

Draw out four cards and place them face-down in a vertical line starting at the bottom.

### Part 1

Turn over the lower two cards (1 & 2).

Read the lower card (1) by saying "I see this situation from my own point of view as …"

Read the second, upper card (2), saying, "However, other people see this situation as …"

Compare the two cards – are they very similar *interpretations* or very different?

How does this explain how people are behaving about the situation?

How does it explain why you are receiving the feedback and responses you want or do not want?

What might you say as a *commentary* on these two cards and their comparison?

## Part 2

Turn over the upper two cards (3 & 4) – only having read as much as possible in the lower two cards.

Read the lower of these two cards (3) by saying "My major attitude about the situation which is not necessary is …"

Read the card as a *distracting hope* if it is generally positive in nature or a *distracting worry* if it is more negative.

Either way, it illustrates something that should now be dropped or released in some way.

Offer a commentary on how this attitude (whether a useless, unrealistic and misguided hope or a depressing, anxious, worry) might be utilised.

Read the uppermost card (4) as an outcome by saying, "So, the outcome will be …"

Interpret that card as a natural consequence of the insights gained from the previous three cards.

Does it offer a warning or a result? Either way, it is the necessary information to be communicated at this time.

Take a moment to look at all four cards and their relationships.

Do you have several Court cards?

## TIPS

Always go back to first principles if you want by using the keywords or the words you chose for challenge/resource/lesson.

Always look at the cards.

Allow yourself to read them as pictures in a book.

## EXAMPLE

### 1 & 2

I see this situation from my own point of view as a lesson [Hierophant]

However, other people see this situation as something I am driving [Chariot].

Commentary: I realise from the difference of these two cards that I need to show more responsibility and accept my agency. That it is not just a lesson for me – it impacts others. Also, that I should share what I am learning with those involved.

The fact that the two cards are Major Arcana shows this situation is a pattern that plays out in other areas and times of my life beyond the present situation and question.

### 3 & 4

My major attitude about the situation which is not necessary is working without reward [Eight of Pentacles]. The outcome will be a fruitful blessing that will grow naturally and with bounty [Empress].

Commentary: Whether I worry about the work and effort or not, the outcome is one which will be rewarding given time. I should also allow it to take a natural course. I can follow the advice that arose from cards 1 & 2 and take the reins that belong to me, as a major lesson in my life.

## Intermediate/Advanced Exercise

You can now read a Celtic Cross.

If you go back to Exercise XII (12) and add this Exercise XVI (16) you will see that we have now learnt the whole Celtic Cross.

Go back to the very first layout of ten cards in Exercise II (2), "There is No Such Thing as an Accidental Oracle" and lay them out in a Celtic Cross if they were not already in that layout.

Read your reading from Exercise 2 using Exercise 12 & 16 and you may now see that there is indeed, no such thing as an accidental oracle.

All is planned to the pattern and you are now prepared to face 10,000 (or more) readings.

In our final five lessons XVII (17) – XXI (21) we will explore further methods for you to put all the principles into your ongoing practice beyond this section of the present book.

## - XVII -

### SPREADS ARE FOR BEGINNERS. LATER, ONE READS ONLY THE CARDS.

Tarot is a lyrical language of the soul's encounter with the Universe.

It arises freely, and like the most dignified dance, allows us to express ourselves in motion to the music of the divine.

The re-arrangement and reading of the deck is as sacred as the most religious ritual or act of love.

Remember then, from the very beginning, to Treasure it. Trust it. Let it divine you.

This will never be any different, from the beginning to the end.

## Extended Commentary

*The tarot deck itself is a sacred artefact. It is a place-holder for our encounter with what we do not yet know in life. As such, when we lay it out in a fixed spread, we constrain it within our own choice and expectation. We assume that we know which spread will be suitable to our situation. Having said that, the oracular moment is sacrosanct, so it likely matters not at all whether you choose a spread.*

*In Tarosophy we seek to follow our cards with one essential attitude; curiosity. This means that sometimes, we will simply read the cards in some manner that does not involve any fixed spread or positions.*

## Practice

In this lesson we will work with one of the many Tarosophy split-deck methods, which goes beyond basic spreads but is easy to perform as a beginner.

We call it "Oracular Sentences" and is good for practice, self-reading, and particularly parties – it is one of the methods for practical readings we cover in *Tarot Face to Face*.

Divide your deck in advance into three piles; Majors (22), Minors (56) and Court cards (16).

Place these three separate piles face-down from left to right on your chair, table or other space available.

These three piles will form the structure of an "oracular sentence" composed of a noun (object), a verb (action) and an adjective (a description).

You may wish to practice this method and then play with your own variations.

Pause and then select the top card from the first pile of Majors.

Turn it upwards and say, in your most oracular voice the name of the card. If for example, you turn over the "Empress", simply say "The Empress".

If you are moved in the moment to say something else, do so – however try and ensure it is a noun, an object, or a thing that you can see on the card, for example, "The Field", or "The Waterfall".

Never deny an oracular moment, always say what tells true to you.

Now select a card from the second pile of Minor cards.

This card is the 'verb' of our Oracular Utterance. This card says what the previous noun or object is doing.

As an example, if we pulled the Two of Swords, we might say "balances" or "weighs up" or even "waits".

Add this verb to your noun and say it out loud, clearly, and deliberately, for example:

"The Empress weighs up…" or "The Waterfall waits …"

Finally select the top card from the third pile of Court Cards.

This gives you the adjective or *descriptive* word for how the verb (action) is being performed, for example, if you pulled the Page of Swords, you might describe this as "carefully", "cleverly", "thoughtfully" or "cautiously".

You can now utter the full oracular sentence in your best soothsaying voice:

"The Empress Weighs up Carefully…"

At this point if you feel moved to do so, add any poetic or divinatory statement, such as:

"The Empress Weighs up Carefully … so be aware that whatever you sow you shall reap".

And that is it. Do not interpret or explain your oracle, even to yourself.

If you do not add any commentary, that is fine too, just state it as a succinct oracle, perhaps stressing a word, such as "The Field Waits Cautiously. That is your oracle. Remember, this is important – The Field WAITS cautiously".

It is meant to be mysterious and enigmatic – but nonetheless, it may be immensely powerful (in *Tarot Face to Face* we share one of many events where this method totally hit home with someone and shocked them into insight).

## TIPS

Make sure you speak in an over-the-top or simply deliberate oracular voice, even if you are doing this method for yourself.

### Intermediate/Advanced Exercise

As an advanced version of this method, when you have practiced your oracular sentences arising from three cards, you can perform this reading by taking the top cards as already described, then adding a "BUT …" and taking the bottom card from each of the three piles and adding that sentence as a prophetic warning or advice.

## EXAMPLE

The Wheel of Fortune + 3 of Wands + Page of Wands.

BUT …

Temperance + 6 of Pentacles + Queen of Pentacles.

*Illus. The Wheel of Fortune, Three of Wands & Page of Wands.*

*Illus. Temperance, Six of Pentacles & Queen of Pentacles.*

## ORACLE

The Centre Looks Out Earnestly
but
The Angel Measures Materially.

Spoken out as:

*"Your Centre may look out earnestly, but your Angel measures you materially".*

## - XVIII -

## LEARN THE MEANINGS WITH PRECISION, READING IS ANOTHER MATTER.

To learn tarot is to learn life.

In life, as tarot, we continuously strive to recognise rules and patterns for prediction based on our observation and experience.

The meanings of each card, whilst multivalent, tend to specific core meanings.

We learn upwards from the core meanings and downwards from connecting the cards to life.

Remember then, from the very beginning, to know what the cards mean and be able to justify your interpretation.

This will never be any different, from the beginning to the end.

### Extended Commentary

*We have seen that cards can mean anything even if they tend to mean something specific. In learning and practising tarot, we experience a constant process of connecting meaning to events and those same events inform our meanings. If we continue to read for many years, perhaps even maintaining and reviewing a journal, we develop a new faculty; predictive hindsight. This is the ability to know and say what you would say about a reading after the situation had developed following the reading itself. The skill is to be able to know what you (would have) will say later and say it before – at the time of the reading.*

### Practice

There is a simple practice for today.

It is to break us out of ever thinking that the meanings of the cards are either beyond our interpretation or fixed in some particular manner.

Shuffle your deck.

Take a card.

List in your mind or write out possible keywords to describe the card, in this specific way:

Start with one Keyword or phrase beginning with the letter A.

Then think of another keyword beginning with B.

Then C.

Then D.

And E ...

That is all for today.

As with many exercises in the approach of Tarosophy, it may appear simple, but it installs a different way of thinking about your cards.

Obviously, do not be too concerned about key-words beginning with Q or Z, etc. or if you find yourself using Q(uest) or any other word for more than one card.

## EXAMPLE

*The Ace of Pentacles.*

*Affluence.*
*Bargain. Beginning.*
*Coin. Cash.*
*Design.*
*Economy.*
*Finance.*

...

## TIPS

Use a dictionary or thesaurus. These are essential tools for a good reader.

### Intermediate/Advanced Exercise

If you come up with more than one word beginning with a particular letter, also make a note of it.

Another good exercise – particularly for beginners - is to look through one Suit of cards at a time, or the Majors, and close your eyes before sleep and try and visualise every card in sequence.

Then see how your visualisation compares with the real cards and keep practising each night until you can run through the entire deck in your mind.

## - XIX -

## SEE THE SPACES BETWEEN THE CARDS.

Tarot is as much about silence as it is about speech.

In a reading there are spaces that make up the spaces outside of the lines.

Tarot shows us not only a map of the land but of the people, the politics, the names of the places as they were and are and will be known.

So, we might see that we can look between the cards and through them, as much as we can look simply at them.

Remember then, from the very beginning, to recognise the vast space that awaits beyond the edges.

This will never be any different, from the beginning to the end.

### Extended Commentary

*There is an idea in art that one can draw a shape, such as a horse, by imagining not the horse itself but the outline of it as being a coastline of the space that is not the horse – the space around the horse that forms in the middle as you draw the lines of the space. This perspective applies as much to tarot as to any situation. What cards are not present in a reading? What Suits are missing? Why did the Court card that most applies to the most significant person in the situation not turn up at all? Ask not what you are missing or have got "wrong" but what the silences and spaces are shouting to you.*

### Practice

In this practice, as we approach the conclusion of the Tarot Principles, we provide a method for daily practice.

I do not teach "one card of the day" as I find it slow and limits the student in later years.

Rather, practice this spread in the morning and review it in the evening.

It is called the Dawn Spread (designed in 1983) and was introduced in *Tarosophy*.

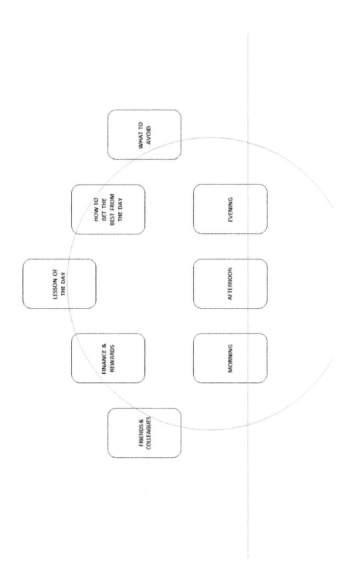

*Illus. Dawn Spread.*

Simply use this spread for your ongoing practice and review.

## TIPS

The practice of this spread will increase your ability to interpret every spread or method for other people.

### Intermediate/Advanced Exercise

In *Tarot Twist* (2013), we published the Sunset Spread, a companion spread for additional use as an evening review once the student has become comfortable with the Dawn Spread.

They can be used together, or switch from the Dawn to the Sunset Spread as you find works for you.

An advanced way of reading the horizon and arch of the Dawn spread is given below, for those already familiar with it from *Tarosophy*.

The 3 Base cards (left to right):

Review – What is the basic lesson I can take from today?
Resolve – What do I need to do differently tomorrow?
Refine – What can I see now that I couldn't see before?

The 5 Arched cards (left to right):

Others – What have I learnt about those around me?
Environment – What have I learnt about the world?
Me – What can I say about myself now?
Problems – What is the nature of the challenges I face?
Solution – Where shall I look for solutions tomorrow?

- XX -

BE SERIOUS IN YOUR STUDY BUT INVENTIVE IN YOUR PRACTICE.


A Tarot reading requires five attitudes, but a sixth is the attitude that it requires whatever it asks.

These attitudes are:

### Congruency

*The attitude that connects the cards to the life of the client and provides messages that support each other and the client.*

### Flow

*The attitude of following the flow of the cards and the state which arises from their reading, generating a compelling narrative to the client.*

### Pacing

*The attitude which allows for information to be presented at the best rate for the client, allowing for pauses, repetition of key points and silences.*

### Intimations of depth

*The attitude which presents the meaning of the reading in such a way that it can be recalled, has impact, and opens many layers of inner activity and response.*

### Curiosity

*The attitude that reveals the whole universe is an act of enquiry, and the reading, the reader, and the client are all partaking of that enquiry in a simultaneous manner.*


We should aspire that our reading is true to the cards as it is to life; that the divination comes to us and is delivered in a powerful flow; that we recognise when to speak and when to hold silence; that we communicate the connection to all things in our narrative; and that we are open to the question as well as to the answer.

So, we might welcome every reading as an opportunity for practice.

Remember then, from the very beginning, to be curious – when we divine, we learn as much as we can teach – this is our calling.

This will never be any different, from the beginning to the end.

## Extended Commentary

*These five (six) attitudes were observed and collated from hundreds of readers at fairs, events, conferences, bars, parties, workshops, and gallery shows, online for free or for dollars per second, an open square in New Orleans and a forest in Switzerland. They were present in readers around a fire in Brazil as they were in a Youth Club in Singapore. They were present in an absolute beginner three decades ago and an experienced reader today. Above all though, we shuffle our cards to remind us that nothing is set in stone forever – we can adopt and adapt what works for us, even these attitudes. Of course, in doing so, we follow them.*

## Practice

Today's practice is our fail-safe method of reading the cards, to assist you in every reading.

Firstly, we know that we only read the cards – at least, in the beginning.

When we get stuck, we should just read the card – but there is more than that, and it is in Kabbalah we find a method which applies to all divination.

In Kabbalah, the system of Jewish mysticism whose Tree of Life diagram is familiar to most esoteric students, when one studies a sacred text, there are four levels of interpretation.

These also apply very well to Tarot:

1. *Peshet*, Simple.

2. *Remez*, Symbolic.

3. *Drosh*, Extended.

4. *Sod*, Secret.

## Level 1: Simple

The first level is the simple description of the text; its length, number of words, any key appearance of particular words and so forth. In Tarot this is the simple and literal description of a card. Try it with this card, starting sentences with "I see…"

[5 of Wands]

*Illus. Five of Wands.*

Notice that you might tend to drift up a level to the "interpretative" or symbolic level. You might say or write, "I see five men arguing" whereas what you actually see is only "five men holding sticks" – the "argument" is an interpretation of the literal images of the card.

## Level 2: Symbolic

The second level is this "symbolic" and interpretative level. This is the level where books of symbols can assist you and any text written by the artist(s) and/or designer(s) of the deck.

At this level we say or write, "On this card are five staves, symbols of the will or values of a person".

## Level 3: Extended

The third level is "extended" which in Kabbalah would look at other sacred texts, make comparisons, and put the studied text into a wider context. In Tarot we do this when we say such things as "So it is like a war …" or "This reminds me of the story of "The Three Little Pigs".

We even do it when we extend our interpretative level to the other person's life or our own; such as "So in your life this is those moments when you feel out of control or at a loss, two aspects of the same problem".

## Level 4: Secret

The fourth and top level is when we have those moments of connection or insight, intuition or conscious realisation and there is a certain sense of "fit" in the reading.

This is that "Aha!" moment, when in the case of this card above we might suddenly see, in context of the other cards in a spread, "So what is really happening is that your previous failures have led you to develop a bad habit, entirely self-destructive, where you never complete anything".

Which Way to Go When You Get Lost – DOWN NOT UP.

Now what happens when readers flounder – and we have watched many hundreds do so at one time or another – is that they always (almost always) go UP the levels of interpretation, usually straight to the symbolic or extended.

Readers start to flounder and generate flourishing metaphors and symbols, clichés, and sayings, such as "So here we can see that like the three little pigs, the wolf is not able to use his breath to blow the stone house down …" and so on.

This does not help the other person.

The best way to deal with a flounder or moment of confusion, is to go straight back down the levels to the absolute literal.

Face the card and let it face you – re-establish your connection on the basic level.

Simply describe what you are seeing in the card. Keep describing it. At some point you will start to naturally rise back up the levels, and there will have been no break in your reading. Also, you will have remained true to the cards.

As an example, one might start to flounder with the above card in a "future" position in a spread and so then start to re-describe the card:

"So … er … I am seeing these five men. They are bearing their staves. One man is looking away whilst the others are looking in other directions. The sky is white. The man looking away is perhaps the leader – ah – so I figure that one particular experience or value in your future is being turned away because of the blankness of your memory, you have forgotten something that is most important to you …"

And off you go again, back up and down the levels. So always remember when stuck, read the card.

Just before we leave this lesson, notice that the first letters of those Hebrew words spell out the word PRDS.

As Hebrew has no vowels, this may not be at first obvious as a word, however, it is the word *Pardes*, meaning "garden".

We are more familiar with it when pronounced and spelt "Paradise".

This is called in Kabbalah the "formula of Paradise" and is a way of opening the secrets of holy texts and re-entering Paradise.

As our Tarot is also, in a sense, a divine text, it is also a key to that same garden.

## TIPS

Read the Cards.

In Tarosophy, the use of Kabbalah underpins most of our techniques and teachings through correspondence, and we recommend further study.

## Intermediate/Advanced Exercise

When dropping down to the literal level, use lots of linking words:

and … then … so … when … as … because … with …

This will create a narrative flow and soon take you into the symbolic, extended and even secret levels of the reading.

## - XXI -

### TAROT IS TO ENGAGE LIFE, NOT ESCAPE IT.

Life is our Temple.

Heaven is Hid in our Images and we Abide in the Sanctuary.

We should use Tarot to Take Us Beyond Ourselves, not See in it an Endless Series of Selfies.

So, at last, we might come to realise that this World is the Answer we have always sought.

Remember then, from the very beginning, we are wayfarers, and our journey takes us to the very end, where we will switch off the lights together.

There is no Escape, simply an Everlasting Day.

This will never be any different, from the beginning to the end.

### Extended Commentary

*The most valuable knowledge has always passed through the most unlikely of hands. The secret can only be hidden in plain sight because it is so simple – tarot is the moving likeness of eternity; it is time in our mind made real. When we consider the past, present and future, we make images and these images are in the cards when we lay them out – past, present, and future. We remain, here and now, looking at the cards, perhaps waiting for revelation. Yet it is this. We are here. This is our temple. It is real.*

### Practice

Welcome to your final lesson of the twenty-one Principles of Tarot.

In Lesson III we used three cards to illustrate our connection to the World.

We now return to that method and add to it a timeline.

This is where we have been leading you, from the Empress (3) to the World (21).

For this reading we draw NINE cards and lay them out FACE DOWN in a 3 x 3 Square.

We first read the centre column. The centre column is the present, with the top card our challenge, the middle card our resource and the bottom card our lesson.

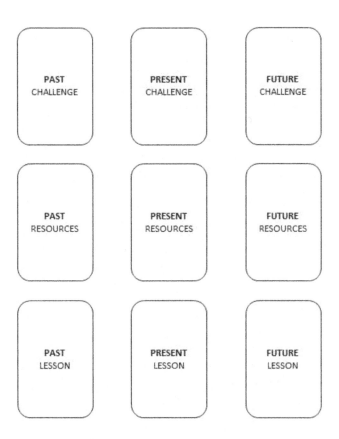

*Illus. Nine Card Grid.*

## THE PRESENT

We read these exactly as we did in the 3rd lesson. You can now go back and review all the lessons if you wish, before conducting this reading.

Turn over the first card, saying … "My present challenge is …"
Interpret this card as a challenge.

Turn over the second card, saying ... "However, I have the resource of ..."

Interpret this card as a resource.

You can also say "This card shows me what I can draw upon and it is telling me I can draw upon ..."

Turn over the third card, saying ... "And when I do, I learn the lesson of ..."

Interpret this card as a lesson.

## THE PAST

We now turn up the three cards in the left column, reading these as the PAST in order to see how the situation has arisen and gain more context.

We do this by simply using the *past tense* in exactly the same sentences:

Turn over the first card, saying ... "My challenge was ..."

Interpret this card as a past challenge.

Turn over the second card, saying ... "However, I had (found) the resource of ..."

Interpret this card as a past resource.

You can also say "This card shows me what I drew upon ..."

Turn over the third card, saying ... "And when I did, I learnt the lesson of ..."

Interpret this card as a past lesson.

## THE FUTURE

We now turn up the three cards in the right column, reading these as the FUTURE in order to see how the situation has arisen and gain more context.

We do this by now using the *future tense* in exactly the same sentences:

Turn over the first card, saying … "My challenge will turn into …"

Interpret this card as a future challenge.

Turn over the second card, saying … "However, I will benefit from the resource of …"

Interpret this card as a future resource.

You can also say "This card shows me what I can draw upon …"

Turn over the third card, saying … "And when I do, the outcome will be (or the problem avoided) …"

Interpret this card as a future outcome or avoidance of problem.

## EXAMPLE

"My present challenge is how to develop my new work [Three of Pentacles]. I have the resource of experience and knowledge of my subject [King of Swords]. And when I do, I learn the lesson of taking delight in it [Ace of Cups]".

"My challenge was that I was over-active and got into conflict [Knight of Rods/Wands]. However, from that, I can now see I found the resource of exposing ignorance [Devil]. And when I did, I learnt the lesson of making clear-cut decisions [Ace of Swords]".

"My challenge in the future will be carrying the responsibilities and not being overburdened [Ten of Wands]. However, I will benefit from the resource of direction – being able to delegate and do one thing at a time [Ace of Wands]. And when I do, the outcome will be success and good leadership [Six of Wands]".

You have now, in your three-week journey, come to understand the twenty-one Principles of Tarot and experience many methods for your practice.

There is just one more thing, nothing really, for those of you who wish to take one little leap.

## - 0 -

AIM IN ALL THINGS TO RESTORE THE SPIRITUAL DIGNITY OF TAROT.

Remember then, from the very beginning, that this is our spiritual journey.

This will never be any different, from the beginning to the end.

### Extended Commentary

*We see the tarot as the language of initiation into the Western Esoteric Initiatory System. The teaching of tarot is to provide a symbolism for a sequence of progressive mystical states and ultimately provoke and communicate those states in an accessible manner. The cards, arrayed on the Tree of Life, illustrate the challenges of the quest, the resources of grace and the lessons of the divine.*[40]

---

[40] If you are interested in this further journey, we invite you into the Crucible Club at www.everlastingday.com.

# - IV -
## FOUNDATIONAL CONCEPTS

## Practice Skill Not Method

We have seen elsewhere in this book that we should practice skills first and methods separately, once we have the skill to conduct the method. In this context, it is good to practice by not doing readings first, but practice making up stories - from the cards.

Take three cards out and say:

"First, there was [say the SCENE/IMAGE from the first card, like "A man with 10 sticks on his back"]

"… then this happened …"

[say EVENT/ACTION from second card, like "everything got shook up"]

"… which meant that …"

[say the SENSE/LESSON from the third card, like "A decision had to be made" or whatever comes to your mind].

*Illus. Ten of Wands, The Tower and the Queen of Swords.*

There is a tendency as a beginner to practice something that is being found difficult by practising the method, which just results in frustration. Practice the skill by itself, with no pressure, no rules, no expectations, or performance, and then go back to the method of reading three cards as a standard reading. You may be surprised by what happens.[41]

---

[41] Advanced readers and teachers will see how this simple practice encourages the student to learn three pivotal points to be linked for any card in any sequence.

## Prediction

> The fox knows many things, but the hedgehog knows one big thing.
> - Archilochus (c. 680–645 BC),

When Dan Gardner looked at the accuracy of predictions in his book, *Future Babble* (2012), he mainly looked at popular media and pundits, concluding that their accuracy was limited and often prone to bias and narrow thinking, amongst other factors. He categorised the lack of accuracy of hedgehogs, who applied one view to predict one outcome, against the foxes, who were wiser with more broad knowledge and awareness of complexity.

Interestingly, he also looked at those "foxes" who were far more able to make precise and accurate predictions, proven over time, and found at least three main factors to their success:

- Aggregation

- Meta-Cognition

- Humility

These three factors should be borne in mind by Tarosophists; the ability to aggregate - gather - all the cards and nuances in a reading, into a consistent whole. The more the details are aligned, until the whole picture fits, the more accurate the reading. This aggregation should include everything the reader knows about psychology, politics, economics, history, philosophy, and every other experience at their disposal. These sides of their life should not be set aside to become a tarot reader - quite the opposite.

The Tarosophist should also be aware of their own ways of thinking and have a removed assessment and review of their own life, i.e., meta-cognition, which we might more broadly term self-knowledge or self-awareness. This is developed over time and by working on oneself, but also through formal counselling or therapy, which I would encourage all towards at some point in their life and more often than for one period of time.

The third quality of humility should be brought to a reading to acknowledge that the reader is not a faultless oracle - unless engaged in an exercise of such nature - but rather brings a curiosity and openness to their reading, alongside the client, viewing it as a map of a journey outside of the map can ever fully explore.

With these three attitudes of experience, self-knowledge and humility, developed constantly, the predictive nature of readings takes on a more subtle and, in a way, accurate nature.

## Which Card Signifies X?

A common question on our social media is in the form of "which card signifies marriage", or "which card shows someone who has an addiction", or even, "which cards show most the sort of person likely to leave for another country". These questions are predicated on a misunderstanding of the multivalent nature of the cards, and the oracular moment. In effect, as we have seen elsewhere in this present book, any card can potentially stand for any event, situation, or person, it is just that certain cards are more (or less) likely to do so.

Also, we must note that a wide question can be answered from any number of different approaches, dealing with different aspects of the question.

If we asked, "which card signifies a road traffic accident", we might be tempted to answer, "the Chariot, reversed". This may seem a fitting and surprisingly easy correspondence - literally, an upturned car. However, the Three of Swords might be a better indication of the precise specificity of the accident; "this card shows an injury, perhaps a broken leg in three places, caused by a car accident which happened because the road was wet with the rain we see in the background of the card".

Further, in conjunction with other cards, it could also be the Three of Cups because someone had been out drinking with their friends, or the Eight of Wands because it was the busy rush hour of traffic all trying to get to the same place at the same time. It could be signified by three cards, or a combination of fifteen cards in a Thoth Tarot reading, or any other variation. The question of which card signifies something is more useful as a means of testing the reader in their ability to interpret multivalent images, and a test of the deck to see which cards might presently and without context better or lesser signify a particular thing, to that reader at that time.

We will consider in the next section which card might signify the losing of a job, in this light.

## The Unemployment Card

We will now demonstrate how any card might be an "unemployment" card, in the context of the previous section. As we have seen, some cards may more closely tend towards a particular meaning than others, and an interpretation will also depend on the question and context. Having noted that, let us now see how every card can be the "X card", where in this case, X is potential unemployment.

## Minor Arcana and Court Cards

This card is the "lose your job" card because:

Ace of Pentacles - you are about to start at the beginning again.
2 of Pentacles - you cannot juggle your finances and lifestyle anymore.
3 of Pentacles - you need to go learn something new, you have outgrown your job.
4 of Pentacles - you have achieved everything you can here and must move on.
5 of Pentacles - there is only poverty ahead in your current job.
6 of Pentacles - you are not being valued properly and giving to much in this job.
7 of Pentacles - you have put all your hopes in one job and now must change it.
8 of Pentacles - you have worked without reward for too long, they do not appreciate you.
9 of Pentacles - you have been successful but are unhappy and need to fly out to a new job.
10 of Pentacles - you are at the end of the road in this job and must look to a new place.
Page of Pentacles - It is time to seek a new way of earning money.
Knight of Pentacles - Your current job is a bore, and you can only stay stuck.
Queen of Pentacles - A better and more fruitful job awaits you.
King of Pentacles - You are already at the top of your game here and must seek other kingdoms.

Ace of Swords - you will lose your job in a sudden cutting of resources and staff.
2 of Swords - there is a decision being made about your job you cannot see, and the tide is changing.
3 of Swords - you are going to be divorced from your job.
4 of Swords - a long extended 'rest break' is on its way from your career.

5 of Swords - someone is plotting against you and you will lose your job.

6 of Swords - time to travel to another job, fast.

7 of Swords - someone is plotting (this time, behind your back) and you will lose your job before you even know it.

8 of Swords - you are bound within this job and will soon be relieved from it.

9 of Swords - prepare for lots of worry and sadness about your lost job and lack of future.

10 of Swords - you will lose your job. It will hurt. Lots.

Page of Swords - Start looking for another job.

Knight of Swords - You will make a rapid move to another job soon.

Queen of Swords - You will be judged and lose your job and must attend interviews.

King of Swords - You might make a better boss than your boss when he tells you that you have lost your job.

Ace of Cups - you must follow your heart, it will soon take you to a new job, because you are about to lose your job.

2 of Cups - when you lose your job, you will be better in a more equal partnership.

3 of Cups - you will lose your job and take time to celebrate your freedom with others.

4 of Cups -Don't refuse any new offer when you lose your current job soon.

5 of Cups - You will feel very bad when you lose your job.

6 of Cups - Your current job is really weird because you have outgrown it. The man in the background walking away is a secret symbol that you are about to ... lose your job.

7 of Cups - Your current job is unreal and you will lose it soon and have to look at many other options.

8 of Cups - You are about to lose your job. Sad.

9 of Cups - You may feel comfortable in your job, but you are about to lose it through self-satisfaction.

10 of Cups - You will soon be spending all your time with your family. Because you are about to lose your job.

Page of Cups - It will come as a complete surprise when you lose your job.

Knight of Cups - You will be going on a quest soon because you are about to lose your job.

Queen of Cups - Whilst you were not keeping an eye on things, you prepared the ground for losing your job.

King of Cups - You are very unsteady in your job and you are trying not to feel it. You will be overwhelmed when you lose your job, despite your armour, because this is the lose your job card.

Ace of Wands - Time to strike out on your own because you -

2 of Wands - start looking for a new job.
3 of Wands - set your sights on a new job.
4 of Wands - accept any invitation to a new job (because, just in case this isn't clear, you are about to lose your current job).
5 of Wands - there is too much confusion in your current job, no-one can agree, there is chaos, nothing is being done and you will soon lose it. Your job. You are going to lose your job.
6 of Wands - You feel very self-accomplished, but that horse has a secret look to that tells me it is going to throw you which means that you are going to lose your job.
7 of Wands - You have fought to hold your position, but it cannot go on, you will lose your job.
8 of Wands - you will rapidly lose your job and must move on.
9 of Wands - You are going to be pushed out of your job and it will wound you.
10 of Wands - you have carried this job for too long and will soon lose the ability to hold it.
Page of Wands - Time for a new job because you are going to lose your job.
Knight of Wands - Ride out to new challenges when you lose your job soon.
Queen of Wands - Look for new values after you have lost your job, which this card signifies (the black cat is "evil" and brings only misfortune, so it means you will lose your job).
King of Wands - You will soon be the boss of yourself - because you will lose your job.

## Major Arcana

Fool - You will lose your job and be free.
Magician - You will lose your job because this is a man stood by himself.
High Priestess - The oracle herself says you will need to lose your job for spiritual discovery.
Empress - There is a new job already waiting for you (she is pregnant with a new child, signifying your new job, anyone can see that).
Emperor - New job. A powerful one. Because you are going to lose your current one. In the Spring because this card corresponds to Aries. So, exactly March 20th.
Hierophant - You are going to be sacked.
Lovers - You are going to be given a choice in your method of redundancy options.
Chariot - You are going to lose your job and move on.
Strength - Someone is going to force you into leaving this job.

Hermit - You are going to lose your job.

Wheel - You are going to lose your job.

Justice - You are going to lose your job.

Hanged Man - You are going to -

Death - You will lose your job.

Temperance - You will lose your job (and move onto another job).

Devil - You will lose your job.

Blasted Tower - Definitely, you will lose your job.

Star - You must look to a new hope because you will lose your job.

Moon - In twenty-eight days, you will lose your job and enter a dark unknown future.

Sun - Within the year, you will be "stripped naked" like the child as you lose your job.

Last Judgement - You will have to get another job and make a new life.

World - It is certain the world awaits you when you are free from the constraints of your current job - which you are about to lose. Which in esotericism brings us back to the Fool, so this is an important part of your journey through the Arcana. You are losing your job, that is.

## Free or Fixed

When looking at a card, consider where it is free and where it is constrained. Where can it move, where is it fixed? Are there more points free or fixed? What is the difference between those points? This gives a lot more detail from a single card and is powerful when reading it across several cards.

## Example

If we have the Page of Pentacles (Waite-Smith Tarot) in a one-card draw, "What do I need to know about Project X?"

*Illus. Page of Pentacles*

We can see that; the BELT is FIXED; the COIN is FREE; the FEET are half-FIXED, half-FREE. The Trees are FIXED; the field is half-FIXED, half-FREE. The Hat is half-FIXED, half-FREE.

Most importantly, the hands are free. We can read more deeply from that card in terms of our possible avenues of action - our agency. We might first consider that the FIXED BELT is the main point of constraint in this card. We might ask, what have we fastened around ourselves that has bound us? Is it an expectation, a promise, a contract?

We can then consider (perhaps with another card, or just considering the situation) how we might loosen that constraint. We might consider too, that our hands are free - what do we want to do with them? If this were part of a three-card reading, we would look at the hands in another card for the answer.

We might also look at the half-free/half-fixed aspects of the card; perhaps we just need to wait until the field is fallow or full. We might only be fixed to its state at this time.

This is one of several ways of looking at a one card reading for greater depth, or when looking at methods to consider several cards together.

And, when we think we have read all the detail in a card, look again - notice how tight his sleeves are around his wrists. We might say, "Why are you wearing a particular set of clothes to make you look like something, when in fact, it is too tight?"

That might be interpreted as another potential constraint; perhaps the person in this reading cannot improve their finances because they are constraining themselves to behave as they think others expect. Also, some things in the landscape are more fixed than others - the mountains more so than trees, the trees more so than the ploughed field. We can then map those symbols to different areas of the situation; what is the field, that can be waited on a little while to grow? What are the mountains in the situation and is there something positive about their nature, even though they have always been there and will continue to be so in the far future?

# - V -
## SKILL DEVELOPMENT EXERCISES

## Tarot Kihon

The Tarosophy approach to teaching tarot is modelled on the traditional manner in which teaching is conducted in martial arts. There is a far older and richer tradition in such teaching than in cartomancy, and much to be learnt, particularly in the way in which mixed ability and experience classes are taught and the grading of experience and skill. Whilst there is a natural reluctance to grade cartomancy, it is apparent that different people have different experience and skills. It is also of interest that - as in tarot - martial arts have many different types and even traditions within each school, so one form of Karate may have variations to another form.

In martial arts, one learns by repetition (*kihon*) and a graduated set of patterns called *Kata* - 'forms'. We do this before we even practice the analysis (*bunkai*) or application (*kumite*). I love the word "Kumite" because it means 'grappling hands', like the 'shuffling' hands of a tarot practitioner.

In Tarosophy, this is how we teach tarot:

- Kihon is the simple, rapid, but powerful split-deck methods.
- Kata are the layouts and use of correspondences.
- Bunkai is the language patterns.
- Kumite is all the reading methods applied in practice.

This may seem at first a little obscure, but it is the fundamental structure of all our unique teaching.

## Example

As an example of Tarot Kihon, shuffle your deck and split it in two, face-down.

Turn face-up the top card on the left.

Say "In answer to your question about starting a new business, this card says ..." and then say something quick.

Now turn face-up the top card on the right.

Say "however ..." and then say something quick from that card.

Place the cards to one side and turn up the next card on the left.

Say "In answer to your question about starting a new business, this card says ..." and again say something quick.

Turn the top card up on the right again, saying "however ..."

Keep repeating the process until you can do it for any card combination easily and fluently.

You have now experienced a *Tarot Kihon*, a training method of repetition, which is also a confidence building exercise and an actual method you can use at the table.

In the following exercises and skill-building techniques we will explore more practices that serve a variety of purposes.

## Connecting Cards I

One of the common challenges which is reported by absolute beginners to tarot is connecting cards to weave a story and address the question. This is in part due to faulty teaching which advises a student to learn "one card a day", installing the idea that cards are separate and deep, which ignores the idea that cards are endlessly deep and better read in relationship to each other, as the universe itself is one whole set of connections.

In this exercise, we keep it simple, as it is better to produce exercises which have steps that are difficult to fail and utilise existing skills - or teach those skills prior to their exercise.

1. Take your deck and simply shuffle.

2. Take out three cards and as you do, say out loud the title of each card like so:

- "Well, it was all a bit [name of first card] until now when it's just …"

- "[name of middle card]" and it looks likely to …"

- "[name of third card]".

You can add your own voice, stresses, sighs, raised eyebrows or any other body language as fits the cards. Do not be concerned about making any interpretation in this exercise, it is a failsafe exercise that can be performed by anyone who can read the name of each card from the card.

## Example

**Cards**: Queen of Pentacles + Ace of Swords + Ten of Pentacles.

*Illus. Queen of Pentacles, Ace of Swords & Ten of Pentacles.*

Sentence: "Well, it was all a bit Queen of Pentacles until now when it's just the Ace of Swords and it looks likely to Ten of Pentacles".

I felt like saying that very positively, picking up to the third card. My tone changed a bit when I said it a second time, dropping a bit on the Queen of Pentacles. The first time it was more neutral on that card.

Pack the cards away and try it again a in a few days, or several times a day or week as you like.

You may notice your actual 3-card readings joining up a bit more. We are just using this *Kihon*, this "drill" to install a language pattern without worrying about the 'interpretation' bit.

## Connecting Cards II

Once we have practised naming three or more cards in some sort of sentence structure, we can utilise our natural skill at interpreting pictures applied within an oracular sentence. In this variation, practice will help your story-telling flow:

- Shuffle and take three cards out from your deck.

- For the first, write (or think of) one action that is shown or suggested by the card, i.e., dancing.

- For the second, select a situation in life that is suggested, i.e., the home, the workplace, friends, etc.

- For the third, think of a state of mind or emotion that the card depicts, i.e., separation.

- Then put the three together in a sentence as follows …

- "I see you [or "myself"] in these cards [action] in the situation of [situation] which results in [state of mind]."

- "I see myself in these cards dancing in the situation of work which results in a state of separation".

*Illus. Three of Cups, Ten of Pentacles, Three of Swords.*

Once we have practised the sentence construction in the present tense, we can also move it into the future. Take three more cards and repeat the same process to come up with another action, situation, and state, and place those three words into the following sentence in the future tense:

- So, these cards show us that you [or "I"] should [action] to bring about [situation] and gain [state of mind]".

*Illus. Two of Pentacles, Four of Cups, Six of Swords.*

In these cards I might say:

> I see myself in these cards juggling in the workplace, resulting in a feeling of boredom. So, I should take time to myself to bring about travel and gain a new enthusiasm.

And there we have it, a six-card format reading to describe and advise upon any question. The more we practice this, the more variations we will think upon, until it becomes extremely easy to speak our own voice and tell a story from our cards.

## An Interval of Riddles

The Tarosophist may find themselves always considering tarot as an endless riddle. Here are six riddles given as an interval, and the reader is encouraged to create their own from the cards.[42]

### Riddle 1

I am the Path into the Unknown.
I am Imagination but not Spirit.
Which card am I?

### Riddle 2

I am on my way yet already there.
I am swift but not a bird.
Which card am I?

### Riddle 3

The Cioppino is fresher than I thought.
Which card am I?

### Riddle 4

I am Change, Unexpected.
I am Change, Again.
I am Change, Transformation.
I am Change, Hidden.
I am Change, Waiting beyond the Fear.
Which Five Majors are We?

### Riddle 5

If I was a thing, I would be a breath of fresh air. What card am I?

### Riddle 6

We'll never get this church built in time. Which two Minor cards are we?

---

[42] Answers at the back of this book.

When these riddles were given to readers of our Facebook group, 'Tarot Professionals', many readers concurred with their answers however sometimes there was leeway to a couple of riddles.[43] This was notable as it was often a choice between a suggestion of a Major card favoured by some as an answer, or a Minor card by others. In some cases, it was two common answers slit between the same Minor or Court card. This demonstrates the resonance pattern between the Majors, Minors and Court Cards, where a particular "interpretation", "energy" or "meaning" exists in one card from each of those three segments of the deck.

A further exercise is then to take any concept and using a split-deck constraint, find the best Major, Minor and Court card to fit that concept.

## Examples

- **Freedom**: The Fool (Major), the Eight of Wands (Minor) and the Page of Wands (Court).

- **Courage**: Strength (Major), Seven of Wands (Minor) and the Knight of Swords (Court).

---

[43] https://www.facebook.com/groups/tarotprofessionals.

## Random Words

To practice your skills of tarot interpretation, it is sometimes better to work backwards rather than forwards. Use a book, dictionary, or online random word generator to select three random words. Then, as quickly as you can, ascribe them as keywords to three Tarot Cards.

## Example

- Monotonous + Porter + Vote.
- We might ascribe those as: Hermit + Chariot + Hierophant.

The cards do not have to be Major Arcana, for example:

- Turret + Airline + Inflated.
- We can ascribe these as: Blasted Tower + Eight of Wands + Nine of Cups.

Once you have practised this several times and can feel confident there is no word in the English language that cannot be roughly assigned to one card or another, add sentence creation to your practice. Simply create a sentence for a reading with the three cards, whether you use the same three words or not.

## Example

Using the first example above:

- Hermit + Chariot + Hierophant.
- "Nothing will change as someone in power casts their vote (at work, maybe)".

In the second example from above:

- Blasted Tower + Eight of Wands + Nine of Cups.
- "Being secure, the airline raises its prices".[44]

---

[44] The Tarot can be as literal as the Lenormand.

## Fire and Fuel

In this exercise, we take a six-card triangle reading and view it in two important parts; the *fire* and the *fuel*. This is a metaphor for actions that need to be taken, supported by resources that also need to be in place. It is a good practice to ensure that every reading (other than oracular ones or those not requiring this pattern) has *both* fire and fuel - clearly defined actions coupled with resources which will support and maintain those actions for the client.

To visualise and practice this structure, create a six-card reading where the bottom three cards are the fuel for the top three cards.

- CARD 1: Aim.
- CARDS 2 + 3: Actions.
- CARDS 4 + 5 + 6: Resources.

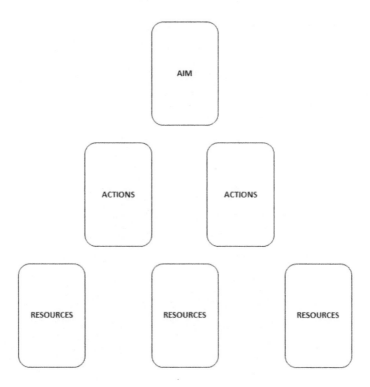

*Illus. Fire & Fuel Six-Card Triangle.*

This can be conducted as a full-deck or split-deck method, in the latter case using Majors for the Fuel of positions 4 + 5 + 6, and the remaining deck of Minors and Court cards for positions 1 + 2 + 3. The blended deck of Minors and Courts (rather than splitting them into two sets) is used as the aim might be best described as behaving, becoming, or acting like a particular person (Court) or best described as taking on specific actions (Minors) - so we would use both sets.

**Example**

> **Aim**: 3 of Wands.
> **Actions (Fire)**: Hierophant + Hermit.
> **Resources (Fuel)**: Queen of Wands + Hanged Man + 3 of Pentacles.

*Illus. Six-Card Triangle Example Reading.*

**Interpretation**: Our aim is to build and set our plans in motion, a positive confirmation of the go-ahead of a project. Our actions, on which we must expend our energy, time, resources, and commitment are two-fold; firstly, to seek advice from professionals (Hierophant), and secondly, to remove ourselves from distractions so we can give the project serious and solitary thought (Hermit). In order to maintain this two-fold and likely time-consuming switch between others and ourselves, we are advised to draw on the following for fuel; the Queen of Wands, somebody who is passionate and driven, and can be invited into the project to cheerlead it; the Hanged Man, ensuring that at every stage our own values are met, and we are prepared to make sacrifice as 'fuel'; and finally, the Three of Pentacles, a plan that is fixed (by the professional with experience) and checked against at regular intervals, reducing stress.

In dividing our triangle up into aim, action and resources, or *fire* and *fuel*, we practice ensuring that we are always looking into the cards to deliver not only advice, ambition, action steps, but also the *resources* the client (or ourselves) requires to support those actions and meet their aim.[45]

---

[45] This practice keys into the Tarosophy 3-minute teaching method for Tarot which sees every card as a resource, challenge, and lesson. It should be familiar to the student of Tarosophy to view cards as resources for the fuel section of this further practice. It builds to increasingly elegant and powerful readings as the client is given a push/pull propulsion system that is easier to follow than a carrot or stick answer from a reading.

**Two Card Draw**

This practice exercise, like most in Tarosophy, can also be used as a divination. It is useful to have methods that are extensively used which also provide practice in the core skills of divination, so every reading builds the ability of the reader as well as providing a divination. Conversely, it ensures that no practice is wasted and always applied to life and real-world events.

In this exercise, we use a two-card draw to pare down the basic concepts of Tarosophy and practice our ability to link two cards in a combined narrative. This method also obliquely practices a skill useful for Lenormand or Oracle card reading.

1. Take a deck.

2. Shuffle.

3. Pick a card:

- If it is a Court Card, think of a person.
- If it is a Major Card, think of a big thing throughout your life.
- If it is a Minor Card, think of a recent event.

4. Accept whatever thought comes to mind as you look at the card, allowing time for a single thought to repeat itself or stabilise in your mind.

5. Shuffle the deck again, leaving the first card on the table.

6. Pick a second card.

Apply the same rules to the second card as the first card.

When you have two separate thoughts for each card, or even as a second thought arises, ask yourself, "What relationship is illustrated between the two cards, if any?"

**Example**

We draw the Two of Swords and think immediately of a recent situation where we had been holding back from a decision, but then the tide turned, and the situation was resolved without us having to make any decision.

We then draw the Fool and after some thought, settle on the theme of not applying personal responsibility to life and too often taking the easy road.

*Illus. Two of Swords & Fool.*

We then consider both cards and see that sometimes it is good to know that you need not be responsible, but the responsible choice is to know when to make a decision or when to leave things as they are in a situation, so that it can resolve itself.

We are immediately reminded of the song, *The Gambler* (1978) by Kenny Rogers, with the chorus line of "you've got to know when to hold 'em/know when to fold 'em". When we look up the lyrics of the song, we find much other relevant advice, smiling in that it is of course, about cards, and a verse that sticks out is "And somewhere in the darkness/The gambler he broke even/But in his final words/I found an ace that I could keep".

We can now see the Two of Swords as a bit of a gamble, particularly with a card like the Fool nearby, and we can also think that the next time the Two of Swords shows up, and we need a decision, we can shuffle the four Aces and take one out to divine what sort of decision will resolve the dilemma and be least risky:

- Ace of Pentacles, a practical decision that involves us.

- Ace of Swords, a change of mind that does not outwardly involve us.

- Ace of Cups, a change of heart that does not outwardly involve us.

- Ace of Wands, a stand on principle that involves us.

We can see in this extension of the original method that now we have more language in which to speak with the cards, and, in this case, a perfect solution for the situations in a reading that come down to whether someone should walk away or stay at the table.

## Genre Exercise

In this exercise, we continue to work on linking cards in their three types; Majors, Minors and Court cards, by utilising a source with which we are already familiar; novels or films. We can then apply the fictional narratives to our real-world divinations.

Take three cards at random from a split-deck, one from each pile. i.e. a Court card, Minor card and Major card.

Apply the three cards as illustrations within the same unique genre of narrative, such as a thriller, horror, sci-fi or fantasy, no matter what deck it is. This works especially well as an exercise to choose a genre that is totally opposite the style of deck, such as a *chicklit* genre to the Thoth, or *gothic horror* to the Gummy Bears Tarot.

Take the Court card as a *character*, the Minor card as a *scene*, and the Major card as the *theme* of that chapter.

## Example

We might draw the King of Cups, Four of Cups and Temperance from the *La Corte dei Tarocchi* by Anna Maria D'Onofrio (pub. Osvaldo Menegazzi, il Meneghello).

We can then Imagine them as the chapter in a *Noir Thriller* book.

We see the King as a policeman, a "copper" (from 'Re di Coppe', perhaps), and he is an established part of the police force; but then that cup looks like it could be a cup of poison - perhaps he is the killer.

The Four of Cups, also pulled entirely at random from the Minors, is then a scene where he is attempting to kill four people - perhaps people with whom he has an emotional issue. We can make it even more noir by assuming they killed his family.

The final card, Temperance, is the theme of becoming what you do - the angel looks as if it is not enjoying being tempered; so, nothing good comes of it.

We can play about with those ideas, but we do not have to do anything else - it sets up a loosening of our thinking for when we next do a reading - it becomes increasingly easier to apply the cards to a real situation, because we have been stretching ourselves in a specific way by applying cards to a genre outside of their own reality.

If we were to apply those cards to a reading, under the same thinking, we might say "There's a guy who has been around a while, but he is offering something that is poisonous to you - take time to think about how it will change you if you accept whatever he is offering".

## Creating Keywords

Once we have some experience in tarot, we should be able to create quick key-words to utilise any deck, even one with an uncommon structure, renamed (or extra) Suits, or other variation of the standard pattern of tarot. In the example below, using a deck based around the film, *Labyrinth* (1986, dir. Jim Henson) we see how simple key-words were suggested by the names of the Suits, such as "Owls" being a Suit of "vision", without forcing the correspondence to the elemental Suits. The numbered Minors bore enough resemblance to a standard one to ten pattern for kabbalistic keywords modified slightly by the theme of the film, such as gifts, temptation, dreaming, fighting, and surrendering. The Court cards were also ascribed key-words to the coming of age phases of life, such as proposing, and - as an adult - considering and deciding. The Major arcana were keyed already to the film characters and situations, so would require knowledge of the film to utilise fully. However, they were forced by the deck designer to fit the existing tarot template, such as the Blasted Tower or the Hermit, and these archetypes could be already read as a common pattern.

### Suits

Orbs = Action
Owls = Vision
Clocks = Time
Books = Knowledge

### Minor Numbers

1 = Plan
2 = Break
3 = Balance
4 = Build
5 = Fight
6 = Surrender
7 = Gift
8 = Take
9 = Dream

$10 = \text{Finish}$

## Court Ranks

Jack = Wait
Cavalier = Propose
Queen = Consider
King = Decide

## Example Reading

**Cards**: 5 of Orbs + 7 of Owls + 4 of Clocks.

**Interpretation**: Fight in all your actions to gift your vision and it will build over time.

We can also practice in reverse, by taking any set of related components and assigning them divinatory meanings, for example, we could make up the *Tarot of the Anemoi*, based on the Greek deities of the Winds and have four Suits, being Boreas, Zephyrus, Notus and Eurus. The Suit of Boreas, then, would have the attributes of storms, cold and a violent energy, being of the north and winter. The Ace of Boreas (or Ace of Storms) would be the north pole from which cold winds might come and carry corresponding interpretative meanings. We could then design the other Suits and even imagine what the cards might look like in such a Tarot.

The reader is encouraged to consider the observed and established patterns in the world, the great myths, legends, metaphors, fables and stories, and recognising their symbolism as a form of tarot; this is the state of mind described by A. E. Waite when he wrote that the "true tarot is symbolism".[46] He meant not that the tarot deck is symbolism, but quite the opposite; all symbolism, all the universe, *is a tarot* - a set of symbols presented to us for our divination and interpretation. We will experience this concept a little further in the next exercise.

---

[46] Arthur Edward Waite, *Pictorial Key to the Tarot* (London: Rider & Company, 1974), p. 4.

## Learn to Read the Universe

Look around you right now. See if you can see three objects that suggest Tarot cards. Read them as advice for your life in the coming week. This method practices intuition, observation, and correspondence, and in particular the link between tarot and real life.

## Example

- Soda Can - Ace of Cups.

- A map on a shelf saying "The World" - The World.

- A book called *The Magus* - The Magician.

**Interpretation**: "This week I should remain emotionally open to see the whole picture and the magic within the world".

In this method we also practice reading the universe as a constant oracle, without it becoming too overwhelming.

## Reversed Cards Practice

In this exercise, we play with a pair of reversed cards using pinpointing and bridging. These are the two essential skills of connecting cards and building narrative. As with all Tarosophy exercises, this is both a practice and a method in itself, in addition to installing a useful unconscious or habitual skill.

1. Take your deck and shuffle whilst thinking of a situation where you need new insight.

2. Take out a card, face-up, turning it upside-down if not already reversed.

3. Look at it, and see which single item sticks out most, like a "hat", or "cat" or "wand" or "river".

4. Write or think "The [item] is upside-down..."

5. Select a second card and turn it also up-side down.

6. Look at it and again see which item sticks out the most.

7. Write or think "… so I must upturn the [item]" as you slowly and deliberately turn that second card the right way up.

You may get something quite surreal, apparently meaningless, or profoundly oracular. It does not matter as your unconscious will do the work. Leave it be. This method can also surprise you by working better with a deck which is very different to those with which you might usually work, so explore any such different, unfamiliar, or barely used decks in your collection.

**Example**

**Cards**: Nine of Wands (rev) + Queen of Pentacles (rev).

*Illus. Nine of Wands (Rev) & Queen of Pentacles (Rev).*

- Symbols: Tallest pole sticking up + Coin (pentacle).

- Oracular Sentence: "The tallest pole is upside-down so I must upturn the coin".

**Interpretation**: When this sentence was said, there was an intuition to say the plural word of "coins" rather than "coin", so we will take that as an oracular moment. The "tallest pole" was immediately noticeable in the Nine of Wands when upside-down, as it looked almost too big, bigger than the others or that held by the figure, who seemed far less important in the reversed image.

The statement of "upturning the coins" and even "the tallest pole" feel as if they do indeed relate to two extremely specific things - a situation where one thing above all is actually causing impact, and a very definite reversal in the way finances are being utilised. We should resist conscious interpretation and allow this message to sink into our unconscious, which will often seek resolution or closure to this "incomplete yet signalled-as-meaningful and important message" by naturally and powerfully directing our actions and behaviour.

## The Man Who Can Read the Clouds

*The man who can read the clouds and divine thereby*
*will say it is truer to reach to heaven.*

*The man who reads the secrets of fate in rocks*
*will say it truer to touch the earth.*

*The woman who reads others*
*will speak of the truth of the heart*
*and she who reads the lines of the face*
*tells the truth of the body which houses the soul.*

*They who read pictures upon cardboard (in all its various configurations)*
*will tell you that only such symbols truly illustrate all that a person may dream.*

*Perhaps it is only true and most certain that nature is true to the divine and not the diviner*
*always true to nature.*

# - VI -

## KABBALAH

## KABBALAH

The Kabbalah is a mystical tradition within Judaism and was adopted by esoteric thinkers, particularly the Tree of Life diagram.[47] We have introduced this subject in several other books and in the first *Tarosophy* but will quickly review it here for ease of reference. One of the main texts of basic Kabbalah is the *Sepher Yetzirah*, 'Book of Formation', which deals with the twenty-two Hebrew letters, their correspondences, and relationships to the divine and to the world. It is upon this text that the corresponds were built to the twenty-two Major Arcana of the Tarot and then the Suits, Minor Arcana and Court cards - in order of the level of direct correspondence.

There are many arguments about correct correspondences, but it is really only a discussion about which type of map might be best for the way in which you are travelling.

In Tarosophy, we consider the ten cards of each Suit as stages of creation, the four Suits as aspects of the world as it manifests, and the Court cards as levels of energy (worlds) within that manifestation. The twenty-two Major Arcana correspond to the paths or relationships between the manifest world, illustrating how we learn from the world as it arises from the divine and make our return ascent.

When we have made these basic correspondences, we can see that the Ten of Cups is the tenth (final) stage in the world of Cups (emotions), so it has concluded – and a new cycle starts. In doing so, when we go on to study Kabbalah, and consider "Malkuth (10) in Briah (Creation)", we will already know how that is illustrated.

In that sense, the Tarot is an illustration of the same universe as described by Kabbalah. Two maps. Same place.

The evidence for the origins of this connection between Kabbalah and Tarot is clear and not at all mysterious or unknown. We have evidence for the origins of Tarot, which originated 1380 - 1440 in Northern Italy depending on which deck we call Tarot or what primary texts we accept as evidence. However it is, the origin and approximate date remains clear, and there is currently no evidence at all for any earlier origin, and certainly not in ancient Egypt.

We have relatively clear evidence for the origins of Kabbalah which was first written down c. 2nd Century, again, depending on what we might specify as Kabbalah.

We have clear evidence for the first written connection between Tarot and Kabbalah (which could have only come after the 15th Century because Tarot did not exist prior) in 1781, when Antoine Court de Gebelin and Comte de

---

[47] See Marcus Katz, *The Magician's Kabbalah* (Keswick: Forge Press, 2016) and Andrea Green, *Kabbalah and Tarot* (Keswick: Forge Press, 2015).

Mellet wrote about the alleged connection (and to Ancient Egypt) in *Le Monde Primitif*.

We then have all the evidence thereafter in which occultists such as Eliphas Levi, Papus, Wirth, and then Mackenzie, Westcott, Woodman and Mathers (Golden Dawn) and then Waite and Crowley all took the connection as meaningful in some way and developed it further.

The Kabbalah proves an invaluable tool in Tarosophy on which to map the tarot, and the tarot proves an invaluable tool through which we can illustrate Kabbalah. And ultimately, both are maps of the world, of which tarot - and the letters - are the language by which it is constructed through correspondence. In our brains, as they create the reality in which we exist. As above, so below.

## Illustrating the World

We have seen that through magical correspondence is revealed the arcana of the world of concepts. We can take any Hebrew word and find it illustrated by Tarot through simple correspondence, illuminating the patterns beneath thought. The Hebrew language works for this as it is a cipher, symbol, and each letter also a number, amongst other characteristics. We might compose a similar set of correspondences for the English language, but it would not carry the same utility and breadth.[48]

We can unveil vast patterns of correspondence with the Majors, such as when we make enquiry into the nature of the World. We take the Hebrew word for 'world', which is *Olam*, as in *Tikkun Olam*, the repairing of the world to its original estate.

This is spelt in full as A'aVLM, Ayin + Vau + Lamed + Mem.

We can then make a correspondence of these letters back to our Major Arcana:

- Ayin: The Devil
- Vau: Hierophant
- Lamed: Justice
- Mem: The Hanged Man

---

[48] A so-called "English Kabbalah" or "English Gematria". These were popular, for example, during the early days of Chaos Magick, as magicians experimenting with 'throwing out the old and bringing in the new', but few systems (if any) caught on as they were limited compared to Hebrew. Further, they were of no use in decrypting earlier writings such as the Golden Dawn and Aleister Crowley, who might be considered the babies in the bathwater of Gematria in this context, which, when one is taken from another leaves us quite a spectacle.

These cards can now be considered as the 'illustration of the world' and the pattern that exists just below the surface of the apparent world. It illustrates the material nature of the world through the Devil, and the relationship of the Devil to the Divine. The Hierophant demonstrates the world as a divine teaching, an interface or exemplar of the divine patterns. Justice further explains the equilibrium or 'truth' in which the world is maintained - some might even see in this the law of Karma. The final letter of Mem, corresponding to the Hanged Man, shows the divine nature 'drowned' upside down in the matter of the world, but ever-present.

This pattern of cards also shows the path of return through the world that we must tread; that we must initiate a complete reversal of our beliefs, learn the patterns of the world, connect to the world as a teaching of the divine, and ultimately face the devil of our ignorance, in order to pass beyond and through the world as it appears on the surface.

We can conduct this analysis for every card, every word and every concept, revealing endless patterns of correspondence and teaching in the everyday patterns of letters and words - through which we construct our universe.[49]

If we were a teacher who wished to know the deeper level of our role, we could look up the word 'school' in Hebrew, which is *Bet Sefer* meaning literally 'house of books'.

In Hebrew characters this is BYTh, Beth + Yod + Tau and SPhR, Samekh + Peh + Resh.

By correspondence, these letters correspond to:

- Beth: Magician
- Yod: Hermit
- Tau: World

With:

- Samekh: Temperance
- Peh: Tower
- Resh: Sun

We can see that the concept of a school, of education, of learning, is illustrated by the tarot as the meanings of those cards, first for how to build the House of learning:

---

[49] See Jorge Luis Borges, 'The God's Script' in *Labyrinths* (London: Penguin, 1989).

- Skills (Magician) + Self-Knowledge (Hermit) + Experience (World)

Or:

- Spoken Instruction (Magician) + Self-Study (Hermit) + Practical Work (World)

Leading to the impact of learning or books:

- Independence (Temperance) + Change (Blasted Tower) + Awareness (Sun)

Or:

- Maturity (Temperance) + Revelation (Blasted Tower) + Confidence (Sun).

We can consider these concepts as the pattern and goals of education, of schools and learning, through analysis of their correspondence in Hebrew letters to tarot.

The reader is encouraged to take their job, role, their place as a mother or father, sister or brother, any location with which they are having issues, any object or action in life, and analyse it through correspondences, breaking the world down into its fundamental patterns. In doing so, we can better understand and align ourselves to the deeper and divine nature of the world.[50]

---

[50] At this level, the Tarosophist should acquire a Hebrew/English Dictionary.

## Central Pillar Method

In this Kabbalistic method, we utilise the fundamental patterns of the Tree of Life as a spread, but with a tarosophical twist - we use split-deck methods to pre-select a range of cards that best suits our question, resulting in far more precise and direct readings. As ever, this method is only one example of the many that the reader can then discern in the branches of the Tree.

Take a question and select a Suit to the context or theme of the situation:

- Pentacles: Material things, resources, time, money, or health.

- Swords: Clarity, education, logic, decisions, learning, confusion.

- Cups: Emotional, relationship, family.

- Wands: Ambitions, will, values, importance, lifestyle, the big picture, self-development or spirituality.

For the Suit you have selected, we further refine it and take out of the deck only the Ace, Six, Nine and Ten of that Suit.

## Example

If it were a job or employment question, particularly involving a financial aspect, we would take the Ace of Pentacles, the Six of Pentacles, the Nine of Pentacles and the Ten of Pentacles.

Lay them out as illustrated in the example, in a vertical column, Ace at the top, Ten at the bottom.

*Illus. Ace, Six, Nine & Ten of Pentacles in Vertical Column.*

What we have laid out is an illustration of the central pillar of the Tree of Life in the most appropriate of the four kabbalistic worlds which concerns our question.

We now look at the pictures on those cards. They will tell us:

- **Ace**: The crown of your situation. Where it comes from. The absolute thing we really need to get from this question.

- **Six**: The *beauty* of the situation. Where we can find balance in it, where it will all make sense and hold together.

- **Nine**: The *foundation* of the situation. Where, in that particular world - of money, of love, of ambition, of decision - we can find stability and get it fixed.

- **Ten**: The *kingdom* of the situation. How we can act, what we can actually do, where the activity must concentrate to manifest and complete it.

Take a moment to look at how those four cards illustrate those things, and if you are using Waite-Smith, a variant, or Thoth, etc., you should see those lessons illustrated to some extent. Other decks may have surprising things to say in their illustration of those numbers.

Now for the Kabbalistic Magick. We take a breath, shuffle the rest of the deck, whilst considering the situation and looking at the four cards. When ready, lay out a card from the shuffled deck on each of those four positions - one card on top of the Ace, one on top of the Six, one on the Nine and one card on the Ten.

Those cards can now be read as Universe telling us how to align ourselves to those four essential creative steps; the card on the Ace will show us what to aim for, the card on the Six how to maintain it in a balanced manner, the card on the Nine how to stabilise it and the card on the Ten how to act and manifest. And all four cards will work together because we are reading them to the most powerful map of all creation.

Even if we do not know any Kabbalah.

In the next section we will look at other potential patterns we can discern on the Tree, particularly regarding the *Sephiroth* and their balance.

## Working with Kabbalah through the Cards

We can work with our Major Arcana cards to represent locations on the Tree of Life and resolve imbalances at the highest levels through their divination. The Tree represents a blueprint of existence as it is; perfect and whole. However, from our perspective, flawed and incomplete in our illusionary separation from the whole, the universe may appear far from perfect.

In such cases, we can take any of the Major Arcana from their location on the Tree and divine them in terms of their relationship to the divine world; the world represented by the unknowable *Sephiroth*. As each Arcana illustrates a path between two *Sephiroth*, we simply draw two cards, one for each of the *Sephiroth*, and interpret their relationship.

## Example 1

1. Select out the Strength Card.

2. Shuffle the remaining deck and place one card to the left and one card to the right of Strength.

3. The left card shows you what you have made 'active' in your life that should be passive and constrained.

4. The right card shows you what you have made 'passive' but should be given free expression without bounds.

In performing this reading, you will be learning about Geburah and Chesed on the Tree of Life, and their relationship illustrated by the correspondence to the Strength card.

## Example 2

1. Select out the High Priestess card.

2. Shuffle the remaining deck and place one card above the High Priestess and one card below her.

3. The upper card tells you what divine lesson is being expressed through your life right now.

4. The lower card tells you how to manifest that in your awareness and actions in the world.

In performing this reading, you will be learning about Kether and Tiphareth and their relationship illustrated through the High Priestess card.

You will also be learning about "intuition" expressed as action in *attunement* to a recognised divine source.

## Applying Kabbalah to a Three Card Reading

In this method, called the Tree of Life Locator, we utilise the Tree of Life map by taking the schema of the Four Worlds, the paths and the Sephiroth, upgrading a simple three-card reading to something far more elegant.

1. Take your deck and consider a situation in your life about which you seek a kabbalistic and spiritual perspective to guide your response.

2. Split the deck into three decks; 22 Majors, 56 Minors and 16 Court Cards.

## Part A. What is actually happening [Court cards]?

1. Take the Court Cards and Shuffle, asking "To which world does this situation actually call me?"

2. Take out one Court Card and consult its rank:

   - King: This situation is coming from the highest world and requires contemplation ….

   - Queen: This situation is coming from the creative world and requires me to create …

   - Knight: This situation is coming from the formative world and requires me to organise …

   - Page: This situation is coming from the world of action and requires me to act …

   "… with regard to [consult Suit of the Court Card drawn] …"

   - Wands: My ambition.
   - Cups: My feelings.
   - Swords: My thoughts and plans.
   - Pentacles: My behaviour.

## Example

We pull the Queen of Pentacles, who says, "This situation requires you to create [new] behaviour". This is a situation that doesn't require contemplation, planning, or organisation, but actual behaviour, and creative … so, in this case, writing new material, not discussing it, thinking – just writing. So that's what I do – I was tempted to respond in a particular situation by a longer-term plan, but the time for that may be later; this reading makes me do stuff instead.

In using this method, the reader will soon start to dynamically and experientially appreciate the Tree of Life model of the four worlds, and the elements, as they are modelled by the Court Cards. This brings Kabbalah into your everyday activity through the map of Tarot.

## Part B. What is the actual problem [Minor Arcana]?

Take the deck of Minors and shuffle, asking, "What is the state of this situation?"

Select one Minor card and consult its number:

1: This situation has only just started and …
2: This situation is full of energy and …
3: This situation is starting to get stuck in a pattern and …
4: This situation is getting out of control and …
5: This situation is getting constrained and …
6: This situation is being balanced and …
7: This situation is going round in circles and …
8: This situation is being focused and …
9: This situation is establishing a foundation for something and …
10: This situation is finished and …

Then consult the Suit of the Minor card and add …

- Wands: is consuming everything.
- Swords: is dividing everything.
- Cups: is splashing over everyone.
- Pentacles: is costing.

## Example

We draw the 3 of Cups and put together that this situation is getting stuck in a pattern and splashing over everyone. That makes sense, although it brings my attention more to that it is becoming a pattern and affecting others – I need to change my behaviour, which is what people respond to, as indicated by the first card! At least I can see that there is no "cost" in this situation, which was a concern. This method also tells you a lot by excluding the other states and situations, alleviating false concerns.

This part of the method teaches you how to use the ten *Sephiroth* in the four worlds via the correspondences of the elements in a real application. You are seeing here how the ten *Sephiroth* flow into creation, from the source (Aces/1) to the manifest world (10). In each of those states are the four worlds again, as the pure divine source flashes down the Tree into the world as we experience it.

## Part C. In what Activity is the Resolution [Major Arcana]?

The Majors are attributed to the 22 "paths" between the 10 Sephiroth, so in effect arise from the activity between them. This is a perfect mapping because it allows us to use them to see what two Sephiroth (aspects of the universe) we really need to balance, resolve, sort, merge, or whatever we have been advised by the previous two parts of this method.

Take your 22 Majors, shuffle, and ask, using the words from the previous two card draw, "What activity will bring the most divine outcome to this situation … [use your words here from the previous two cards, in my example, "which requires me to create new behaviour and [was] getting stuck in a pattern and splashing over everyone?"]

For each major card, for reference, I have given the numbers of the Sephiroth [i.e., 5-6 is Geburah and Tiphareth] so intermediate students can see which two Sephiroth are being worked with by the corresponding Tarot card on the path between them.

I have also repeated the Tree of Life diagram here for ease of reference. Consult the card:

0. Fool [1-2] Doing something new, novel, totally unexpected. But doing it with a leap of faith.

1. Magician [1-3] Get everything together, out where everyone can see it. Exposure.

2. High Priestess [1-6] Withdraw, find your own centre and source. Remind yourself what the point is.

3. Empress [2-3] Weigh up and balance what you are putting in and what you are getting out. That's it.

4.  Emperor [2-6] Look at one particular thing on which to focus all your energy and effort. Do that.

5.  Hierophant [2-4] Other people can give you advice to expand from where you are. You need help.

6.  Lovers [3-6] Only associate and work with things that are harmonious. Make choices.

7.  Chariot [3-5] Use a set plan to rein in what is happening. Stick to the rules. Drive safe.

8.  Strength [4-5] This is a card of perfect reconciliation. There is only one working solution. Find it. No grey lines or areas allowed.

9.  Hermit [4-6] As you expand, you must keep everything in balance. Take some time off and away from it. Don't get dragged down below.

10. Wheel of Fortune [4-7] There is an obvious pattern here, again. Do something that changes it. Anything. Take a chance.

11. Justice [5-6] It is up to you – the power is with you. Make the best decision you can, no-one else can.

12. Hanged Man [5-8] You are being asked to raise the stakes. Take a step up, don't hang around.

13. Death [6-7] Transform. Everything changes, you must accept that and go with it now. You've done it before, you'll do it again. So, do it now.

14. Temperance [6-9] Everything needs to be in the mix – include everything and everyone, no matter how difficult.

15. Devil [6-8] You must be the bad guy to get what you want, in holding people to their word. Do not allow them to hide in the shadows, stick to what was agreed.

16. Blasted Tower [7-8] There is no simple resolution, let it all fall where it may and get ready to rebuild.

17. Star [7-9] Sticking to what is important, keeping that vision, even through change, wait for a while, and then continue.

18. Moon [7-10] Go back over it and repeat. Repeat again, keep on going on.

19. Sun [8-9] Clarity is what will resolve this situation once and for all, even if it burns someone.

20. Last Judgement [8-10] Decide, shake things up a bit, and call on others to change. You are the one who knocks!

21. World [9-10] Resolution comes from completing everything, take on nothing new, close the doors, and get everything tidied once and for all. It is almost done.

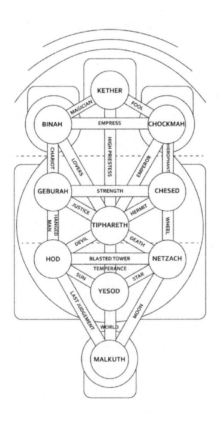

*Illus. Tree of Life with Major Arcana Correspondences to Paths.*

## Example

We pull the Hermit, between Chesed and Tiphareth, the Sephirah of Giving and Balancing. I am advised that I need to take a break from being dragged into the situation – the same one I have been told by the previous reading which is splashing over others and requires new behaviour. That behaviour is even more obvious now, given the third card, it is not to engage but to get away – and take time to create new things. That is the course of action I choose, thanks to this method.

Also notice (according to kabbalah) that the advice also counsels and suggests not doing the opposite, as that is likely the temptation. As an example, if you had the Magician, you may have tended to try and resolve the situation by keeping secrets, hiding things, not calling someone out on their behaviour.

The reader may find this three-card reading a powerful method of applying complex Kabbalah to their life through tarot. And even though it is not necessary, the more you learn Kabbalah, the more powerful this method will prove.

# - VII -
## NLP SKILLS & TALISMANS

## NLP & Tarot

Asking about the "most useful" method of NLP in Tarot highlights several methods which are useful.[51] The first one is the approach of "incorporation and utilisation" which I have taken from the pioneering work of Milton Erickson. You can see that I have already "incorporated" the exact phrase used by the question, rather than re-word or re-purpose it to my own design; I am going to use "most useful".

Now I am going to utilise it in a demonstration of the very thing I am explaining. This is also NLP – as Richard Bandler said, "We go there first", we always enter the state first in which we want to move our client. We aim for *congruency* – in our language, body movements, tonality – everything.

A tarot reading gives us a lot of opportunity to do this, as we can adopt the poses and tones of voice suitable to each card, providing non-verbal anchors for each message from each card.

Anyhow, back to the point, which is "most useful". When we say "most" or "least" in a phrase, it generates what is termed a "trans-derivational" search in the other person, which happens in the unconscious. They must go through a list of all the methods (in this case) to determine the "most" or "least".

Knowing that, the most useful thing to say to a client is "think of the time you were most happy" not "think of a time when you were happy".

## Representational Systems

It is interesting from an NLP point of view that a lot of tarot readers say things like, "OK, I will *see* what the cards *say*" (a visual representation of hearing something). Some readers say, "the cards just aren't *talking* to me today" or "I'm not *seeing* anything in this reading". Other people will say, "I'm getting the strong *feeling* that this card is *telling* you to ..."

Everyone has their own unique way of using their representational systems, it's interesting to develop all of them. Another interesting thing is that most people switch their main "system" when they go into an altered state, whether it is a trance or a panic, etc.

Someone who changes their state when using divination tools will go from a usually "auditory" person to a very "visual" person, etc.

---

[51] I have since covered NLP in Marcus Katz, *NLP Magick* (Keswick: Forge Press, 2020).

## Incorporate and Utilise

In *NLP Magick*, I introduced the concept of "incorporation and utilisation" from the work of Milton H. Erickson. This attitude allows the practitioner to appreciate all communication as meaningful and that even an apparently resistant response is still a positive response. There is no such thing as not communicating. In Tarosophy, we take this even further in that we perceive the entire universe as a constant flow of communication, divining our state within it as a mode of relationship. In this state of awareness, it is only natural, in fact, inevitable, that we will incorporate our surroundings within a formal divination. We can utilise the arising and spontaneous emergence of events as a constant synchronicity in this oracular state.

This includes the apparently mundane events or aspects of a situation, none of which should be ignored. In fact, the entering of this state will often provoke unusual or remarkable events in the surroundings.

The natural circumstances can provide a timely and precise spread in answer to an unspoken question. If the client is silent but has spoken about some past event, and there are five worn-in coffee cup stains on the table, we will use them as the pentagram positions of a "The Soul is Stained with Experience" spread to see what old patterns are worn into the soul of the client. The table and the stains become a living metaphor in real-time, using the cards as illustration and interface, allowing deep conversation and change.

If we are sat near a quiet staircase, and a client has asked us about motivation, we might use the first three steps of the staircase as a "Getting Up One Step at a Time" spread, with three cards on each step. This will lead to further discovery and an easy communication of the interpretation, as we all recognise what walking upstairs feels like as a common experience.

If our client is sitting on a wobbly chair, we might lay out two cards on each arm, either side of them, and ask them to keep steady whilst we read "The Cards of Gaining Life Balance".

If there is a net curtain behind us, we can place one card behind it for the end of the reading as the card which "Unveils the Secret".

The World is a Living Oracle. Divine it.

## State Generation

In NLP, we learn to use conversational language patterns as part of our overall communication.[52] In a client reading, one example of this I would call "framing preamble". In our opening conversation with the client, if it feels natural and appropriate, we can introduce a range of themes that might come up in the reading. These are general themes that are likely to apply in any

---

[52] See Marcus Katz, *NLP Magick* (Keswick: Forge Press, 2020).

reading, rather than anything specific. In a sense, this is the opposite of cold reading; we are setting a framework for the divination to call upon if it further serves the interpretation of the cards.

It is also a useful approach because it encourages the reader – as would it an NLP Practitioner – to have a conscious set of "resource states" to hand. In Tarosophy, we might recognise these "resource states" as one of the three contexts for the three-minute learning method, being "resource", "challenge" and "lesson".

Every card contains a wealth of resources, and it is often such that many readers will pick up on during a reading, when you observe many readings. The Ace of Cups, for example, contains the resources of "spiritual connection", "deep emotions", "grace", "generosity" and so on.

The more general themes that we can usefully seed in our preamble include, but are by no means limited to:

- Change
- Recovery
- Healing
- Openness
- Curiosity
- Determination
- Positive Thinking
- Patience

To seed these themes in our preamble, we might talk about how fast the weather has *changed* recently, or how the days are getting *lighter* – or we are finding more *comfort* as the evenings draw in during winter. We might even pick up on the smallest thing and amplify it slightly, again, in context, such as "it was *good thinking* for you to park your car there, it is much cheaper".

We might reply to the client's initial presentation of their situation or question with stated curiosity and openness, also modelling these states for the client. We might say "that's really interesting and I'm sure there's a lot more going on than you can easily say. However, that's what I find the cards can sometimes *surprise* me with, when you're *open* to them – a new side of the situation or a new solution".

Notice also in that casual sentence a Me/You switch, embedded between the two seed words, which is a form of Ericksonian Language pattern.

We might refer to something odd and then explain it, such as a little mystery like "I never knew what was in that shop next door – did you?" which will directly elicit curiosity in the client. Again, we are not planting ideas in the head of the client, we are merely laying out positive resource states that will frame our interpretation of the cards.

Of course, the reader might also consider what positive resource states they are best in when conducting a reading, and how they can move themselves into those states at will.

## Rapport Skills

A recent study of a range of therapeutic modalities suggested that the *type* of therapy counted far less to successful outcomes than the *relationship* between the therapist and the client. In tarot, it is also the relationship we establish between the cards and client's life that is of utmost importance, and the increasing of congruity, comprehension, and consistency in their consciousness.

One way of building rapport - or certainly, not losing it - is by speaking to the client's own meta-pattern of big picture or little picture. This is sometimes called "big picture thinker" and "detailed thinker". We can discover which part of that spectrum is natural to the client, and then deliver the reading in a more easily received manner, maintaining rapport.

We should discern whether the client likes lots of detail or do they prefer a general overview? Do they get overwhelmed with detail or do they get uneasy with too vague a description? We can tell quite quickly whether someone is "big picture" or "little picture"; listen to how they describe their world or themselves. This works a bit with email enquiries too.

Do they tell us about their journey to get to see you in lots of detail? Or do they just say, "It was fine"? We can also watch how they arrange things or their gestures. Do they make lots of small precise gestures, or a few sweeping ones?

Often someone who is opposite in their pattern to you (you are "big picture" naturally and they are "little picture") you might find annoying, frustrating, or confusing, or just not "get".

Another way of telling is to watch in the corner of your eye which way they unconsciously move when you put the cards out on the table. If they move slightly back to see the whole layout, they are a "big picture" person, and if they move forwards to look at the cards, they are a "little picture" person - or have poor eyesight, you always need to check in several ways before jumping to a conclusion.

Once you know if they are particularly big/little picture, deliver your reading with that in mind - to help them. If they are big picture, use lots of general stories, metaphors, keep providing a summary and overview - don't get lost in detail. If they are little picture, use lists, details, pick out different points in the cards and symbols - they can handle it.

When you finish the reading, summarise it in general terms for the big picture person like so "So, overall, there are positive currents when you use the things you have done in the past ..." and for the little picture person, summarise it in a list of precise details like so, "As I mentioned with the Four of Cups and the Fish on the Page of Cups, you will be twice as successful in your business if you take the four creative steps of ..."

The best practice for all these skills is listening to people in your life with the concept in your mind. Make an exercise to find someone who is a really big picture thinker and someone who is a really small picture thinker - they may be obvious when you see them in this way.

Also ask what are they good at, both approaches, and what not so good? What eases them, what disrupts them? And... which one are you? How can you change your thinking and language to be flexible in both modes?

## Impossible Questions

In Tarosophy, we adopt the NLP Magick principle of "Incorporate and Utilise", which itself draws on the approach of psychiatrist and hypnotherapist Milton H. Erickson (1901 - 1980).[53] In the case of incorporation, we accept all communication in a session, be it a hypnotherapy session, counselling session, tarot reading or conversation on a train. Any confusion, conflict, or challenge is simply met as a communication which can be utilised, rather than an obstacle.

This approach works to make a tarot reading a far more dynamic and interactive experience for both reader and sitter. It also applies to just about any situation that will ever arise and prompt creative solutions in real-time, rather than a rule-book which cannot answer every possible issue.

Sometimes, for example, if we take the whole notion of divination to the extreme, there could well be a totally impossible question presented to us. I am not sure what this might be, but let us presume it could be something such as "how does God(ess) work?"

Firstly, if it is impossible to answer, we do not attempt to answer it, but rather we do incorporate it as a useful situation. As we are tarot readers, with the spirit of curiosity that is the hallmark of Tarosophists, we might want to know *why* the question is impossible to answer. That does sound like a question we can ask our tarot.

We draw a few cards, dependent on our usual style. We then interpret them to get an understanding of *why* the question is impossible to ask or answer through the tarot.

## Example

**Actual Question**: "*Why* is it *impossible* for the tarot to answer, 'how does God(ess) work?'"

---

[53] See Marcus Katz, *NLP Magick* (Keswick: Forge Press, 2020), pp. 48-9.

**Cards**: Judgement card, crossed by the Six of Cups, with a clarifier card of the Five of Swords.

**Interpretation**: To awaken this question, it is as if you are asking a question that can only be understood from a new life. It is blocked by spiritual immaturity and exceeds the boundaries of your expectations.[54]

Once we have that answer, we can then further utilise it by continuing to accept (incorporate) the impossibility of an answer, in asking "what can we do (if anything) to make the question possible to answer?"

We can then draw one or a few cards dependent on our usual style and interpret the cards as an action we can take, or a new way of thinking about the question.

## Example

**Cards**: Two of Pentacles crossed by Nine of Cups, a clarifier card of Three of Cups.

**Interpretation**: We must organise the physical practice (Two of Pentacles) of our spiritual life into a more harmonious (Three of Cups) way of celebrating the divine and not just sit on our bench (Nine of Cups) imagining we might be able to ask that question. Then, the answer to making the question possible, requires it to be part of a fully engaged spiritual life, not just a one-off question in the middle of the other stuff of life.

We then set about actually doing the actions as suggested by the reading. We can eventually then satisfy the bounds of the impossible and make something possible. Once we have done so, we might re-ask the original question in some new light, phrasing or from an entirely different perspective.

If we do not understand the answer even from the new perspective, we can ask the tarot a similarly incorporated and gently curious question as to what we can do to understand the answer. Once we get that tarot is a language, we can talk to it about anything.

---

[54] Using references from Tali Goodwin & Marcus Katz, *Tarot Flip* (Keswick: Forge Press, 2020).

## Defusing a Bomb

When we might have issues interpretating Court cards in a reading, particularly when they are buried in the middle of a spread, we can often get more information by taking the cards to an extreme. As we might be having issues interpreting their characters, behaviour, nature or even energy, rather than trying to take that limited knowledge to an extreme, we take a situation they could be in to an extreme. In fiction writing, it is sometimes said that a character is best revealed by their reactions to challenges rather than simply a description of their traits. And of course, a narrative is best constructed by constantly providing increasing challenges to your protagonist.

If we take an extreme situation and drop our somewhat uninspired, insipid or sketched-out characters, into the middle of it, we often discover a lot more about them than we might have guessed. My personal go-to situation is posed as a simple question, particularly when it is a pair of Court cards:

- How would they defuse a ticking bomb with only moments to go?

This is from a real reading where I was struggling to get a lot of detail about how a Court card representing the client and another Court card had come up, representing a work colleague, regarding a project which had a tight deadline. I simply made the situation a bit more extreme so I could dig more detail out of the two Court cards.

If the question had been "is X the right partner for me?", we might look at the two Court card(s) in a reading, and say instead, "How would these two investigators work out if Mr. Normal is the serial killer or not?" When we have answered that question, it will throw more light on the way in which the client will work with their prospective partner, whether they go into crime-fighting or otherwise!

A question about a work project with a one-card draw producing a difficult-to-read Court Card becomes "We have a month before global disaster, what does this Court card invent that no-one has considered, to save the day?"

We always make the scenario ludicrously extreme so we can test the character and draw out what we already unconsciously know about 'that sort of person' who is a Knight of Wands, and how they would react coupled with a Queen of Cups in a plunging elevator.

That is the first trick with this technique of extreme thinking, then there is a twist.

If we take any truculent or recurring question, we can conduct a reading by using a split-deck of just the Court cards, drawing out one or two cards. We then turn the question into a dramatic scenario and resolve it in some fictional or narrative manner with the court card or cards.

Then we simply wait a few days without attempting to read the Court card in any more detail or as an answer to the actual question. We have already processed the answer unconsciously, by "chunking it up" to an extreme - the actual solution to our question often then arrives naturally and suddenly in our conscious mind after a few days. It may also come to us upon wakening, in a weird synchronicity or in a dream - it is quite a magical technique. Sometimes it may even come as a weird change in the situation or event that you could not have possibly influenced.

This NLP-based practice will also help you practice the 'extreme' exercise skill which will kick in unconsciously whenever court cards come up in a reading or any spread. Our best Tarosophy exercises install new patterns in our unconscious, which it will often take on board as easily as a new habit.

## Dreams and Tarot

In Tarosophy we take a generally Jungian approach to dreams, particularly inspired by the work of James A. Hall M.D.[55]

People in dreams are either a part of oneself that is consciously recognisable, in the case of a known person in the dream, i.e., our mother, a friend, or Taylor Swift, etc., or, if it is an unknown person, i.e., "a young woman wearing a black dress" then it represents a part of oneself that is unconscious. The characteristics of that person, known or unknown, correspond to the part of the self being expressed, for example, if you thought that Taylor Swift was an "independent and creative woman", it would be that independent and creative part of yourself - a conscious part - that was being active in the dream.

Their behaviour, role, or relationship to others in the dream will indicate their position and function in the psyche. If you were dreaming that Taylor Swift was arguing with someone, that would possibly represent an internal conflict from your independent and creative side of the psyche. This will often relate to an external cause which is activating this conflict.[56]

A building in a dream often represents the whole psyche, such as a house or home. If we are in the attic, it is a "higher" part of the psyche, and the basement will be a "lower" part. The "living room" will be a symbol of our daily life, etc. A school building specifically represents our sense of education or a Church symbolises our beliefs.

A person in a dream can be assigned a Court card and a place can be assigned a Major Arcana card. We can then assign a Minor card to the activity of the dream; if it were a celebration, we could assign the Three of Cups or the Four of Wands, for example.

When we have assigned a set of cards to a dream, we can draw them out of the deck and then shuffle the remainder of the deck, asking, "What is the message of this dream, in terms of tarot?" We can then draw 3-5 cards to further analyse the dream.

In fact, we can then have those cards next to our bed and seek to enter them in our dreams, creating a constant feedback of symbols between life, dream and divination.

There is no division between cards, dream, and reality; they are all merely aspects of our relationship to divinity. This much we can learn each time they coincide with each other.[57]

---

[55] See James A. Hall, *Jungian Dream Interpretation* (Toronto: Inner City Books, 1983).

[56] See Michael Conforti, *Field, Form and Fate* (Sheridan: Fisher King Press, 1999).

[57] For work on dreams and tarot, see Tali Goodwin & Marcus Katz, *Tarot Temple* (Keswick: Forge Press, 2014).

## Tarot Talismans

The twenty-two Major Arcana of the Tarot are illustrations of archetypes, or fundamental patterns and forces that project the world and in turn, are projected by us back into the world. As a result, they can be powerful communication tools in a reading and serve as a profound magical tool to generate change in our reality.

One of the simplest ways in which we can utilise the Arcana as a magical tool is by creating a talisman. These talismans are somewhat like sigils but are designed to be a long-standing and constant energy rather than a sharp burst of intent to achieve some immediate result.

As it is often "lust of result" that gets in the way of magical acts, we can go some way to remove this by stacking tarot cards in a talisman. This helps us submerge the initial intent in layers of symbolism, freeing us from obsessing upon the result and allowing us to concentrate on the pure will, "unassuaged of purpose".[58]

## Creating a Talisman

We first select two Major Arcana cards that serve our *purpose*; that embody the nature of the change we wish to bring about. In this example case, we are going to look at protective talismans. Protective talismans are a good exercise for beginners as they are "passive" in a sense and serve to protect only the caster but can also bring about noticeable positive consequences.

If we were in a situation where someone was misusing their authority against us, for example, we might select the Magician and the Hierophant. One is about control and power, the other is about authority and respect.

Another example might be the Blasted Tower and the Devil card; together they would create a talisman which protected you from sudden shocks – shocks which might result in being chained to something unwanted in your life.

A third example might be to create a talisman protecting your family, which would be the Empress and the Emperor, perhaps, for balance too, or the Empress and the Sun, for better luck.

## Suggested Talismanic Powers of the Major Arcana

Fool: Freedom, Choice, Liberation, Space to Breath.
Magician: Chance to Speak, Success, Accomplishment.
High Priestess: Protection from Ill Speaking, Keeping under the Radar.

---

[58] "For pure will, unassuaged of purpose, delivered from the lust of result, is every way perfect", Aleister Crowley, *Liber Al* [1:44].

Empress: Family Protection, Growth of all Projects and Work.

Emperor: Power, Energy, Authority, Recognition, Control.

Hierophant: Courage of your own Commitments, Attracting Experts.

Lovers: Love, Choice, Passion.

Chariot: Victory, Triumph over Odds.

Strength: Strength, Courage.

Hermit: Simplification, Clarity, Leadership (with Emperor).

Wheel: Good Luck, Revolution, Change of Fortune, Finances.

Justice: Fair Play, Balance, Resolution of Work/Life Split.

Hanged Man: Exposure of what is Hidden.

Death: Change, Letting Go of Old Habits, etc.

Temperance: Grace, Favour, Divine Guidance.

Devil: Pleasure, Facing Your Shadow, Fearlessness.

Blasted Tower: Acceleration, Sudden Change, Clearing the Air.

Star: Ideas, Inspiration, making your own future, following of a vision.

Moon: A talisman to encourage divinatory dreams.

Sun: A talisman to bring success.

Last Judgement: A talisman for entering a new life, stepping into a new job, etc.

World: Binding, Finishing and Starting Anew, general protection.

To create a Tarot Talisman, select two appropriate cards, choose a specific symbol from each, and draw them together or on top of each other, such as a lightning flash and a chain for the Blasted Tower and the Devil.

Draw them how you feel is most appropriate.

In the case of the Empress and the Sun, the talisman might be a sheaf of wheat and a sun symbol.

Then *seal* the talisman with a third Major Arcana card, which should be chosen to represent the strength or resources *available to you already*, no matter how weak or small. This is the Tarosophy tweak with talismans, in that we have found it best to always leverage your current situation and amplify the archetypal patterns from where you are presently. This avoids merely trying to create a talisman (or sigil) that is entirely constructed of future components, and not at all grounded or earthed in anything of the present.[59]

If you are unsure, choose the Strength card.

Another example would be that if you had already some amount of time available to you, you could choose the Wheel of Fortune, or if you had expert advice already to hand, the Hierophant.

You can choose a card already used within the pair of cards if it is

---

[59] As with much of the magical practice of Tarosophy, this approach is grounded from analysis and experimentation of systems from the Golden Dawn, Aleister Crowley and many others, to derive the fundamental working model.

appropriate, simply choose the same - or a different - symbol from the same card.

Next draw a shape around the two central symbols using a symbol from the third card. In the case of the Wheel, simply draw a Wheel in a circle around the symbols.

In the case of the Hierophant, perhaps a triangle of Keys or a Circle of Crosses. Use the symbol most fitting to you and in the shape that conveys most protection.

## Using Your Talisman

Place your talisman under your pillow, in your garage, car, pocket or at your place of work, etc., wherever most appropriate for the talisman to function.

- Those with an esoteric background or training might utilise other means of activating or charging the talisman to most effect.

- Those with astrological background might choose a specific time to create the talisman.

- Those drawn to colour and correspondences might choose specific colours.

- Those with knowledge of numerology or divine architecture might choose a specific number of symbols to draw as a seal on the talisman.

- Those experienced in ceremony and ritual might use the talisman itself to inspire a whole ceremony or unique ritual.

- Those skilled with oils and incenses can blend a particular and corresponding scent.

- Those who work with pantheons can select out the appropriate and corresponding deities to bless the talisman, such as Zeus (Wheel) and Hestia (Empress).

Have the talisman active in whatever chosen manner for a specific period, i.e., a lunar month or until the threat has passed.

Whatever happens, destroy the talisman after a set period. You do not want to remain attached to an outworn protection.

To destroy the talisman, burn it or bury it, throw it in a river or cut it into pieces and fling it into the air, depending on the elemental nature of the two Major Arcana chosen for the talisman.

Experiment, play, and discover combinations that work for you.

# - VIII -
## THE MAJOR ARCANA

## Reading the Majors (A 32-Day Course)

A student of Tarosophy is encouraged to learn to read using only the twenty-two Major Arcana. Ideally, we should be able to conduct a spread such as the Celtic Cross using the Majors and reversals, and divine from these cards not only the thematic patterns but also granular detail and practical advice in the situation.[60]

With just a few Major Arcana we can often get to the heart of any situation and discover the *lesson* we are being encouraged to learn from the *challenge* of the situation – and what *resources* are best employed to meet that challenge and learn that lesson.[61] This makes the Major-only reading a very direct and practical approach, although it is often said that tarot cannot do this in comparison to Lenormand, for example.

The methods we give in this book for Majors-Only readings can also be usefully employed with a Tarot de Marseille (TdM) deck or one of the readers preferred Majors-Only Deck - I have provided a brief outline of some of my own favourite Majors-Only decks at the conclusion of this book.

We can consider that Major Arcana cards are nexus points, placeholders of patterns, somewhat like the junctions that turn roads into journeys. They work together to illustrate that our experience is a series of relationships, which create the specific journey – a "Fool's Journey" if you like – of each individual. It is not only what happens to us that creates the journey but how we respond to it.[62]

1. Take the twenty-two Majors out of your deck or use a Majors-only deck.

2. Shuffle whilst thinking of the situation or question.

3. Take the top card and the bottom card of the pile.

4. Place them side-to-side, the bottom card on the left, the top to the right.

---

[60] I started reading tarot when I was 13 and used only a photocopied deck of twenty-two IJJ Swiss cards, with reversals, and the Celtic Cross, as it was the only spread I knew. As no-one told me that might be difficult, I never learnt that it was difficult and comfortably read that way for over two years before buying a seventy-eight card deck. I then initially found it more difficult to read using Minor cards rather than reverting to just using the Major Arcana.

[61] This is, in part, why we teach these three aspects in our three-minute beginner method. It means that the student has already learnt and practised the heart of Majors-only reading by the time they are ready to try it.

[62] See *Fearless* (1993), dir. Peter Weir.

5. Say to yourself, "Everything is going from [name of left card] towards [name of right card]".

We might say, "Everything is going from the Tower to the Sun" or "Everything is going from the Devil to the Hermit".

That may already give you some idea of the situation, but do not try to interpret the cards.

As these two cards are describing the flow of the tide, we now need to know what to do.

· With the Majors we may not immediately get a "straight" answer, we get something we must learn, in the face of a challenge by drawing on implied resources. We take it that we are never given more than with we which can deal.

6. To discover the lesson, shuffle the remaining twenty cards whilst considering the two-card sentence.

7. Pick out one card from those twenty cards from anywhere in the stack and place it above the two cards already laid out.

8. Say "In order that [or "so that"] I can recognise [name of card]".

We might say, "In order that I can recognise the Chariot" or "In order that I can recognise the World".

In our example, then, we might have "Everything is going from the Tower to the Sun so that I can recognise the Chariot".

Now we can simply interpret that oracular utterance straight from our reaction to the images, use our normal reading experience, or even look up key-words and replace them in the sentences:

- "Everything is going from sudden change to expansion so that I can recognise my own direction".

(or)

- "Everything is going from shock to growth so that I can recognise limits".

Every interpretation will likely work because the Major cards are images of big patterns and particular junctions.

Also, we all naturally have been taught to learn lessons in th
our parents, peers and education; "learn to stick up for you
patience, save your money", and so on.

Now it is time to learn for ourselves - with our tarot deck to help us.

We would then know in our example above that we can learn the lesson
by being clear about our direction or making boundaries. We would not be
served by going with the flow or blindly agreeing with something. The
reading advises that we are in a good position to be more direct and state our
case, etc.

The Majors show us the currents underneath all situations and what we
are being taught in order to get the most out of that current.

This is also why Majors-only readings will work for even the most
apparently mundane situation; everything arises from these basic principles –
the Devil followed by the Tower may just be the loss of a favourite item of
clothing to which you were attached, to learn the lesson of the Hermit, i.e.,
not getting attached to things.

## Majors Only Method

Another problem that many new readers have with the Major Arcana is that
they feel that they are "big picture" things, archetypes, majors, even!
Unfortunately, we tend to consolidate that fact, equating them to archetypes,
cosmic themes, the gods and goddesses, and other abstract concepts. What
happens when we try and apply that to "Should I buy a new car or repair my
current car?" type questions, of a mundane nature?

What we can do is ask one question of the Major Arcana card; "What does
it do for me?"

As an exercise, for each Major Arcana, fill in the blank word at the end of
this sentence:

- THE [MAJOR CARD] MAKES ... [Your Word Here].

## Examples

- The Magician MAKES magick.
- The High Priestess MAKES mystery.
- The Hermit MAKES his way.
- The Chariot MAKES tracks.
- The Hanged Man MAKES sacrifice.
- The Devil MAKES mischief.
- The Tower MAKES change.

ın completing this simple sentence, we automatically, naturally, quickly, and easily communicate with the archetype, tune into it, condense everything we have learnt about the card and discover the core of it - the *function*.

The function of the archetype that is illustrated by the Magician is to carry "magick" in the world and our relationship to it. The function of the archetype that is illustrated by the Tower is to hold all notions, concepts and examples of sudden change or shock.

Having made this simple sentence, we can apply it straight to our question by asking:

- What ACTION would MAKE the same thing as the CARD?

**Example**

If I pulled the Magician, for my question about buying a new car, I would have to ask, what action (buying a new car OR keeping my current car) would also make magick, i.e., serve the same function as the Magician does in the deck?

To me, making magick is about changing things, at the very least, so that function would be served by buying a new car. The fact that Mercury corresponds to the Magician, etc., backs that up, but is not necessary to know.

If I got the DEVIL card for the same question, I would realise that keeping my current car would be quite mischievous, rather than buying something brand new and obvious. The fact that the Devil has chains and signifies something we are attached to is useful, but again, not necessary to know.

For different readers, it might be the other way round, but this method is about your relationship to the universe through the archetypes, so should differ from every reader.

Here is my list for possible inspiration:

The Fool makes fun.
The Magician makes magic.
The High Priestess makes mystery.
The Empress makes plenty.
The Emperor makes boundaries.
The Hierophant makes tradition.
The Lovers makes union.
The Chariot makes tracks.
Strength makes endurance.
The Hermit makes his way.

The Wheel of Fortune makes movement/revolution.
Justice makes laws.
The Hanged Man makes sacrifice.
Death makes transformation.
Temperance makes tolerance.
The Devil makes mischief.
The Tower makes change.
The Star makes clarity.
The Moon makes reflection.
The Sun makes will.
The Last Judgment makes awareness.
The World makes evolution.

We will now work through all twenty-two Major Arcana with a lesson taught by each card in sequence. The cards will be given as overlapping from one end of the sequence to the other, to demonstrate that they are best considered always in a mobile dance with each other. We will start with the Magician (I) and the World (XXI) as a pair, and then move inwards, with the High Priestess (II) and the Last Judgement (XX), etc. This will also demonstrate how to create single key-words and concepts for pairs of Majors.

We will also see how each card reacts in reversals, as the Fool takes a journey through all the Major Arcana as reversed images, shedding his necessity to find the true meaning of the soul's journey.

It is recommended that the student of Tarosophy take each lesson as a daily contemplation, for a working which will last thirty-two days, with an extra summary day, lasting about a month. This inbuilt course can be taken following the Tarot Principles earlier in this book, in a similar manner, providing an intermediate or advanced two-month practice.

# Lesson 1

~

THE MAGICIAN MET THE WORLD AND SAID,
MY WILL IS THE SAME AS YOUR WILL -
LET US CALL IT NATURE.

~

We begin by pairing the cards in a particular sequence so we can learn how they compare or contrast. In this first lesson we pair the Magician (I) and the World (XXI). If we imagine that they are having a conversation, one possible topic they might discuss is their sense and meaning of Will.

The Magician has an individual Will, skill and intent to manipulate, particularly given the correspondence to Mercury. The World, in contrast, is the complete Will of all things, all four elements acting together as a whole. They both share these four elements, in fact – the Magician has them on his table, ready for his use, whereas the World dances within their quarters.

They also share a duality; the World sometimes carries two wands signifying duality, and the Magician likewise carries a wand and points to the above and below. In this symbolism, they both say to us, from One comes Two, from Two comes One, and from One and Two comes All.

Together, we might consider their keyword to be 'Nature'.

They are nature as our interaction with it, and it with us – when we pour salt on our meal, we are the Magician; when we cry at a sunset, we are the World.

When these two cards come up together, they signify a highly connected point in time, where we take full responsibility for what happens – everything (the World) hinges on our decision (Magician). Whatever the question, these two cards are going to show it is "natural" for it to be, or what follows. In Love, this would show a willing coming together, but possible manipulation (depending on other cards) or in Business and other matters, the power to change the outcome.

This pair, in a sense, is both beginning and end, and so a shorthand for everything in between – our mind is set on the outcome, and so it is most likely to arise as we desire.

**Lesson 2**

~

THE HIGH PRIESTESS WAS CALLED TO THE LAST JUDGEMENT
AND SAID,
WHAT I KEEP SECRET YOU HAVE CALLED TO ALL -
LET US CALL IT REVELATION.

~

In this second pair, we have a contrast rather than a comparison – one card is about secrets and mystery whilst the other card is about every secret becoming known to God in the Last Judgement. They are truly opposite – one is the inner world of the individual, and one is the new world shared by all humankind. One is the inner intuition, and one is the universal calling.

Yet they are both a form of communication; the deep psychic well of personal connection on one hand; and the wide sense of common shared experience on the other. When these cards are together, they illustrate how we judge ourselves and others, and how that judgement tells us more about ourselves than it can ever tell us of another.

We are not our own mystery – the mystery is other people, and yet in this we all share the same common veil in our connection to others. The only thing we know for sure is that we reflect upon ourselves (the Moon corresponds to the High Priestess) and we sense that others do likewise.

There is a Revelation in this pair of cards, in everyday terms it would be a secret (High Priestess) revealed (Last Judgement). It would also be an immediate and powerful call to action, a trumpet blast of awakening to something we sort-of-sensed was already the case.

In Love, this would be a confession, a sudden truth, a demand for honesty, in business and other matters, likewise. It might also manifest as a private matter of inner insight to what one must do – how one might act in an authentic sense, true to self and the circumstances to which one is called. We might also notice the equal-armed cross in both cards and perhaps suggest that one card is simply "keep silent" and the other is "speak out".

# Lesson 3

~

## THE EMPRESS MET THE SUN AND SAID,
## WHAT I NURTURE, YOU EMPOWER -
## LET US CALL IT LIFE.

~

Next, we look at a pair of Major Arcana that could be seen to supplement each other more than they could be said to compare or contrast.

The Empress and the Sun are two cards usually seen as being extremely positive; in *Tarot Flip* we discovered that the unconscious keywords by actual readers for these two cards is 'cultivation' (Empress) and 'demonstration' (Sun).[63] That might seem a strange word for the Sun but consider how expansive and growth-promoting is the Sun; and those Solar Gods like to demonstrate their power – in fact, they cannot hold it back.

The Empress is gradual growth, promoted by the energy of the Sun and together they are life itself. All that lives, lives. This much is true – and we are part of the garden in whatever role we find ourselves.

In fact, let us consider that the earthy Empress is *matter* as much as *mother*, and the Sun (our father) is Light. Is not everything a matter of light as much as it is a light matter?

Together in a reading then, this pair would be wonderful – literally, full of wonder, and opportunity. It would signify that there is inevitable and good growth; whether it be in love, business, education, or travel – there is time (a solar year) to develop the situation.

And this is life, is it not – a moment of time measured in years in which we are born from the mother and make our way back to the light of the Sun?

If we consider their reversals, the Sun keyword (in *Tarot Flip*) is "concealment", and the Empress is "harm". It is unnatural in both cases; the mother should not harm her offspring, and the Sun should not be hidden – a fact which perturbed our ancestors greatly upon an eclipse. Yet there is something wonderful even here; suppose we had them both reversed and accepted those meanings? They would say to us "a harm is being concealed". In fact, they would tell us to be aware of such harm and bring it to light. Even reversed, these two cards cannot help but do good and promote growth and light.

---

[63] Tali Goodwin & Marcus Katz, *Tarot Flip* (Keswick: Forge Press, 2020), p. 40 & p. 45.

## Lesson 4

~

THE EMPEROR MET THE MOON AND SAID,
WHAT I RULE, YOU CHANGE -
LET US CALL IT ADAPTABILITY.

~

Now we see a very opposite pair to our prior pair, in the Emperor and the Moon, rather than the Empress and the Sun. The Major cards themselves are illustrations of the biggest patterns in life, to which we adapt; this might also be considered the teaching of the Empress and the Sun ("life") with the Emperor and the Moon ("adaptability").

If we had to come up with one word which was defined by "big patterns to which we adapt in life", or "life, adapting" almost the first word we might think is "evolution". This is an example of how we can take four cards together and combine their singular keywords into one word – a technique my co-author Tali Goodwin calls the "Keyword Kaleidoscope".[64]

- Life + Adaptability = Evolution.

When we now consider how the Empress and Emperor are the female and male energies, the mother and father, form, and force; and the Sun and Moon are the very life-giving and controlling factors of time and the tide from which we emerged, these four cards are indeed a perfect illustration of evolution. Even better, whenever any of these four cards comes up in a reading, we might see them as a quarter of the pattern of "evolution" and this may tell us something important.

The Moon in a 'past' position might suggest that the person's evolution was in the past and had been a somewhat dark experience but had brought about change to the present point. The Sun in an 'obstacle' position might suggest that the person's evolution was their present challenge and they needed to "demonstrate" their evolution to meet that challenge.

A fifteen-card reading with the Empress and Emperor in it could show us that their evolution was connected to their own patterns inherited from their parents.

We can contemplate how a combination between a fixed card such as the Emperor and a flexible card such as the Moon can provide a very energetic

---

[64] Tali Goodwin & Marcus Katz, *Around the Tarot in Seventy-Eight Days* (Woodbury: Llewellyn Publications, 2012), pp. 20-3.

and positive pair. Consider also that we have already learnt that we "compare, contrast or combine" any pair of cards, and now we can also add that a Major card can be loosely categorized as "fixed" or "flexible".

In the next lesson, we will pair the Hierophant (V) and the Star (XVII) and see how these simple pairings and basic categories can lead us easily to read Major-Arcana-only spreads.

## Lesson 5

~

THE HIEROPHANT MET THE STAR AND SAID,
WHERE I TEACH, YOU GUIDE –
LET US CALL THAT ENLIGHTENMENT.
THE STAR REPLIED
SOME MIGHT CALL IT INDOCTRINATION.

~

When we communicate, we teach, and the world is communicating its teaching to us all the time. This is called "exemplarism" in mystical philosophy. The way in which we learn is equal in part to the way we are taught. This is the process of education. All education in any subject is the passing of information from one person or situation to another. This is communication.

We are all doctors in this sense – healers; the word 'doctor' comes from *docere*, meaning 'to teach'. It is where we also get 'indoctrination'. When we indoctrinate, as the Star accuses the Hierophant, we attempt to teach without any critical thought on behalf of the student.

The Star is our individual will in this sense; "every man and every woman is a star".[65]

The Hierophant is the 'common belief' in this sense; Hierophant means 'revealer of the sacred'.

Sometimes belief allows us to see something in the world for ourselves, sometimes it allows us to see the world as others see it. But our path is to the Star; it shines ahead in sight all the time like a navigation beacon. We swim across the ocean of belief towards it.

The Hierophant is our example of teaching; an expert, experience, professional, outside advice, power to another, belief, common thinking, rules and regulations, guidelines, taking the expected course. And the Star is our example of enlightenment; our own core principles, our individualism, our

---

[65] Aleister Crowley, *Liber Al* [I.3].

will, our inner desire, direction, unique thinking, our course in life, vision, taking the road less travelled.

They are two sides of a universal philosophy:

The Hierophant really says, "do as you would have others do unto you".

The Star really says, "do what thou wilt".

Both can be selfish, wrong, and misguided as much as they can be selfless, right and guiding. The Star may be naked truth, but that can make us blind to consequences; the Hierophant is the truth delivered in a manner we can comprehend. They are both essential elements of every situation where we interact with the world, which is communication.

Let us seek to be an example, then - as much as the world provides us all the examples we require.

The cards merely teach us; they should not be tools of our own further indoctrination.

In our next lesson the Lovers arrive at the Tower and we receive (as we might by now expect) a "shocking revelation."

## Lesson 6

~

THE LOVERS MET THE TOWER AND SAID,
WHAT WE HAVE BROUGHT TOGETHER
YOU HAVE PULLED APART –
LET US CALL IT CREATION.

~

When a couple tell me about their young child, whether it be friends or family, I always ask a simple question; "Are they a builder or a breaker, or a bit of both?" Children are closer to their creation and tend to exhibit one of these two fundamental principles, and it is usually with a laugh that both parents reply together, "Oh! A Breaker! Definitely!" or "Ah! A Builder, I would say". But these two things, building and breaking, like many of the lessons we see in the Major Arcana, are two sides of the same coin, the sides of union and division.

The Lovers card is all about union, for sure. Whether it be literal love and marriage or the signing of a house contract, it is the bringing together of two parties in binding agreement – perhaps.

Because the chance for union is also the chance for division. To put it in reverse, again quoting Crowley, here channeling a divine spirit speaking on behalf of the whole Universe; "For I am divided for love's sake, for the chance of union".[66]

That Blasted Tower, the 'house of god' struck by lightning, is always waiting to break things apart.

Who would build a machine without a reset button? Not even God, despite us believing "those whom God hath joined together let no man put asunder". It is the process of creation, the expulsion of everything from its source and the fall into matter.

The Lovers is also choice (particularly so in earlier decks), free will, and its consequences, illustrated by the Tower, the destruction of what was once considered perfect.

But nothing is perfect, says the serpent.

Nothing is built forever, says the lightning.

And these two things; the serpent crawling back to the garden and the lightning striking down the tree are Creation itself – both, together.

The DNA coils of which we are constructed brick by brick like a tower; the electricity that charges our chemicals to make us love or feel lonely, even the machines built of sand which has been fused into silicon and again across which electricity runs, trembling soft lightning into the echoing dust – everything is just a matter of building and breaking.

It can be a shocking revelation, that we must break to return home, to find the hill of heart's desire. We must fall, be mistaken, be wrong sometimes.[67] The tarot tells us many things, and the Majors tell us the most profound truth – everything is an echo of one story, the story of creation.

Whether the question is "will I get the promotion" to "should I go to war?", whether it is "what is the risk of moving to a new house?" or "should I invest in learning the trombone?" the story is the same. And the answer is either Love or Lightning; the Lovers or the Tower; build it or break it.

**Lesson 7**

~

THE CHARIOT MET THE DEVIL AND SAID,
WHERE I DRIVE FORWARD, YOU HOLD BACK -
LET US CALL IT REACTION.

~

In this lesson, we compare and contrast the designs of the Chariot and the Devil, for are they not amongst the most similar? A central figure, an altar of

---

[66] Aleister Crowley, *Liber Al* [I. 29].
[67] See Mark Townsend, *The Gospel of Falling Down* (Alresford: O-Books, 2007).

sorts, and two creatures in states of attachment? A. E. Waite said of the Chariot that "He has led captivity captive".[68]

This is a biblical quote:

7. Now to each one of us grace has been given according to the measure of the gift of Christ. 8. Therefore it says: "When He ascended on high, He led captives away, and gave gifts to men." 9. What does "He ascended" mean, except that He also descended to the lower parts of the earth?
[Ephesians 4:8]

Of the Devil he says, "Hereof is the chain and fatality of the material life" and compares it to the Lovers, which we have chosen to call "union" in our earlier lesson of that card.[69] The Devil is the way the Union of the Lovers was dissolved - by a deliberate and willed separation, by pride, selfishness and divisive thought, or the fall to act upon some temptation - or contempt.[70]

Further, the Chariot is the power of the mind, intellect, and rationality. It is a world in which there is only black and white, one way or the other. We answer the riddle of the Sphinx by thinking about it. The Chariot is a resolution and clarity of mind, by which we can get so far.

The Devil is the opposing force, the ignorance by which we also enslave ourselves and keep ourselves captive – by the deliberate and reasoned perversion of the truth.

It could be that we really want to say something, but do not. It could be that we really want to do something, but do not. It could be that we really want to be someone else but cannot.

The Chariot is reason applied to liberation and the Devil is reason applied to oppression.

They are the push and pull of the Universe, and their presence in a reading shows how the energy is being pushed forwards or is being pulled back.

When they are together in a reading, we must see in which positions they fall to see where the core conflict is playing out in the situation. Something in the past against something in the future; something for which we hope against someone supposedly supporting us?

Together they are reaction; a reaction to something, inside or outside, which is dictated by the other cards in the reading. The Chariot is good for pressing ahead, the Devil is good for holding us back - sometimes from a terrible mistake. The Chariot is bad for pressing us ahead, sometimes into a terrible mistake, and the Devil is bad for holding us back.

---

[68] Arthur Edward Waite, *The Pictorial Key to the Tarot* (London: Rider & Company, 1974), p. 96.

[69] *Ibid*, p. 128.

[70] Interestingly, according to one relationship expert, the main feeling that he proposed as a key significator ahead of unreconcilable break-ups in relationships was not hatred, mistrust, or anything but *contempt*. Once one partner (or both) had *contempt* for the other, it could be that the relationship is irretrievable from that point.

The Major Arcana are neither good nor bad in themselves for they all illustrate essential functions in creation. Now that we have three pairs remaining to discover, and a card which stands justly alone, let us look at a simple four-card reading using the Majors we have already explored.

## The Cross of Conversation.

1. Shuffle the 22 cards whilst considering a situation and lay four cards out in a cross; top, bottom, left and right.

2. If you wish you can first lay down a Court Card for your Significator, and then lay the four Major Arcana in a cross about the Significator.

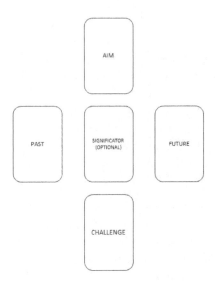

*Illus. The Cross of Conversation.*

3. The positions are:

Top: The highest thing to which you should aspire (i.e., the "advice" or "aim" card).

Bottom: The thing which is most bound to hold you back (i.e., the "challenge" card).

*However, the top card may also be blinding us to the present, and the bottom card may have much to teach us, so we should consider them as a pair. In their conversation we can find more information.*

Left: That which must be done to gain release (i.e., the "past" card).

Right: That which is coming and which we must utilize (i.e., the "fortune-telling" or "future" card).

Again, that which is coming (right) and that to which we aspire (top) may be usefully compared or contrasted in conversation as a pair.

*That which is to be released (left) and that which is holding us back (bottom) may also have a conversation in which their pairing can tell us a great deal.*

## Example

**Question**: "What should we do about X? Should we ignore it, support it or compete with it?"

**Cards**:

- Top (aim): Chariot.
- Bottom (challenge): World.
- Left (past): Star.
- Right (future): Devil.

*Illus. Conversational Cross Reading Example.*

Briefly then, we should aim to reason it out, be rational (and not emotional). We should certainly move ahead and not hold back [Chariot]. The challenge is that "everything" [The World] is holding us back, it might even feel like everything is against us. How can the Chariot ride away from the whole World? The release must come from the Star; so, doing our own Will, enlightenment, guiding and teaching. What we must utilize is the Devil; to put ourselves in a deliberately 'shackled' position.

All of which sounds strange but makes much sense in the real situation for which these cards were drawn. In effect, a situation we might have chosen to simply ignore we are being advised instead to walk into, fully accepting the constraints. It is like Daniel in the Lion's Den or putting the fox amongst the chickens.

For the reader taking these lessons as a daily contemplation, today practice this four-card reading.

In our next lesson we will look further at the possible pairings of these four cards and conduct another reading to show how even the most mundane questions can be answered directly with Major Arcana.

## Lesson 8

~

STRENGTH MET TEMPERANCE AND SAID,
WHERE I AM FORCE, YOU ARE FLOW –
LET US CALL IT CALL IT POWER.

~

The Tarot Major Arcana are the big things, but these things apply to everything, even the little things. When a client asks the reader to interpret the cards for an apparently mundane question, such as "Where did I leave my house keys?" it is already part of a bigger story. And we cannot ever decide what is "mundane" and what might be "magical" as we are not the judge of our own history. Neither do we know everything.

The location of the car keys, or the journey to locate them, may be the little bit of the story that becomes "It's funny how I met my lifetime partner – I was just looking for my keys".

Imagine that and recall those moments in life that were big but had small bits; you bought a newspaper that day and found a job or inspiration to change your life or travel, instead of buying it another day. Someone played you a piece of music that turned you onto a new path.

Strength is the force that encourages us all to face the lion which is life. We might try and close its jaws in fear or open them in daring, or we might simply try and hold on for dear life. But it roars. Temperance is sometimes more like the tempering of steel than the temperate nature; it perhaps says, "What does not kill me makes me stronger", although tempering can produce brittleness as well as it produces sharpness.

They are both cards about a balancing of power – and their positions on the Golden Dawn version of the Tree of Life correspondences illustrate this better than words:

Too much tempering, you eventually lose your temper, and everything spills out.

Too much strength, you eventually become weak and get eaten by it.
Too little tempering, there is only overwhelming anger.
Too little strength, there is only defeat.

We must locate our power in the middle of these cards, where the Angel's hands hold the cups at just the right angle, and the Maiden's hands hold the jaws of the Lion, just so.

Fulton J. Sheen (1895 - 1979), a Catholic bishop, said this of power:

> *Patience is power.*
> *Patience is not an absence of action;*
> *rather it is "timing"*
> *it waits on the right time to act,*
> *for the right principles*
> *and in the right way.*

And in fact, we are half-tempted to refer to this pairing of cards as "time" rather than "power", but perhaps they are, in the end, much the same thing.

Let us briefly return to our example reading in lesson seven and see another aspect of the pairing of those cards, which were:

- Top (aim): Chariot.
- Bottom (challenge): World.
- Left (past): Star.
- Right (future): Devil.

Let us imagine we pair "that which is coming" (the Devil) and "that to which we must aspire" (Chariot), or our future and our aim. We have already seen what the Devil would say to the Chariot, and that their pairing is "reaction". We can tell from this reading that the whole situation is a "reaction" to something. It is a deeper reaction (in the real case) to one example of many situations and a reaction that needs to be understood and resolved at a wider level.

We might advise the client – ourselves in this case – that we must not over-react as it is something that is pushing our buttons. In doing so we can go deeper into the cause of that reaction beyond the present question and be more profound in our reading.

Let us imagine that we must "release" the Star to meet the "challenge" of the World by pairing those two cards. We know from our key-words that the Star is being considered as "guidance" and the World is being considered as "Will" (universal Will rather than individual). We know that the Star is one-half of a pair considered as "enlightenment" and the World is one-half of the pair we have called "Nature".

There is a deeper guidance going on here, that the person (ourselves) must release our ability to guide to be true to nature; we must go into the situation as a student, not presume to be a teacher. And there is a deeper teaching in this reading too, that sometimes our roles change, and we can surrender our Will sometimes to be true to the situation, honest and authentic.

We might even imagine the conversation of that pair, as we have done for the pattern of pairs we are following in this section:

The Star met the World and said
Where I am distant, you are here –
Let us call it the Way.

Next the Hermit will meet Death but perhaps the reader following these lessons over a period of contemplation can now choose a pair of Major Arcana that are not part of our sequence and have them converse in this three-line manner as an exercise for their own journal.

## Lesson 9

~

THE HERMIT MET DEATH AND SAID,
WHERE I REMOVE MYSELF, YOU REMOVE OTHERS,
LET US CALL IT RELOCATION, RELOCATION, RELOCATION.

~

Even the Hermit and Death have some sense of humor, it seems.

My teacher once told me that the Hermit was no longer following the Way, he had *become* the Way. It took years for me to even remotely understand this, but it is true. When we live our beliefs with no gaps, there is only what we do that tells us (and others) about who we are. This is the Hermit – someone who is themselves.

When we remove ourselves from the opinions of others; our parents, siblings, friends, colleagues, and society, we become our true being and wear such opinions as rags are worn by a hermit.

It is not for us that we carry these vestiges, but for the sake of others who still believe in them. And Death does the same to us, whether symbolic or literal. It is indeed a great transformation, an initiation, a beginning as much as an end within one endless journey.

The Hermit and Death are both alone because they are illustrations of our true state – we are part of one thing, alone and not even ourselves. These cards in a reading illustrate that the person must be true to their transformation. They must accept their true nature (Hermit) or accept that it is being exposed to them (Death). Death comes to remove our attachments – the Hermit discards them. We all prefer the path of the Hermit, but it is sometimes actually easier to let Death do His Work.

In terms of relocation, these two cards fix us to a precise position - our self. The word "locate" comes from a "placing" to a specific space. The Hermit places us squarely in ourselves; it is our own job, our own responsibility, no-one else is to blame, etc. Death places us squarely in our changing; it is our own job, our own responsibility, no-one else is to blame, etc.

Hence relocation, relocation.

Let us now add to our practice a three-card 'non-positional-meaning' Majors-only reading, where the central card is 'enhanced' by the two cards to either side of it.

This is three cards without any meaning to their positions other than as an answer to the question and with the central card as the straight answer, modified by the two cards either side.

If we had the Temperance card, "flow", with the Hermit and Death, we would read:

- FLOW (Temperance) modified by RELOCATION (Hermit + Death).

We might speak this as "There is a power in finding the right time to act, in the meantime you must go with the flow. You will find the action you are considering to be significantly transformative and will not only call on you to be true to yourself, but events will unfold that support this change". In simple terms, "Yes. Do It. But Not Just Now. Because it is going to be a Humdinger".

**Example**

**Question**: What can I do to help my cat make a recovery from his surgery?

**Cards**: Strength (in the middle) + Lovers (left side) + Empress (right side).

*Illus. The Lovers, Strength & The Empress.*

Strength we have associated already with "patience is power" and the force being applied "just so". The main answer is not taking any extreme action, but almost holding one's breath. The Lovers card we have as "union" and choice, as part of the pair meaning 'creation'. Empress we have as "nurturing" and gradual growth, as part of the pair meaning 'life'.

The heart of this reading is that those cards are all about (as we have seen) taking time, nurturing, gradual growth and not taking any extreme action. We would suggest the client resisting their natural inclination to intervene in recovery, to assist him, to make exceptions for him, or anything else other than wait for him and prepare a safe space.

This question and reading, like all in Tarosophy, is based on an actual client or personal experience and in this case, was about my own cat, Alex. He had a severe wound, possibly caused by a dog attack.[71] When he came back from a major operation, he was fine from the surgery after weeks, but psychologically he would not return to the house. Based in part on this reading, as well as veterinary advice, we waited, in love and patience, without 'caring' for him.

We left the door open but did not 'force' him indoors.

We put food out, and patiently threw it away when he did not come to eat it.

And it took almost nine weeks.

Then he just came in and stayed in, and the following day, returned to his annoying habits of sleeping on every clean, fresh surface, eating more than he could eat, and generally being Alex.

Sometimes, as the reading said quite clearly, Love (Lovers) is choosing to

---

[71] Alex said it was a "bloody great werewolf", but we only have his word for that.

be Strong (Strength) enough to simply allow Nature (Empress) to take its course.

The reader following this section as an exercise is now encouraged to conduct a three-card Majors-only reading for yourself and follow the rule of keeping it simple.

In our next pairing of cards, we have a revolution on our hands, as things get turned upside-down again.

**Lesson 10**

~

THE WHEEL OF FORTUNE MET THE HANGED MAN AND SAID,
I AM ROTATION WHERE YOU ARE SUSPENSION –
LET US CALL IT CHANGE.

~

When we look at this pair of Major Arcana, which are the closest to each other in our sequence - which uses Justice as the central card - we see their clearly opposite nature. The Wheel is all about revolution, rotation, change for better and worse, luck and fate. The Hanged Man is all about stillness, suspension, even sacrifice and living to one's values. Yet both are equally about change – the Wheel turns everything upside down in our outer life, whether for good or bad, and the Hanged Man turns everything upside down from inside.

Both leave us looking at things differently, both change everything and reboot our awareness.

Without change (and time, which again we could just as easily call this pair as most other Major Arcana) there would be unending nothingness – a solid state. We must come to terms with these cards as much as (if not more than) all the other Major Arcana.

In our readings the appearance of these cards reminds us that we are on a moving platform, that stability is a brief illusion, and the only constant is change.

The Wheel allows us a moment to elegantly prepare or recover from a significant life change as the Hanged Man encourages us to initiate such a change. In both cases there must be a sacrifice; something hung from the gallows or bound to the Wheel. And that sacrifice is (as Gurdjieff said) of the only thing we truly possess, our suffering. Our suffering comes only from our attachment, what is bound to the Wheel of life or what we have bound inside ourselves – our values, belief, experience, and memory. The Wheel is everything, and the Hanged Man is our upside-down mirror of everything -

244

our awareness.

We are not bound to either, really, but merely suspended between them, like an axle. A. E. Waite placed the Wheel at the very top of the Tree of Life in his secret Fellowship of the Rosy Cross correspondence to the Kabbalah. He considered it the most sublime of the great symbols of the paths – the term he gave the Major Arcana. He saw the Majors as symbols of the paths of the Tree of Life, as illustrations of the great lessons in life, whether spiritual or mundane.

The Hanged Man he viewed (following the Golden Dawn tradition) as a 'drowned giant'; the divine spirit submerged in matter, and asleep to itself. The Wheel he viewed as the symbol of divine unity, the unification of spirit with the divine and the realization of the mystical path.

These cards are both sublime and yet immediate; every moment of our life is enacting out their mysteries; we live, we change, we live some more, in everything we do.

When these cards are present in a reading, we should ask of ourselves or our client – what is it that you want to change, what it is that you value?

They are indeed reminders of our divine nature, whether the question be about moving to a new house or how to deal with a work colleague.

Now that we have met all but one of the Major Arcana - who stands justly alone and waits for us to meet her next - let us again look at a reading, particularly for those readers following this section as a series of daily exercises.

We will now read five cards, using the same approach as we did for three cards, taking the central card as significant and the two outside pairs as adding more information.

The question is a general question, "What do I need to know most right now in my life?"

The five cards drawn are:

- Wheel + Last Judgement + Empress + Chariot + Moon.

*Illus. The Wheel of Fortune, Judgement, The Empress, The Chariot & The Moon.*

Taking the Empress as the central card, we are being advised to allow time and nurture to take place – perhaps of ourselves. Take nothing new on and tend to what we have already.

We then look at the cards immediately either side of the Empress, being the Last Judgement and Chariot. We have already seen these as "revelation" and "reason", or a calling and a pressing forward. If we paired the Last Judgement and the Chariot, we would get a 'reasonable revelation', so to speak – or in plainer language, 'think the obvious'.

The Last Judgement is our calling, and the Chariot is our vehicle to get us to where we are being called. However, there is no still no need indicated by those two cards to "do" anything, other than think it through, take time to consider our options, and listen to what calls us. We might be reminded of Fagin's song in "Oliver"; 'I'm Reviewing the Situation'.

Usually, when a song comes to mind during a reading, we should look up the full lyrics or ask our client to do so after the reading. It is often an oracular happenstance of some significance.

We then pair the Wheel and the Moon on the outside of the spread, and we have just seen the Wheel as "rotation" and as we have seen in earlier pairs, we view the Moon as "change" which is the same keyword we have just given the pair of the Wheel and the Hanged Man. The Wheel and Moon are about a cycle of change occurring outside the bounds of the question; and perhaps this is why we are cautioned to look to nothing new.

"Time's are a-changing," that pair states clearly, and you are within it, "so hold on (to what you got)". Often the Major Arcana can be explained by song lyrics and film scenes because they are all illustrating the same big narratives in our lives.

In this reading then, just at a basic glance for now – we are being advised to take time as a cycle of change wheels around us. After we have met Justice next, who stands alone, our following lessons will go deeper into reading with the Major Arcana, using different decks, reversals, spreads and new methods.

## Lesson 11

~

JUSTICE MET HERSELF AND SAID,
I AM THE MEASURE OF ALL THAT I MEASURE -
LET US CALL IT JUSTICE.

~

In the center of our sequence, where we have paired the Major Arcana from the first to the last, we have one which stands alone, as it should – Justice.

We have not yet met the Fool, for he stands unnumbered and zero, so we will meet him next as he takes us on another journey into the Majors.

Justice (in many contemporary decks) is numbered 11, and thus even the number bears witness to its character – two 1's – a double unity, symbolized by two pillars. The mystical number 111 is the single self "I" in the center of these two pillars, separate but the same – the outer and inner world and the resolution of all duality. And Justice herself corresponds to the Ancient Egyptian deity, Ma'at, who symbolizes rightness, cosmic justice, harmony, order, law, measurement, and rule. Ma'at presided over the judgment of the Soul in the underworld; it is against her feather that the heart was weighed before it could pass into the eternal fields of the afterlife. She presided in the Hall of Double Truth. This was a hall of two chambers, where firstly the heart was "assessed" and in the second chamber, weighed against the truth.

We all face these two truths in the scales of justice – the equilibrium between our inner world and our outer world, between what we say (or think) and how we actually act. The center of the scales is authenticity, being true – to oneself or any other measure, it matters not so long as one is true.

Now we have reached the center of the Major Arcana we can begin to look at reversals. In this section, we will consider them simply as misalignments or opposites, even warnings or attention-alerts.

If we take Justice as a card symbolizing fairness, equity, or "you will get what you put in", or "the right thing will happen for all", etc. then we can use these meanings to look at its reversal.

When Justice is reversed, the scales are tipped over; something is misaligned, unfair, wrong, unequal, and totally untrue. Depending on the position, this could be negative or positive; in a reading where it is the outcome of a court case, it is probably most negative as we could easily imagine.

How could it be positive, even if reversed? Imagine that someone in a situation has been lying, and this card came out as the outcome card – it might suggest that the lie would become very apparent. Reversals give us nuances into the overall reading and rarely overturn the entire interpretation, unless you have a lot of reversals.

Sometimes, if there are many reversals in a reading, I take the message that the question itself is upside-down and ask the client to ask the opposite question. I then ask them to re-shuffle so I can re-read the necessary question, not the one which was presented.

Next we will meet, at last, the Fool, and he will be the start of a new journey into the reversed Majors, for he is unnumbered, and neither at the end or the beginning – he is a reminder of true freedom.

## Reading Reversals (Majors)

## Lesson 12

~

THE FOOL MET THE MAGICIAN (REVERSED) AND SAID,
I AM FREE FROM YOUR CEASELESS TRICKERY –
YOU CAN CALL ME FREEDOM (BUT I HAVE NO NAME).

~

In the next twenty-one we are going to look at the reversals of the Major Arcana, but through the eyes of the Fool. This is because the Fool is freedom and the soul's journey of exile from the places of pestilence. The true initiatory journey of the Fool is through the *reversals* of the Major Arcana. What do we mean by this, really? We mean that the Fool is the only truly "spiritual" card in the deck because he is the illustration of unnumbered (or Zero) matter – boundless and free.[72]

Even the Major Arcana are "corrupted" (an original meaning of 'pestilence') by existence – they are the archetypal patterns that create all existence, so they have a part in it. In this regard, we can recall Agent Smith's entirely Gnostic speech to Morpheus in *The Matrix*, where he complains about his own imprisonment, even though he is the jailer:

> I'm going to be honest with you. I hate this place, this zoo, this prison, this reality, whatever you want to call it. I can't stand it any longer. It's the smell, if there is such a thing. I feel saturated by it. I can taste your stink. And every time I do I feel I have somehow been infected by it. It's repulsive, isn't it? I must get out of here. I must get free and in this mind is the key, my key.[73]

When we say a "plague on all your houses", those houses are the Major Arcana (plague is the original meaning of the word 'pestilence'). The Fool must not take on a lesson from each of these cards, he must learn what he must lose and sacrifice. The Major Arcana are the Houses of Pestilence from which he must escape. This is what Waite refers to when he says of this card,

---

[72] In the Order of Everlasting Day, this journey of reversals is called *via mutationem fortunae*, the path of reversing (or changing) fortune.
[73] *The Matrix* (dir. the Wachowskis, 1999).

"...as if earth and its trammels had little power to restrain him".[74]

Waite also writes, "He is a prince of the other world on his travels through this one..." signifying indeed that there is something vastly different about this card.[75] In fact, in Waite's second tarot set, ten years after his work with Pamela Colman Smith, it is explicit that the Fool is the Christ – a secret he could only intimate in his outer deck, the Waite-Smith.[76]

Whilst admitting the Major Arcana have much to teach us, we must also see them each in reverse to appreciate their shadow side. The Fool, being utterly free, and signifying spirit, freedom, the journey, wandering, movement and all such things in a reading, can see through all the trammels – attachments – of the world. His appearance in a reading says we must be free; usually of whatever position he appears in a fixed position spread, such as the 'past'. If he appears in a 'future' position, we must be free of our thoughts of the future, etc.

The Major Arcana, reversed, can signify the attachments by which we are bound and of which the Fool is free. When the Fool meets the mercurial Magician, then, he sees only the trickery and deviousness, the lies and cheating of the mind. The Magician, reversed, in this sense, is the lies we tell ourselves, the negative thinking, that positive thinking even which is not real – and never will be.

The reversed Magician is more like the earlier depictions of the card as a trickster, a charlatan, sliding the cups of choice around but there is no pea beneath any of them – it is always a loser's game.

Every moment we think, we entrap ourselves – this is the nature of thought. It has its limits, for we can never know everything, and so all our thinking is in some part wrong. Meditation, ecstasy, trance, and other methods aim to transcend this limitation – even dancing to music or barking like a dog – the reversed Magician must be overcome.

In fact, we may appear foolish to do so, to realize the limitation of logic and rationality. We have built our whole world from such thinking. But it can only take us so far and is only part of the journey – and in the different, spiritual journey, it has a place, but must, like everything, be utterly transcended.

To summarize, then, the Magician (reversed) is bad thinking, erroneous thought, self-trickery, or manipulation – this last, particularly when in a position such as "the other person". In our next lesson on the reversed Major Arcana, we will see what the Fool makes of the High Priestess.

---

[74] Arthur Edward Waite, *The Pictorial Key to the Tarot* (London: Rider & Company, 1974), p. 152.

[75] *Ibid.*

[76] For more on A. E. Waite's second tarot images, held secret for a century, see Tali Goodwin & Marcus Katz, *Abiding in the Sanctuary* (Keswick: Forge Press, 2011).

## Lesson 13

~

### THE FOOL MET THE HIGH PRIESTESS (REVERSED) AND SAID, I AM FREE FROM YOUR ENIGMA – YOU CAN CALL ME REALITY (BUT I HAVE NO NAME).

~

The High Priestess, reversed, is about concealment – she veils, rather than reveals. She becomes a secret, and her words are spoken stealthily as an unreliable oracle. This is when intuition serves us badly, as it can do sometimes. It becomes nothing more than a guess, biased to our hope of an unlikely outcome.[77]

The word 'enigma' also has a slightly stealthy trail. It comes indirectly via the Latin from the Greek *ainigma*, which comes from *ainissesthai*, to 'speak allusively', which in turn is from the root *ainos*, meaning 'fable'. The reversed High Priestess is indeed 'absolutely fabulous', but fabulous in its most original sense of "as in a fable", i.e., totally untrue and not taken to represent reality.

Our unconscious, our intuition, even our oracular utterances, or daily speech, are a representation of the world – a story we construct and nothing more. Our dreams are like our reality; something that happens deeply and darkly in our head without us having any idea how it actually happens. Our world is merely but actually a reflection of reality – hence the correspondence of the High Priestess to the astrological Moon.

When the High Priestess is upright, she speaks of the connection between that deep knowledge and the truth; when she is reversed, she shows a disconnection of the same. We are lying to ourselves, when she is reversed, and we may not even know it, or accept it. She is a riddle we do not care to undo.

Consider what might be meant by the omens of a reversed moon, or the shattered pillars of a great temple, or a veil rent in half. Perhaps we can consider the pomegranate, the symbol of being captured and taken into the underworld, or a broken cross, and a scroll of "law" torn into pieces.

The High Priestess is the final symbol which holds back the truth of existence illustrated by the Magician, and if the Fool were heading back this way from the World card, we would see this even more clearly. When we start our sequence back from the World, in which the Fool finds himself, as we will do following this section of twenty-one lessons, each card becomes a challenge and a method of liberation. We work from the World to find our

---

[77] See Malcolm Gladwell, *Blink* (New York: Back Bay Books, 2007).

Spirit, the Fool, and our final two challenges and methods are the Magician and the High Priestess – truth and reality.

These first few cards of the Major Arcana reversed are almost beyond conception, because they are pernicious and all-encompassing of our experience. They are illustrations of archetypes, the very core of our human perception and model of the world – every culture has a trickster god, every culture has some form of divine (or exiled) feminine.

The Fool, as he works through this sequence, will find many ambushes along the way, and he must be always aware that everything is working against a simple truth – freedom. The siren call of the dark High Priestess is one to which many succumb, even those who have escaped the trickery of the Magician.

"Let us not think", say they – "let us feel and be free". And in that moment, all is lost, for everything is a trap; replacing one shackle for another is the only freedom they have won for themselves. The reversed High Priestess is the shame and guilt of living an untruth and a powerful catalyst for change if we, like the Fool, overturn her and accept nothing more than reality.

Her veil of light is fabulous, all these unspoken untruths, promises, lies, misconceptions, guesses, fuzzy thinking, all that come from the greatest of all our unspoken untruths; "I do not know". And it is the last trap of all, that we mistake that glorious light for the source of the light itself and bask in its radiant prison.

In the next lesson we move on to the Empress and begin to build up our reading methods with reversed Major Arcana being applied to details within an everyday situation.

## Lesson 14

~

THE FOOL MET THE EMPRESS (REVERSED) AND SAID,
I AM FREE FROM YOUR HOLD –
YOU CAN CALL ME TRESPASS (BUT I HAVE NO NAME).

~

In everyday readings, the Fool often signifies a form of movement, in the general sense of freedom or specifically and more literally as "get out of there, even if you have to go to the edge". When he meets the Empress who is reversed, he can only see Her nature as the cloying, grasping, possessive mother – the cancerous and harmful aspect of nature. She is literally "unnatural" in her reversed form; although, truly, nothing is unnatural as we are all part of nature, as is every aspect of Nature.

Here the Fool then becomes trespass – he must go across this phase of life and realize it is natural. The word trespass means to "pass across" or "pass over". When the reversed Empress appears, then, we must imagine it in our reading as a swamp, a marsh, a dismal place that was once happy and fruitful. It is something that has gone sour, is rotting, is nature taking its course in a way we would rather it not.

We will now begin to look at a variety of everyday readings to see how a reversed card might indicate specific detail.

Let us take "Where is my missing cat?" which often comes up online, although less rarely do cat owners think to appeal to tarot readers in real life, in my experience. If this card, the Empress, *reversed*, came out as a one-card draw then it would be an interesting answer, because it is so specific. The cat was out of her known territory, somewhere "unnatural" for him or her – perhaps they had been attracted to some "unnatural" change in the environment.

In this case, we would ask the client to locate such a change and be unsurprised perhaps to hear that a building site had started up in the neighborhood. A building site could also be considered as a reversed Empress as whilst it is construction, it is man-made and therefore 'against nature' in the sense of replacing the 'natural' habitat.

That all comes directly from the "unnatural" keyword for that aspect of the reversed Empress.

We might also enquire as to whether the cat had shown any "unnatural" behavior of late – an obvious question, to be sure, but we have a specific answer already. If the owner said that actually, the cat had been coming back later for a few days before it had vanished, this would also suggest that the building site was the cause and not an unrelated or sudden accident.

If we then pulled one Major card for "What to Do" and received the Blasted Tower, this would appear (like the reversed Empress) somewhat negative on first glance.

But we have seen that the Tower is about the "breaking" pattern and forces, energies, and aspects of the entire Universe, so this card is giving us direct advice. We must break whatever we are doing to search for the cat and do something totally different. If we have been handing out flyers, we should instead put something on the internet. If we have been searching by car, we should search by foot; if we have been looking in one direction, we should look in another.

Again, it may seem obvious, but when the owner goes to the actual building site (which was far out of the cats expected range) and finds their cat in the workman's hut, enjoying their sandwiches, our cards will have done a great and specific service.

Further, we might smile when the owner talks with the builders and they point to a large pile of bricks, and joke that the cat had been getting mice that had escaped when they "brought that old tower building" down.

Whilst we might consider the Major Arcana these "big things" in life, the Fool can see through them all the way down to the ground; they are everywhere and everything, even the literal. A two-card reading with the reversed Empress and the Blasted Tower may not appear to bode well at first glance, our reading of it should always be focused on a positive outcome.

However, if we had sensed in our reading of those two cards that they are 'negative', then we should also be unafraid to go with that and consider that the cards are being more brutal.

In the more negative case, the cards may be telling us that the cat was dead (reversed Empress as the opposite of "life" and "nature") and that the owner should be prepared for a shock (Tower). Usually, it is often the subtler reading of the cards, their more complex nature, that turns out to be true rather than the simple stark "This card is Death, so it means death" sort of reading. Otherwise, everyone would be able to read tarot and they would be right all of time – or we would all simply use cards with "Yes", "No", "Horse 7 in the Grand National" and "Dwayne will come back to you on Thursday at 3:00pm, following a 60-word text message that morning" written on them.

But as tarot card readers we must be able to go down to the literal from the complex, not simply stick with the simplest reading as our only method – like the Fool, we must be able to go everywhere in search of the answer.

The "oracular moment is sacrosanct" as we say, and this is why the reader is encouraged to also listen to their growing experience with the cards as well as learn all their associations and methods of reading.

Next, we will meet the Emperor and see a whole range of things that he might mean in mundane readings, and how the Fool might shirk such responsibilities in his Quest.

## Lesson 15

~

THE FOOL MET THE EMPEROR (REVERSED) AND SAID,
I AM FREE FROM YOUR TYRANNY –
YOU CAN CALL ME EVERYONE (BUT I HAVE NO NAME).

~

When we meet the Emperor, reversed, we see immediately that it is a simple case of power upturned, either against oneself or others. Tyranny, absolutism, seizing of power both wrongly and undeserved, dictatorship, enslavement to a person or ideal, and all that is the corruption of power.

In a reading, the reversed Emperor is going to tell us that we are not in control, that we are not empowered.

But we do it to ourselves; suppression, repression, and oppression; these are all what the mystic Gurdjieff called "buffers", that project us away from the true power of our own authentic self. Similarly, depression; when we depress something that is arising in us. This takes all the energy we hold and disempowers us even further.

The Emperor is about our relationship to ourselves as it is to others, for how we relate to others is merely a projection of how we relate to ourselves.

Those people who manipulate others? Imagine how much they must manipulate themselves, and then perhaps spare a moment of sympathy for the childhood that led them to have to do such a thing. Those people who bully others? Imagine how much they are bullying themselves, and then spare a moment of empathy for the life that led them to have to do such a thing.

This is not an excuse for such behavior, but a seeking to best understand it to stand on our own feet in the face of such activity, which often seeks to disempower us.

A good Emperor stands for his or her people, a reversed Emperor treads upon them. The reversed Emperor is showing us this aspect of the Universe; that someone (or ourselves) is disempowered, is selfish, is plain horrible.

The Fool knows that this is folly, for we all die alone, and we must live with others until that point. Also, the Fool knows that control itself is an illusion, because it requires the erroneous thought that any one thing is different to another – you must have two things for control; one to control the other. If there is only unity and one thing, in the transcended freedom of spiritual progression, then there can be no control nor even any concept of it.

The Fool frees themselves of tyranny by simply being themselves and recognizing that everyone is also being themselves, no matter how that self is presented. At the same time, we are all in this together, whether we like it or not – we were all born, had parents, and live on a ball of rock orbiting a sun with little means of escape and many reasons to celebrate together.

The Fool then offers in the face of the reversed Emperor a true Democracy, from the Greek, meaning 'the people rule'; *demos* meaning people and *kratos* meaning "power". Literally, "power to the people".

When the reversed Emperor is present, we must find democracy, a sharing, a generous nature to our own self and conflicts, or that of others – whilst being ourselves. Often, what we hate in others is merely a projection of what is most hated inside ourselves, which makes it almost impossible to bear and imperative to project out into someone else.

The reversed Emperor asks, "What do you hate about yourself?" more than telling you tyrannically, "Let's find out who to blame". We must never let any Emperor sit on our own throne.

In *Tarot Flip*, we discovered that the Emperor keyword was often seen as "endurance" and reversed, "instability", and it is no surprise that such internal conflict can lead to unstable behavior. We will look now at how a *reversed* Emperor might be briefly interpreted and succinctly stated in all ten positions of a Celtic Cross:

- Situation: "You have given your power to someone else, or others".
- Challenge: "What is happening now is an opportunity to reclaim your own power".
- Immediate Past (left card in cross): "You once were under some control".
- Immediate Future (right card in cross): "You will be facing a chance to see your own control issues".
- Aim (top card in cross): "You might seek to recognize how power is placed with yourself and others".
- Resources (bottom card): "You can draw upon your experience to take better control of your life".
- How you see Yourself: "You are in conflict with what you must recognize and above which you must rise".
- How others see You: "Others presently see you as trying to dominate the situation".
- Concerns: "You are concerned that you have given away your power, but this is not the case".
- Outcome: "This situation, without change as a result of this reading, will lead to the wrong person being in charge".

These are merely suggestions and would always be modified by the other cards and the language we might choose to best communicate to a particular client – or ourselves.[78]

In our next card, we meet the reversed Hierophant, and compare and contrast these reversals of power, particularly in relationship readings.

---

[78] For more information on how we read a Celtic Cross and its background, see the original *Tarosophy* and the later booklet, Tali Goodwin & Marcus Katz, *Secrets of the Celtic Cross* (Keswick: Forge Press, 2016).

## Lesson 16

~

THE FOOL MET THE HIEROPHANT (REVERSED) AND SAID,
I AM FREE FROM YOUR PRESCRIPTION –
YOU CAN CALL ME CHAOS (BUT I HAVE NO NAME).

~

When the Star met the Hierophant, in lesson five, we saw the first example of a reversed card, as the Star called out the Hierophant for signifying "indoctrination". The Star will always guide true and is a useful card in any reading because it shows in its position where we must concentrate our awareness to find our way.

If the Star is in "the past", that is where the answer lies; if it is in the "challenge", similarly – and if in the position of "others" we must sort the situation out with other people first, not within ourselves.

The Star saw the Hierophant's shadow, then, or reversed meaning; indoctrination – a lesson being taught without openness to question.

One of my friends who was studying philosophy at college told me that they had come up with the idea of a "rhetorical answer" rather than a "rhetorical question"; and by that they meant an answer not meant to be questioned, rather than a question asked idly and not meant to be answered. The reversed Hierophant is often a "rhetorical answer", something not meant to be questioned. It can be something authoritative for the sake of it, even, at a mundane level, a "jobs-worth"; someone doing something because of the "rules", not because it makes sense.

This could be as simple as not letting you get on the train because your ticket has been misprinted, to putting you on a train going to a concentration camp.

It is a card that on a social scale shows what happens when the system swallows us, when the computer says "no" to credit, to access, to services or treatment, even, no matter what people think. It is also taboo; and political correctness, and saying the wrong thing at the wrong time, causing offence – it is everything that happens when we are simply not simple and straight-forward.

It is robes on top of robes, sound and fury, signifying nothing.

It is the horrible feeling you get when someone gleefully refers to "their tribe" when they do not know that a tribe – by definition - is a group with a set code of rules, a single chief in charge, authoritarian principles, and people who will be included and excluded in a hierarchy of acceptance.

There is a good and natural hierarchy in nature, which is illustrated by the Hierophant, but when he is reversed, it signifies that not everything is in the natural order, the right place.

This card when upside-down sets boundaries that we do not need, and is another form of manipulation, such as the Emperor reversed; here it is prescription – a writing down of behavior which must be followed without question.

The Fool, of course, must remove these boundaries; of belief, of religion, of self-indoctrination, to be truly free of all constraints; socially, morally, legally, attitudinally.

The Fool then replies to the reversed Hierophant that they are Chaos. They are the unexpected, the surprise, the Joker in the pack, the Court Jester. They can say what they want without recrimination and reprisal – the reversed Hierophant is the opposite; it shows when you cannot say anything without consequence.

In a relationship, whether romantic or workplace, friend, or family, online or for real, this reversed Hierophant is illustrating a very negative influence. In a relationship reading, let us see how it might be read in a selection of spread positions:

- Past: You are moving away from a situation where you could never say the right thing without consequence, and you just did not understand the rules by which you were being constrained.
- Future: You are heading towards a situation where it will become increasingly difficult to gain any freedom of action, behavior or speech.
- Obstacle: You are cautioned to become more aware of how you are setting expectations based on your own beliefs and that you are not being open to the beliefs of your partner.
- Family: The way in which your family set its own rules is now playing out in your relationship.
- Aim/Outcome: Without injecting a bit of chaos and surprise in this relationship, it is likely to become a very fixed, boring, and unchanging situation.

Now that we have looked at a few cards in reverse, next we will also start to mix them up a bit with upright cards so we can continue to learn Majors-Only Readings.

**Lesson 17**

~

THE FOOL MET THE LOVERS (REVERSED) AND SAID,
I AM FREE FROM YOUR SEPARATION –
YOU CAN CALL ME UNITY (BUT I HAVE NO NAME).

~

The mystic Adi da Samraj (Franklin Jones, 1939 – 2008) provided a self-enquiry mantra to students for one stage of his work, which was simply "Avoiding Relationship?" He spoke of the way the process of ego separates us from reality, from union, and how that arises as conscious seeking for such union.

The Lovers card is an illustration of the most obvious form of union, that of a man and woman. There are many other forms of union, all arising from separateness.

The reversed Lovers is the pattern of separation; one thing from another, one person from another. It could appear in the workplace as a break-up between a team, who should be sharing a vision or process, but have separate ideas which may be in conflict.

It could appear in a question about taking a course, illustrating that the person will have to separate themselves from their domestic life during the time of study, and this could cause conflict.

It could appear in a relationship question as actual, potential, or past separation, such as two people who have drifted apart in their development, ambitions, and lifestyles.

The Fool has already transcended this sense of separateness, for he is no longer avoiding relationship with anything at all. Ah, to be free of all seeking, all conflict, all contraction of the self to anything at all. That is the Fool.

In our readings, then, we are always addressing some separation, often between what is imagined and what is reality. Our readings should aim to bring unity, wholeness, healing to a situation, by illustrating the possibilities in every situation to enter a more engaged relationship with reality.

The Lovers sometimes denotes a "choice" or "decision point" in a reading, and its reversed aspect is that of ourselves putting ourselves in a position where there appears no choice at all.

It is an unquestionable relationship that must in fact be questioned, whether with a spouse or a boss, whether with a pet or an Aunt. It is certainly a card where we might like to look to other cards for more information as to how we should go about undoing this knot of self-contraction.

Let us look at a three-card reading, with the Lovers (Reversed) in the middle.

The question would be too easy to have as "Is the man I have just met the right man for me?"

We will have as a question, "Is it the right time for me to move to a new house?"

The three cards (Majors only) are: Magician, Lovers (Reversed) and Empress (reversed).

We have seen that the Lovers (Reversed) is separation, but always one of self-contraction. The person does indeed want to move to a new house but is holding themselves back from doing so. It is not a question or situation of practical, financial, rational, or emotional consideration; it is a psychological issue.

We look at the Magician, whom we have already met both upright and reversed, and see that this is a card illustrating "individual Will". That is curious, as in *Tarot Flip*, we saw how readers see this card as usually denoting some "success" as the Magician has the skills, channel, and elements on his side.

But let us keep it to this course, where we simply take the card as the "Will" of the individual, their ambition and ability to work towards it.

In this reading is a powerful drive to move to a new house. Something within the person really does want to move. Again, there is no 'external' cause or consequence to this situation – it is all down to the person.

We can now talk in the reading about this, perhaps confirming or revealing that there is no concern externally about it being the "right time". They should neither rush or wait, it matters not in terms of finances or timing. And then we have the Empress (reversed), which we have seen in an earlier lesson as "hold", and an "unnatural" aspect of life – something rotted, gone wrong, a dismal swamp in a once perfect place. Perhaps now the reading makes sense.

When they originally moved to their present location, it was perfect for them, but they have outgrown it. It no longer serves to hold them, perhaps they had a child there (Empress) that has now left. Perhaps indeed they moved into their deceased mother's house. Perhaps rather, they no longer feel that the house is holding or protecting their current situation.

In this reading we can now develop the original question "Is it the right time?" to "How should I look for the House that is a better garden for me now to further grow?"

We might even offer to do another reading for that question, either then or in a following appointment once the person had processed this new information and moved on in their own enquiries.

The reversed Lovers is the card that illustrated the flip side of our mythic expulsion from the perfect garden; and the flip side is that we can go back by realizing we never left.

Next, we will continue to develop three-card Majors-only readings with reversals, when we meet the reversed Chariot.

**Lesson 18**

~

THE FOOL MET THE CHARIOT (REVERSED) AND SAID,
I AM FREE FROM YOUR NECESSITY –
YOU CAN CALL ME STILLNESS (BUT I HAVE NO NAME).

~

In the upright Chariot, we of course see movement, momentum, and a sense of victory. This is ambition personified, a willed direction. However, when reversed, we see all the consequences of such ambition if undertaken for anything other than the journey itself – the Chariot is over-turned. We can recall the collision scenes in *Ben Hur* as one fast-moving Chariot hits another at speed – and recall what it is like when "all the wheels come off" in our life.

This is the Chariot reversed – something escalating out of all proportion, a compulsion, drive, or obsession even, which looks still on the outside but is furiously active on the inside.

The Fool is free from such recklessness because he is everywhere at all times, so has nowhere he needs to go. He is free from all necessity. The drive to do, to be, to go, has run its course in the Chariot reversed; there is no chance of victory, only surrender to the moment.

At least it may be over quickly, particularly if accompanied by another transitional card such as the Blasted Tower or Death.

Or at least it may be about someone else's project or ambition.

Or at least it may be about a small matter, such as whether you will find a decorator quickly or not.

When the Chariot appears reversed, there is usually a conflict of time, or of something happening too quickly, or not at all – particularly when seen with the Hanged Man. One must remain still and quiet when the Chariot is upside-down, and hope not to get too bruised as all the horses, wheels, carts and sand eventually hit the stadium wall.

If we now take a five-card Majors-only reading with a typical geometric spread such as a Pentagram (Star) Spread, we can start to see how cards might relate to each other.

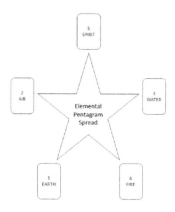

*Illus. Elemental Pentagram Spread.*

Here the positions are based on the elements:

1. Earth = Money & Resources.
2. Air = Education & Communication.
3. Water = Emotions & Dreams.
4. Fire = Ambitions & Lifestyle.
5. Spirit = Spiritual & Philosophical.

We might ask a question about a bout of insomnia which appears to have no known cause.

We shuffle and draw the cards as follows:

1. Earth = Money & Resources: 5 Hierophant (Reversed).
2. Air = Education & Communication: 13 Death.
3. Water = Emotions & Dreams: 19 Sun.
4. Fire = Ambitions & Lifestyle: 12 Hanged Man.
5. Spirit = Spiritual & Philosophical: 2 High Priestess (Reversed).

If we look at the two reversed cards first, and perhaps start with the spiritual aspect of the situation, we see that the High Priestess is over-turned, and this immediately answers the question.

The client is not able to sleep (or awakening from sleep) because of an unconscious conflict between how she wants the world to be and how it is. This is severe enough to disrupt her sleep, but it is not conscious, as the High Priestess is concealing it for some reason.

We might even look at the other reversed card to see if this will denote what the High Priestess is concealing. This is the Hierophant (reversed) in the position of Money. There is an unspoken expectation about earning and wealth going on here.

We might discuss this with the client and hear immediately that indeed they are feeling stuck in their current job, but this was "not really causing any problem because it was a perfectly safe position". It is that very 'safeness' that the Hierophant is bringing to the surface. The client might have unconscious drives to success and an idea of 'wealth' that is not being met, even though they are "safe".

We can now look at the 'Emotions' position, perhaps, to see if there is a specific reason this emotional disturbance is happening now. We find the Sun card in that position. The Sun, we have seen, is "empowerment" and all good things, and part of a pair we saw as "life" itself.

There is likely a slowly diminishing sense of personal power in the "safe" role, which is starting to conflict with a threshold held in the unconscious as to what the client will find comfortable or not.

It is like the Sun has dawned, gone up … and up … and been high … and now it is going down. It is casting a shadow into the client's sleep, causing them to awaken to its message.

We might next turn to the 'Ambitions & Lifestyle' (Fire) position, to see what we might best advise the client in response to this situation. There we see the Hanged Man, which on immediate glance is perhaps not exactly the card we might want in that position.

However, we recall from our lesson on the Hanged Man that he is part of a "reboot of awareness" and a "sleeping giant", so he is calling the person to awaken to their own values and self-worth. To hang themselves higher and tighter to their own sense of worth, pull themselves up by their own bootstraps, and sacrifice something – in this case, likely their sense of comfortable safety.

We would at that point be within a few seconds of advising the client to walk boldly into their boss's office, sit down, and say, "I've been in the company for quite a while now, and it is starting to feel a bit too comfortable – can we discuss more responsibility and how I might work to get a pay-rise?"

But let us look at the final card before we say anything.

Death. In the position of 'Education and Communication'. Here it is then, they must totally transform themselves because the world is asking them to do so. That is why they cannot sleep – they must make a change.

The change is to risk sacrificing their comfort, so is literally uncomfortable and something the High Priestess within wants to protect them from – but the Hierophant wants to reveal. The High Priestess and Hierophant are waging war, up-side-down with each other, inside the client.

In this reading we can illustrate and illuminate all that for the first time to the client, and they can take action to get on a new training program at work

(Death/transformation in Education position).

In this example we can see how practical (and in a sense, literal) the Major Arcana can be, even with a health or psychological situation, in this case, insomnia. The reader is encouraged to practice this five-card method, using Majors-only and reversals, referring back to this whole section for reference if necessary.

Next, we will look at Strength reversed and how we might further weave our Major cards together.

**Lesson 19**

~

THE FOOL MET STRENGTH (REVERSED) AND SAID,
I AM FREE FROM YOUR FIGHT –
YOU CAN CALL ME SILENCE (BUT I HAVE NO NAME).

~

It is true that we become that which we fight.

When we engage in any combat, we adapt our stance to defend ourselves or attack our adversary. This can be in speech or action, in emotion or thought. Our empathy, even our very brain, through mirror neurons, is re-tracked, re-purposed, and takes on the shape appropriate for the fight.

However, whether we win or lose, draw or mutually surrender, we have already lost something – our previous state of mind. And we have won a new track in our brain; one more likely to be followed the next time, and the time after that – and for a long time if we consider the infinity symbol above the maiden's head.

Silence, the Foolish response to conflict, can have its cost, but it is rarely *our* cost. If others wish to fight, let them – Gandhi not only said "Strength does not come from physical capacity. It comes from an indomitable will" but also "A man is but the product of his thoughts; what he thinks, he becomes".

In *Tarot Flip* we saw that the Strength card unconsciously indicated "Action" in most tarot readers' minds; in whatever way they expressed it, the card was a place-holder for "action" and "doing something". Strength reversed then, is a place-holder for "rest", taking time-out, disengagement, letting go of the Lion, or padding away from the Maiden holding your jaws.

When the Fool has transcended this card and sacrificed the illusionary fight, he is only silent. As we have seen before in this journey, control (and conflict) is based on an illusion of separateness.

If you allow the infinity symbol to be *in* your mind, not *above it*, everything is connected in a loop and all control, all conflict – vanishes. There is only everything.

When Strength reversed is in the past, it perhaps indicates emerging from that silence and now acting and speaking out. It would ask the question, "What strength did you discover in that time?"

When Strength reversed is in the future, it perhaps indicates entering a state of silent withdrawal. It would ask the question, "Can you stay removed from that fight?"

When Strength reversed is in the present, it perhaps indicates that it is time for silence now – take a rest from the battle, it is serving neither woman nor beast.

If we were to weave this card (or any other) with another, perhaps the upright Chariot, we might want to bridge (connect) across the symbols.

**Example**

Let us say we have a simple two-card spread, "Do This / Don't Do This".

- The "Do This" is the Chariot.

- The "Don't Do This" is Strength (Reversed).

*Illus. Chariot & Strength (Rev).*

The Chariot is pressing us ahead, it is the triumph of thought, reining in all that it surveys, mastering all paradox, confusion, and division. It says, briefly in one sentence, in that position, "Do take time to think it through".

Strength reversed says, in the position of "Don't Do this", "Do not take a rest, surrender, dis-engage". We must bridge those two meanings, and our mind might struggle to interpret and say both "take time to think" and also "don't take a rest" at the same time.

In these cases, let us always look back at the two cards and do what we should – read the cards.

As we gaze over both cards, we see right in the middle the hand positions of each, and how different but similar they are – just like our answer. We can incorporate and utilize these images.

We could say:

You are in a tight position, for sure – you need to do two things at the same time to get through this time. You need to think it through before you do anything, but you also need to stay engaged and as you know, you cannot take a break from it. It is like holding two things at the same time, just like these pictures show – can you see how the guy in the Chariot appears to be in control but isn't even holding any reins? His hand looks as if it is, but there is nothing there – it is just that the Sphinxes are trained enough to know what to do without him really having to even have the reins now. So, you must go through the motions, but keep your mind on thinking it through, go onto 'auto-pilot' if you will, because everyone else will continue to act as if nothing had changed. But you know it is changing, you are thinking it through – you still have your rod in the other hand, your own self-determination, and this decision to make a change. Just not yet. And in Strength, when she is upside-down, it is like she is trying to stop things falling out of his mouth isn't it? The challenge is not to say anything at all until you are ready and have thought it all out. These two cards are about planning in secret and not doing anything until the whole course is set out.

That last sentence (in the real example) did not come until the reading was spoken out and through bridging the two hand symbols – and it seems a reasonable summary of the reading, demonstrating how bridging can generate much more than the sum of two symbols.

Next, we will look at the Hermit reversed and what the Fool must leave behind as he passes that way on the mountain. We will also continue to look at Majors-Only methods of reading.

And finally, to return to Gandhi, the Strength card reversed, and as the Fool alone truly knows, "The best way to find yourself is to lose yourself in the service of others".

**Lesson 20**

~

THE FOOL MET THE HERMIT (REVERSED) AND SAID,
I AM FREE FROM A SELF –
YOU CAN CALL ME NOTHING (AS I HAVE NO NAME).

~

This most mystical of meetings is a critical one for the journey of the Fool into nothingness – as he discards all the entrapments offered by the Major Arcana, illustrated by their reversal.

Here the Fool is offered by the Hermit the very thing that we feel is not on offer – ourselves.

The Hermit, as we saw in an earlier lesson, is our sense of self and signifies in a reading the loneliness of the self as independent from others, setting an example by your own behavior, doing what is right for oneself, etc.

However, when reversed, the Star that he carries in his Lantern is being subsumed – it is simply not the right thing that is going on inside. Our ability to hold more than one belief, multiple visions and hopes, like a single star radiating many rays of light, can be our undoing.

Sometimes those beliefs contradict each other, sometimes those hopes are utterly unrealistic or at the forefront of our minds at the most inappropriate and useless time. The reversed Hermit is "all over the place" in the worst way. He knows not where he is really going, what he is really doing, or even who he (or she) really is.

The Fool has simply transcended this mess by stepping around the sense of self altogether – he is everywhere already, and nowhere, so has no self at all. There is no self-reflection in the Fool to be confused because there is no self to reflect.

The reversed Hermit illustrates what happens when this sense of self is fragmented and plays out in the world – we become blind to our own projections of light, not guided by them. It is a card that shows when reversed that whatever the client is saying about other people, their family, their friends, their work colleagues, their whole situation, is more likely about them.

This is always the case, but the reversed Hermit calls it to our attention even more for the oracle to speak.

This card can also show a sense of self-contraction, selfishness, and self-obsession at worst.

We really need to look for the Hanged Man in a reading with the reversed

Hermit, or any other card that might show some way of getting out of this apparently self-destructive place, as the person is perched precariously on the mountain top of their own delusion.

In fact, it would be better if it did indicate self-destructiveness because at least that would reboot the cycle. Unfortunately, whilst the card might appear in a situation that is apparently self-destructive, often it is actually building up the ego and personality structures of the client, either in little inconsequential ways, or a big inflation that will just keep getting brighter.

Sometimes "woe is me" is actually "look at me".

In a reading we might look to the cards as they are laid out and see where that lantern light is pointing in the other cards – we should always try and use the pictures as they are presented to us. Perhaps next to the reversed Hermit, where the lantern is closest, is the reversed Hierophant, holding his three-barred staff on that side of the card.

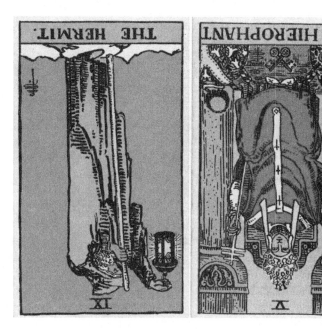

*Illus. The Hermit (rev) & The Hierophant (rev).*

This symbol is the Papal Cross, and one of its meanings is to denote that the Pope is appointed to mete out punishment – in the way that the crozier symbol of the shepherd's crook shows he can gather the flock. What might this mean if we are reading the cards with a knowledge of such symbolism?

It would tell us that the person is punishing themselves for something by their selfish activity (reversed Hermit near to reversed Hierophant, bridging the Lantern and Papal Cross symbols).

We would look to the 'past' card, perhaps, and see there (most likely) would be a card which would tell us – and the client – why they were punishing themselves. And of course, we would look to the 'future' card for a solution, or even draw an extra card from the Majors to indicate more about this behavior and a potential solution.

This would be quite a deep reading, psychologically, but the Hermit is a card which illustrates our self and our psychology, so it would be no surprise.

Next, we will move on to the Wheel, and go around our lessons all over again. Let us hope we find some way to escape the Wheel as we follow the Fool.

## Lesson 21

~

THE FOOL MET THE WHEEL (REVERSED) AND SAID,
I AM FREE FROM THE REVOLUTION –
YOU CAN CALL ME SINGULAR (BUT I HAVE NO UNIFORM).

~

At this stage in the Way, the Fool arrives in the center of the Arcana, having transcended each of the prior cards in his journey to - at last - meet the great Wheel. He has declared – through each previous card - his freedom; his reality; and his trespass; he has become everyone; he has passed through chaos to unity; and come through stillness and silence to nothing.

And now he becomes singular, but not uniform, as he takes his leave of even the Wheel of time and fortune, the life both divine and mundane. This Wheel is a symbol of cause and effect, and the connection of all things are illustrated by its spokes. It is also an illustration of liberation from the cycles of rebirth, in Buddhist philosophy.

We might consider the turning of the Wheel which moves the entire Island in the TV series *Lost*. The Wheel is a universal symbol of vast transformation and the transcendence of time and space.

Is there anything, then, which is *not* this Wheel? Is it not rather an illustration of a rotating black iron prison, which remains invisible to us as we rise and fall on its yoke? The Wheel reversed barely seems any different to that illustrated by its upright position, other than the location of the creatures bound upon it.

And therein is the clue to the Fool's transcendence; it is only in differentiation that time is real; only in separation that space has meaning. When the Fool is nothing but singular, and singularly nothing, there is nothing but the Zero of the Wheel. He empties it entirely by seeing it for what it is – true and infinite, edgeless, without definition.

The Wheel reversed in our readings is likely the most powerful emblem of change possible in any situation. We must reverse everything, turn it upside-down, enact a revolution – by doing nothing other than seeing the truth. It is illustrative of the paradox of being, of life and death, fate, destiny, and fortune, exactly as they are in reality – meaningless yet present.

How to explain this in a reading for a family relationship question, or other common question? Let us imagine it is in the future position of a reading for "Should I contact my sister again?" We might say that whatever the present situation is, the future will neither be worse nor better – it will be whatever is made of it. The card tells us that whilst it appears a big decision now, it is not a particular decision in the grand scheme of things.

We might say to the client that "You can take this Wheel and move it yourself at this point, and it will go whichever way you choose. There is no fated answer, just your choice in how you communicate with your sister. Your present choice is a communication just as would be speaking with her".

The reversed Wheel also tells us that whatever is going on in life of the client's sister is bound to the client, despite there being no apparent connection. It would turn out that should the client contact their sister, the sister would be going through something specifically meaningful to the client. The Wheel does not recognize linear time nor specific causality other than everything arises at the same time as everything else, so it is all one.

The Fool sees this and rejoices in both the unity of all things and the apparent diversity of appearance – he does not even see it all as one thing, a uniform bright light, but as nothing – full of everything. In reaching this point, the Fool can now begin to transcend the other Arcana, next releasing any sense of balance and equilibrium as he approaches the following card in the way of reversals, Justice.

## Lesson 22

~

THE FOOL MET JUSTICE (REVERSED) AND SAID,
I AM FREE FROM MEASUREMENT –
YOU CAN CALL ME BOUNDLESS (BUT I HAVE NO NAME).

~

Having become nothing and singular, the Fool now becomes everything, when he transcends all measurement, all definition, all rules, and expectations of reality.

We have seen how Justice stands alone in the center of the Major Arcana pairings, now we see again how She is everything, by her making of difference between one thing and another. The scales of Justice, the double-edged Sword, both are symbols of duality. We can only measure ourselves against others when we consider that others are different. If everything is the same, as it is, there is nothing to measure or by which to measure.

This is reversed Justice, then, a freedom from the law of comparison. It signifies in a reading that any ideas of natural order are upturned, that the situation is free to go anywhere. This may be welcome or unwelcome, depending on the situation, the reversed Justice card is the Honey Badger of the tarot – it really does not care.

There is a blindness to this justice when reversed, but it is a blindness to any difference, cause, excuse, or consequence. It is purely what will happen will happen. We cannot do anything with Justice when it is reversed, even if we rail against it, our argument falls on deaf ears and an unceasing inevitability.

This is truly the card – when reversed - of instant *Karma*, payback, and even, although it is never justified, nor does it actually exist (for everyone is connected) – vengeance and retribution. Reversed Justice in a reading should make you draw a breath, whether you are reading for someone else or yourself – it means that this stuff just got real, or it is about to go down for real.

And it does not even see you.

We continue the Fool's retro-journey in our next lesson with the Hanged Man, which is confusingly, but fittingly for this second half of the *via mutationem fortunae*, already upside-down.

## Lesson 23

~

THE FOOL MET THE HANGED MAN (REVERSED) AND SAID,
I AM FREE FROM VALUES –
YOU CAN CALL ME EMPTY (BUT I HAVE NO NAME).

~

There is really no opposite to the Hanged Man, for he is the illustration of eternal suspension and sacrifice. It is fitting then that there is really no fitting antonym for "Martyr", a word which is often associated with the card. If we have transcended values because we have transcended a personal self, then we can neither be a martyr or selfish, we can neither be saint or tyrant.

We hang in awareness, which is sacrifice enough – it is a place devoid of attachment but devoid of meaning, as empty of the divine as it is as empty of self.

Our client does not need to know this when the reversed Hanged Man appears in their reading – they just want to know if they should complain about the bad job done by the plumber by taking them to court or lose all their money and pay someone else to fix the mess.

But all questions and answers are the same – they are just being seen on different levels.

Every plumber is sacrificing their time, even to make a bad job.

The transactions of life live in the patterns of the archetypes, literally and by definition. We live inside the Major Arcana – they are not illustrations of complex ideas; it is we who are the complex illustration of their simplicity.

The plumber, the plumbing, and the customer, who is presently sat in front of us, wanting to know about the way they should progress from their $3,000 mess, are all arising from the Major Arcana. And when the Hanged Man is reversed, either in the future position, the outcome position, or as a one-card answer, it means nothing. It literally means that the situation is empty of meaning, it is nothing. There is nothing you can do.

In the case of the plumbing disaster, you are not going to be able to turn the Hanged Man around – the sacrifice has been made, and now you can only do something else.

In short, get someone else to fix the mess, there is nothing to be gained by pursuit of the past.

Perhaps we might even pull another card – and receive the Hierophant; so, someone with experience, a bigger company, more established and reputable (and yes, more expensive).

But the Hierophant has value, the reversed Hanged Man has none.

When a card arises and it causes confusion, speak from that sense of confusion. Do not be a sham reader, presenting a presentation – speak from the cards.

I might say, "Well, this card is upside-down and shows an upside-down figure. It always confuses me, and I really do not know what to say when it turns up that way up. And that is exactly what is happening in your situation – you feel like you should say something, but there is nothing to be said. So, the card is telling us that we should perhaps accept that there is nothing to be said or done and move on".

Notice in that example how we transition through "this card > me > I > your > you > us > we" in our delivery of the card. Nothing is by accident when we speak from the cards through ourselves to the other person. We should always speak from the card, through ourselves, to (or even with) the other person. This is how Oracles communicate – by presaging the future from the present – the unknown to the unknown, the universal to the singular.

We hang between the meaning of life and the meaning of the card and find how they communicate, then we communicate that to another, even if that other is ourselves. There is a divine dialogue when we turn ourselves upside-down again, then right-way up to speak, as every shaman understands when they return from a journey.

Never be afraid to be empty and walk in that emptiness with your words. You can, you know.

The Fool teaches us that we can move beyond getting bound up by our own value and get out of our own way – we must release ourselves even from our self. Perhaps it is the reversed Hanged Man that is the significator card of the Oracles, as much as the High Priestess.

And next, the Fool meets and transcends Death.

## Lesson 24

~

THE FOOL MET DEATH (REVERSED) AND SAID,
I AM FREE FROM LIFE –
YOU CAN CALL ME TIMELESS (BUT I HAVE NO NAME).

~

If Death is *transformation*, when Death is reversed, we would imagine it would be read as *preservation*, the exact opposite.

And perhaps we can see that preservation is in the nature of the card when reversed – a true conservativism, where everything is maintained as it is and was – forever. There is no change when Death is reversed, but worse – there is no potential for change. There is an active element in the situation that is holding things as they are in the present.

We might look to other cards to reveal the agent or agency of this preservation, someone or something deliberately working to keep things the same. Imagine we had a reading which was to answer the question, "Does it look likely that my trip abroad will lead to romance?"

We draw three cards: Temperance + Death (reversed) + Sun.

We read (in this case) the central card first and see that there will be no change to the current situation – the person is unlikely to find romance or should not expect much change to come from the travel. Temperance on the left adds to this interpretation because she is about "flow" as we have seen in a prior lesson, and "tempering" as in the sense of life experience "tempering" us like steel is tempered.

Temperance suggests that whilst going with the flow, a balance will be maintained, and the experience will make the person stronger for it. To make more sense of that, we turn to the Sun card and see that the card is all about "empowerment", and opportunity – we also mentioned the word "demonstration" in our earlier lesson on the Sun. Whilst the travel may not deliver new romance, it will demonstrate to the person, if they go with the flow, how empowered they can be – and this, one imagines, will set them up to be a more different person when they return; a person more likely even to find romance.

We would then read those three cards as an overall positive in the long-term, but a negative in the short-term and in the response to the presented question. When we reverse Death, we hold back time, put things into limbo, which is ultimately an unsustainable state and utterly unnatural.

This might be a great thing if we want a pause in our life and take stock, but we must not be fooled into thinking that anything can stay the same – Death inevitably will return to finish his Work.

The Fool transcends both transformation and preservation by freeing himself from all notion of time. He - or She - enters the everlasting day and abides in the sanctuary thereof. In terms of magical, mystical, or spiritual progress, the reversed Death card is an emblem of the Fool becoming eternally initiated in the mysteries.

He has plucked the white flower from the flag of Death and carries it in endless transformation. As he ascends back up the Tree of Life, at this stage, he overcomes the linear perception of time, becoming awareness dwelling in a timeless realm. As such he is as free from death as he is from despair; for he knows everything is arising all the time, and that everything is alive forever, even as it is dead already.

The Fool turns his back on child, priest, and king – these three ways of engaging with life; innocently, through belief or through rules – and the Fool goes beyond.

And in the moment after Death, he meets his Angel, who we will next encounter together.

## Lesson 25

~

THE FOOL MET TEMPERANCE (REVERSED) AND SAID,
I AM FREE FROM YOUR ALCHEMY –
YOU CAN CALL ME PERFECTION (FOR I AM THE STONE OF THE WISE).

~

In Jung's magnum opus, *Alchemical Symbolism*, he explores in one section the "Vision of Zosimos". This is an ancient alchemical text which narrates the story of an initiatory journey.

The character undergoing the trials of this vision-journey encounters a dazzling white-clad figure named the "Meridian of the Sun" and Jung equates this figure with an Angel also described in other visions. He says that this angel "bears the mysterious elixir on its head and, by his relationship to the meridian, makes it clear that he is a kind of solar genius or messenger of the sun who brings 'illumination', that is, an enhancement and expansion of consciousness".[79]

We can see the upright Temperance not only as a process of tempering, but ultimately as a process of consciousness expansion.

Reversed, then, there is a negative alchemy, or a bad alchemy, an imperfect mixture, a terrible mistake, a horrible combination. We can easily see how this might be applied in every type of reading – the reversed Temperance signifies that there is a bad mix at play.

It can also be in the mind of the client or ourselves; we are trying to hold two values, beliefs, hopes or ideas that are causing each other conflict or spillage into worry, uncertainty and even depression. What should be flowing is stuck, locked, and worse – being corrupted or spoiled.

I am reminded of a gathering of salesmen that I was involved with many years ago when I was a young technology consultant. We were all at a bar in Chicago and the salesmen innocently suggested a "cement mixer" cocktail. The bartender lined it up for me. I was instructed to drink it in a particular way; first, the gorgeous smooth Baileys Irish Cream. I was encouraged to swirl this around my mouth, like a "washing machine".

Then, still swirling, I was told to drink the shot of liquor on the bar.

I did so, and something truly terrible happened in my mouth.

The "liquor" was lime juice – and it instantly curdled the cream elements in the Baileys and equally instantaneously curdled the entire inside of my mouth to which the Bailey's had been coated. I was horrified to find myself swirling around in my mouth some form or glutinous, chunky, slimy mess, whilst my jaw clenched against the effect of the lime on every part of the inside of my mouth.

At this point, the sales guys, bless their cotton socks, laughing in uproar, started chanting loudly, "Spit or Swallow?! Spit or Swallow?!" Several people at the bar also joined in - obviously, this was a common occurrence in the initiation ritual pertinent to that place and time.

That, my friends, is a cement mixer.

I swallowed - in the knowledge that at least now I knew what it was like to experience bad alchemy. The reversed Temperance is that very thing; two or more things that in themselves may be very pleasant, but together are horrible medicine – leaving a bad taste in your mouth.

---

[79] Carl Jung, *Alchemical Studies, Collected Works of C. G. Jung, Vol. 13* (Princeton: Princeton University Press, 1967), p. 81.

We do not want to see Angels upside-down in our readings any more than we should trust salesmen in a bar.

**Lesson 26**

~

THE FOOL MET THE DEVIL (REVERSED) AND SAID,
I AM FREE FROM YOUR SHADOW –
YOU CAN CALL ME LIGHT (BUT I HAVE NO NAME).

~

The Devil reversed is still the Devil, only doubly dangerous. He is a shadow being cast by an object getting in the way of light, which seeks out an object upon which to reflect or be absorbed.

In a psychological appreciation of this reversed card, we might see it as the projection of the shadow. If the Devil is the dark shadow, then reversed, he is the projection of the same. When we experience a sense of moral or ethical, psychological or spiritual lack in another person, particularly when it is a visceral, singular, immediate and almost automatic response, it is often a projection of our shadow.

The Devil whispers, where we cannot hear him, "Yes, you hate it, but why can't you be like that and get away with it?" The reversed Devil in a reading shows that there is the possibility that the situation is being projected from a darker or repressed side of the client or ourselves.

Sometimes the reversed Devil can hold a light in that darker space, that unconscious and chaotic night, from which dreams and creativity arise. When he is recognized and observed, with a particular type of distance, he can be extremely creative and spark new ideas of freedom from our former self.

But our shadow is taller than our soul and we must be wary that we are not engulfed in the pleasures and performance of an endless lack of license. The presence of the reversed Devil is somewhat more useful than the upright Devil, for the most part – it shows at least that the shadow is being projected out and is probably facing us right in the question.

It is also an important way-marker along the path of the Fool; as he has cycled around the archetypes illustrated by the Major Arcana, he now comes at last to recognize and free himself from his own shadow.

Jung said that the path of individuation "exhibits a certain formal regularity. Its signposts and milestones are various archetypal symbols, marking its stages; and of these the first stage leads to the experience of the

Shadow".[80]

In encountering, experiencing, partially-integrating, and then releasing the shadow, we become, like the Fool, pure light – awareness. Thus, the Devil satisfies himself as Lucifer, the bringer of that Light.

There will be detail in the other cards of a reading when the reversed Devil shows up, which provide the "surface" onto which the shadow is being projected.

## Example

Let us examine a personal question, such as "How can I cope with my ex-partner, John, saying such terrible things about me and taking all my friends to his side?"

We draw two cards, and get the Devil reversed for the first, indicating this shadow projection. We might look to the second card for more practical detail, in which the Devil will be discovered.

We look at the second card and it is the Hermit - also reversed.

This would be truly ironic, because we have already seen in this journey these lessons for the reversed Hermit:

The reversed Hermit illustrates what happens when this sense of self is fragmented and plays out in the world – we become blind to our own projections of light, not guided by them.

and

It is a card that shows when reversed that whatever the client is saying about other people, their family, their friends, their work colleagues, their whole situation, is more likely about them.

We now look to see where the light (and shadow) is going in these two cards. It is an interesting method when reading Majors-only to look at the positions and gestures of the hands in each card (if hands are included in the particular cards) or the light sources and their comparisons or contrasts between each card.

---

[80] Jolande Jacobi, *The Psychology of C. G. Jung* (London: Routledge and Kegan Paul, 1951), p. 102.

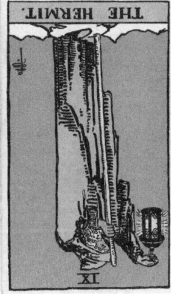

*Illus. The Devil (rev) & The Hermit (rev).*

It may be almost impossibly hard for the person to hear this, but their feelings about John and their friends are all about them alone. We see how the Hermit has turned his back against the Devil with his open hand – he has rejected the devil he knew and the attachment of that card.

The only light that shines is the lantern – away from the reversed Devil, even away from the Hermit himself. It is a combination that points to deep lessons about one's own attachments, fear of loneliness and in the widest sense – the existential angst of being an individual.

Yet this pair, despite their overall lack of light and their reversal, offer a huge reward should we take it. That light, that lantern, points to a whole new world outside the old situation – and even beyond the old self. There has been much learnt (of what to avoid) in the reversed Devil, so it is unlikely to be repeated.

John was a torch upturned and then upturned again in reflection of the client's own psychology. He taught her many things about herself, which she was not ready to see inside herself. Now she has that opportunity, and instead of seeing it played out with her friends, who still believe in the old situation, she can become someone literally new.

She will need to walk away on her own path, even away from these "friends" that she once had – they may be more comfortable with the old self she has now outgrown. It will be hard, but it is an incredible opportunity, and as Jung said, a "milestone". We might even lay out a few more cards to illustrate the path upon which that lantern now shines.

Next, we will look at another powerful agent of change – reversed – as the Fool ascends the Tower.

## Lesson 27

~

THE FOOL MET THE TOWER (REVERSED) AND SAID,
I AM FREE FROM YOUR QUEST –
YOU CAN CALL ME CONTINUUM (BUT I HAVE NO NAME).

~

Many of the interpretations of the reversed Tower are that is signifies some variant of the change, stress or shock that is usually illustrated by its upright position. Some write that it means the change will be for the good, others write that it signifies stress in the workplace; some write that it is a status quo, where there is a deliberate avoidance of change.

The Fool, in his journey of transcendence, steps lightly over the rubble and toppled crowns of the Tower, which has gravitated to the ground, and frees himself from all such construction. The upright Tower is often a symbol of ego, pride and hubris, the folly of attempting to communicate with the divine realm by building a temple made of hands and brick. The divine realm is communicated in a temple not made of hands, an invisible college, everywhere seen.

There is a recognition being struck then, when the Tower is reversed, that what was built was not even relevant, that the signification is to move on and recognize the only constant is change – but there is no change. The reversed Tower, as it should be, is a paradox. It is the riddle that we create for ourselves when we try and think things through, speak what is on our minds - yet all to no avail.

In an everyday reading, it means that there was not such a change – that things are much the same, same as they ever were, and the only task is to recognize the connection of the situation to the change within the client or ourselves.

If the question were about the risk of a new project, the reversed Tower would suggest that the risk was in seeing the project as a big change, when in fact it was an inevitable consequence of a particular stage in the life of the client. We would want to explore how the project related to events and decisions in the recent past and make such a connection clear to the client – or ourselves.

If we had the upright Lovers in the past position, we would connect the project to the client's stage in relating to other people; perhaps they could even deal with the risk by developing the project in the context of their work on relationships. We might also look at their decision-making in the past and choices (Lovers), and whether that was reversing the Tower and making them hesitant when there was yet no need for such self-defeat.

There is no question of ambition or construction when the Tower is reversed, it is rather more a matter of perspective; ensuring that we do not again place the crown in the wrong place. As does the Fool, we skip lightly across the rubble and recognize there is no change – just the continuation of what is always already happening.

## Example

Let us now, at this stage of our lessons, consider a three-card Majors-only reading which we will read in a linear fashion, left to right, as if we were reading a sentence.

The question is: "Will my contact with Debra lead to anything long-term?"

And to make things interesting, we draw three reversed cards:

- Justice (reversed) + Hierophant (reversed) + Blasted Tower (reversed).

*Illus. Justice, The Hierophant, The Tower (all reversed).*

If we refer to our previous lessons, we can see that the first card, Justice (reversed) means that "all bets are off". Whatever is expected, the experiences of the past, and the present moment, are upside-down. There is no certainty in the first card – it is an open situation. We would express this to the client and suggest that there is unlikely to be any intent to commitment at this stage.

The reversed Hierophant is likely to be the other person, Debra.

We saw in our earlier lesson on the reversal of that card stated in the future-tense that; "You are heading towards a situation where it will become increasingly difficult to gain any freedom of action, behavior or speech".

With Justice reversed already, that would also signify a highly 'irregular' or 'unusual' relationship, in terms of normal expectations. And not in a good way, we would suspect, from the reversal of all three cards. Even if we read it as entirely positive, it is going to be a head-turner.

The Blasted Tower, reversed, would conclude that the new contact with Debra was actually just a continuation of past contacts with other people – the same pattern, just being presented as a new face.

Weaving those together, we might say it a little in reverse, starting from the last card:

Whilst this appears to be something new in your life, it may simply be a continuation of old patterns. There may be a lot of old ground you will tread in this relationship, which you should observe as it happens. The other person, Debra, may have a lot of unstated expectations and rules or be vastly different to how they first present themselves. This could lead to an unbalanced and unsettling relationship, where what seemed an open book full of possibilities turns into a familiar straitjacket.

We could then look at the cards upright and discover if there were means by which this situation could be more pro-actively and positively developed. We would usually turn them upright and then lay a new card on each one as a divination for the three aspects of the situation indicated by the first cards:

- For the Justice card we would ask "How might the client establish a better balance in this or other contacts and relationships?"
- For the Hierophant, we would ask, "How might the client get closer to the actual truth of themselves and others in relationship?"
- And for the Blasted Tower, "How might the client better see such contacts in the wider landscape of their life?"

Briefly, let us look at what we might say with three cards for those new questions:

- For the first position of Justice, we might draw the Chariot (reversed).
- For the position of Hierophant, the Hermit.

- For the position of the Blasted Tower, the World.

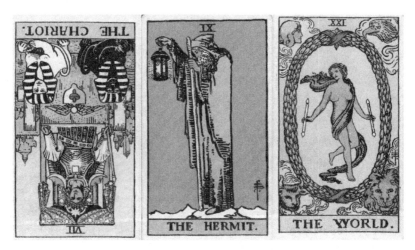

*Illus. The Chariot (Rev), The Hermit & The World.*

Briefly, this might be interpreted as:

To get a better balance (Justice), you should have a wider sense of time, and rein in your expectations which are causing you conflict (Chariot, reversed). There is more time than you might think, and it is important not to rush headlong into something which will be out of balance.

To get closer to the truth of this contact and your relationships (Hierophant), you should remove yourself from the beliefs, expectations and opinions of your family and peers (Hermit). It may be that you are currently be prompted by the universe to sort yourself out and get down to what you want, rather than what you have always thought you wanted, based on your background.

To get a wider perspective (Blasted Tower) you might consider how your contacts arise from your expression of your own true nature in the world (World). Perhaps allow contacts to arise from your activities and engagements rather than seeking them out as things in themselves.

That will be quite a lot to discuss in the reading. We will leave this shake-up reading for now and in our next lesson see what happens as the Fool follows (and then transcends) the Star.

**Lesson 28**

~

THE FOOL MET THE STAR (REVERSED) AND SAID,
I AM FREE FROM YOUR SINGULARITY –
YOU CAN CALL ME RENUNCIATION (BUT I HAVE NO NAME).

~

At this stage of his journey through the reversals, the Fool has little to do other than surrender to the final celestial lights of existence – illustrated by the Star, Moon, Sun and World – with the Last Judgement indicating the whole process of resurrection into the new life of transcendence.

The Fool must give up all hope and all self; two keywords associated with the Star – the nature of "hope" and the "guidance" that the self provides itself through vision. As these concepts are both based on a linear notion of time, which the Fool has long overcome, they are meaningless and at this point have merely been retained as convenient habits of behavior.

The Fool now, with one star in sight, renounces the singular sense of Self.

The word 'renunciation' comes from a Latin root, meaning 'to protest against'. This is not surrender nor sacrifice, it is a pro-active (pro-test) renouncement of illusion in the face of truth. We cannot sacrifice that which we do not possess. We cannot come to truth by way of illusion.

We cannot free ourselves by taking on more shackles or collecting keys.

Our task is to escape the prison, not decorate the walls of our cell.

The reversed Star is indication that our vision, our hope, will not serve us other than to maintain dashed expectations. We are deliberately suppressing the light of truth. This is the ego sometimes protecting itself, resisting inevitable change, against which it is naturally structured to protest. But in legal terms, renunciation is absolute – we abandon a right or position, either explicitly or tacitly, and often without assigning it to anyone or anything else.

The Fool has learnt that he must walk away, saying nothing, leaving nothing, but taking nothing.

The reversed Star says that we must walk into the darkness, that what has served us as a guiding principle for so long is now not only overturned but has likely been that way for some time. It is a card, in its reversal, equally bright as upright – it is realization.

We must make real what we know to be true, we must acknowledge that a singular hope, dream, ambition – even the sense of ourselves as a particular person – no longer corresponds to our observation or experience. The Star reversed is a truly terrifying card for most clients and us, for they (and we) already know what has consumed that old lie and what former brightness must now fail.

Sometimes it is not so bad – there is a sense of relief that the cards have confirmed the state. There can also be a minor situation in which this card is arising upside-down:

- So, I no longer need to feel guilty about what I said about that dress.
- Well, I am not usually a nasty person, it was just that one time.
- Yeah, I know, I gave up on that hope about people a long time ago.
- That company, you are right, I guess it does not owe me anything after all this time.

The Star, like its companions the Moon, Sun, and World, signify the passing of time, and consequences, even when reversed. Oftentimes when upright, they mean something incoming in the time-stream, and reversed they signify something that must be jettisoned into it.

## Example

One way of reading the Majors only is to lay out a triangle spread with three cards, one at the top, and two underneath it. The top card provides a one-word answer, and the two bottom cards provide a sentence which relates to the answer-word. We can of course much extend that reading, but for now we keep it simple.

Let us take a question such as "Should I return from this assignment abroad? I feel like I could stay just the few days remaining and hope the situation home is not as bad as I think." and lay out three cards.

The top card is the Star (reversed), so the one-word answer is "no". The card advises that the situation has already lost hope whatever happens. The two bottom cards might be the World (upright) and the Hermit (upright).

*Illus. The Star (rev), The World, The Hermit in Triangle Spread.*

The sentence we could construct from this is "Nature will take its course whilst you stay here alone". That is to say, the World that you knew is concluding, and you might feel alone but that is the point of the present experience, dealing with things as individuals. If the Star had been upright and those two cards the other side of each other, then the reading would indicate the opposite answer – and other alternatives are possible.

The reader may wish to get those three cards and arrange them in different ways in that triangle, with different combinations of reversals and uprights, and speak out the variations of answer they can provide to a chosen question.

It is like a language drill where you have to practice "We did, He did, She did, They didn't, We didn't, You didn't …" And as we see so often in Tarosophy, the tarot is the language of everything.

Tomorrow the Fool comes to the Moon, reversed, and everything we have learnt so far is reflected back at us, upside-down.

**Lesson 29**

~

THE FOOL MET THE MOON (REVERSED) AND SAID,
I AM FREE FROM YOUR REFLECTION –
YOU CAN CALL ME ENLIGHTENED (BUT I HAVE NO NAME).

~

The Moon, as we know, is mysterious. She rules the night, our dreams, and our fears. She is the mother of the dark and draws unseen tides. She is the passage of time. The Moon is also a mirror and symbolic of all forms of reflection. It has no light, no energy, no radiance, it is merely a polished surface presented to us by the light of the Sun.

When eclipsed, or if there were no light upon it, we would only know it by that which it hides – the stars would vanish and re-appear behind it as it spanned the night sky. The Moon is in part an occlusion, and occult by virtue. It is hidden when we do not shine a light upon it. Again, it returns to mystery.

And there is no greater mystery than the nature of our own existence – our perception, our reflected vision of reality we know to be uncertain. It is even a mystery to us – we rarely understand how our own experience processes what is happening until something fails in it, or something is provoked.

When the Moon is reversed, then, a great secret is revealed – something hidden comes to light. It is revelation, awareness and all the things of the Sun, in a fashion. The Moon reversed is not the Sun, it is the sudden awareness that it is not the Sun, not the light, neither truth nor secret.

It is a great relief to see this card reversed, for it often means that what was feared whilst hidden is coming to light and can no longer be feared in the same way. In fact, it may even be the first light of action.

As we have previously suggested, we can also look to where the light of the card is shining as to what might be the lesson or direction of this secret being revealed. In the case of the Moon, this is the card above it, should there be one in the spread.

The Moon is also a timing card, like the Star, Sun and World, being of the celestial realm. In this case, the reversed Moon is a secret that is revealed within a month – should that be applicable to the question. The reversed Moon is also indicative of a secret that we have held within ourselves that is seeking enlightenment – perhaps this is manifesting as depression, which is becoming obvious in the life of the querent. It can also be the presage of a darker period of self-discovery, even shadow-work, that is now coming to a successful conclusion and demanding action based on the revelations of the previous time.

A "shift" in awareness, at its basic core cartomantic meaning, is the Moon, reversed.

On the highest level, it is enlightenment — the Fool has now passed so far in his journey of rejection, absolution, confession, and exhaustion of all possibilities that he can only live within light. He is true, now. It is true. And there is light. He is fearless in that truth, for there is no reflection, because there is nothing left upon which the light might reflect — there is only the light.

In the next card, the Sun — reversed, and we see what happens beyond even the light of an everlasting day.

## Lesson 30

~

THE FOOL MET THE SUN (REVERSED) AND SAID,
I AM FREE FROM YOUR GAZE —
YOU CAN CALL ME APPARENT (BUT I HAVE NO NAME).

~

The Sun card, upright, illustrates our center, and psychologically the symbol of our self — the burning core of our being that radiates out into appearance as our persona through the ego process. In terms of the Kabbalah, it corresponds not only to a particular path on the Tree of Life, but as the Sun to *Tiphareth*, the central *Sephirah* or emanation of the Tree.

In terms of Astrology, it is the solar aspect of our natal chart which defines core attributes of our personality — and the expression of that through whichever House in which it is located.

In terms of Numerology, the Sun is numbered 19. Which resolves to $1 + 9 = 10 = 1 + 0 = 1$, the number of unity and singularity — and of the Self.

In whatever way we choose to look at it, the Sun is important — even in the humble Lenormand deck the Sun is the most favorable card of "big luck" and "happiness and pleasure". It is warned that if the Sun is far away from the Sitter, then it is "misfortune", as "without the Sun, nothing can grow".[81]

The Sun is the center of our awareness, our planetary system, and our sense of being — from it we radiate. This is perhaps why the unconscious keyword in *Tarot Flip* was "demonstrate" for the upright card.[82] When it turns up in a reading, it is "demonstration" in the sense of being obviously central,

---

[81] Andrea Green, *7-Day Lenormand* (Keswick: Forge Press, 2018), p. 105.
[82] Tali Goodwin & Marcus Katz, *Tarot Flip* (Keswick: Forge Press, 2020), p. 45.

bright, and suggesting the client expresses themselves freely, as the innocent child which is often illustrated on the card.

There is even a bigger secret in the Sun card within the Waite-Smith deck, for the Child on the White Horse holds a very specific meaning to Waite – it is also the only card where his text mentions a specific color.[83] The color is "red", and it is for the banner the Child holds upon the horse. The reason it is a red banner is because the Child is Christ, and the reference is to Revelations when Christ returns "clothed with a robe dipped in blood".[84] The sweet innocent child on the little horse in that deck is also the vengeful Christ coming back after the apocalypse to "strike the nations" and "rule them with a rod of iron".[85]

Yet the card as a savior can be seen in a more positive light - the upright Sun is our true inner self, revealed in all its unique glory, yet inevitably to be sacrificed in the initiatory journey. It is Osiris as much as Christ, Superman as much as every one of us.

When the Sun itself is reversed, the Fool has burnt in his life and exhausted his core – there is nothing left to burn. His rose is now white and pure and no longer red with blood and matter. Pure spirit is what remains when everything else has been destroyed. The spiritual life is a process of subtraction. Not addition.

When reversed, then, the Sun is still central but now everything is apparent – it is an obvious truth that has been turned into a convenient lie. It is much like the reversed Moon in some senses, as both are paired and related in relationship.

It is the action that must arise, like a new dawn, from that obvious truth – it is a push to surface, a push to move on, a powerful drive and energy that can tapped through decision and action. It is like a volcano that is about to erupt, and there is nothing that can be done to stop it.

The reversed Sun is a card of powerful emotion, pent-up expression, that should be carefully directed through the other cards to harness its full potential. If this card is ignored, there will be trouble, which will likely be seen in other cards around it. When we see this card, reversed, in readings, we might get the sense that the other cards near to it are quietly trying to slide themselves just a bit away from it, without being noticed. They know it is trouble.

---

[83] Arthur Edward Waite, *The Pictorial Key to the Tarot* (London: Rider & Company, 1974), p. 144.
[84] Revelations [19:13].
[85] Revelations [19:15].

## Example

Let us consider a four-card Cross reading for a business project, where the four cards relate as follows:

Top: Ideal Aim.
Bottom: Best Resource.
Left: What (old) to Leave Behind/Not Do.
Right: What (new) to Take On/Do.

We draw:

- The Wheel, Hanged Man (rev), Hierophant (rev) and Sun (rev).

*Illus. Four-Card Cross Reading.*

**Aim** – Wheel: The project must be revolutionary, or it will fail – or be worthless. It must aim to turn a new cycle of change, take what exists and turn it around. It does not need to be entirely opposite to what has gone before (that would be the Hanged Man) but rather a new turn on an existing thing.

**Resource** – Hanged Man (Rev): There is literally nothing stopping you – or helping you – in this project. It is entirely on its head already, so you may lack motivation or confidence. You might want to turn this around (as we have seen with the Wheel) by getting some values pinned down for the project. Hang them up somewhere where you can see them.

**Not Do** – Hierophant (rev): You must not set expectations and rules for the sake of it, make a show of things just because you can, and for no reason. You must not try and set boundaries, or any goals based on what has gone before. Again, we see that you have to break free, whilst acknowledging some importance of the past in this project. It is going to be a difficult one to get right.

**Do** – Sun (rev): The client really must express themselves through this project, take full responsibility, lead from the front, have their name all over it, and so on. There must be no hiding – they must be utterly apparent.

We can see in these brief and cursory interpretations that the three reversed cards are providing us a lot of nuance and detail in the reading. There is something about this project that must be both "new" but not locked into the past. It can be a steady project, but there is something missing in its value. It might be a case where the person feels like they are literally "re-inventing the wheel" and will be suspended in doing so for no return. The reversed Sun is interesting because it shows that with nothing much to lose or gain, the client can make this project their own "pet project" and stamp their name on it. This will likely give them an asset for something beyond this present situation, and that is its own value.

Next, we will look at the Last Judgement reversed, when the end of the world comes into sight.

**Lesson 31**

~

THE FOOL MET THE LAST JUDGEMENT (REVERSED) AND SAID,
I AM FREE FROM YOUR DETERMINATION –
YOU CAN CALL ME ETERNITY (BUT I HAVE NO NAME).

~

To be without beginning or end is the quality of the unnumbered Fool, as it is the quality of the divine. Plato defined time as the "moving likeness of eternity", a similitude of the divine, arising through time, which is equally one of its manifestations.[86]

The Last Judgement signals the end of time and a final determination, an action, or a decision. In everyday readings this plays out as a calling to decide, an ultimatum, or literally – a deadline.

When reversed, this moment is being stalled – it is a case where the client (or ourself) is deliberately turning away from what must be done, what must be decided. The call to action still resounds, but the new life will not be entered until it is answered.

This reversal is in many ways similar (but different) to the upright Hanged Man. However, in the case of the reversed Last Judgement, it is an external cause that is generating the action which is being avoided rather than something arising from inside the client.

We might like to look at other cards to see any other reversals which may illustrate the mechanism by which the person is avoiding their decision or action – and the reasons by which they are supporting the avoidance.

The Fool, in his journey of transcendence, is now ready to enter a final union. He has answered the call to finality and passes it by in his realization of eternal life. He knows that everything is always already happening and rejoices. There is neither end nor beginning, there just is an eternal moment that lasts not only forever, but in a way that transcends time. It is an everlasting day.

The client may see in the reversed Last Judgement that they have upturned their opportunity or chance to enter a new phase of their life, but the call will not go unanswered. They may even think they have "missed their chance" because of some "external" change. But it is not the case. The door is still open, it is they who have turned away from it.

It is a card, when reversed, that still operates – it cannot be avoided and

---

[86] Plato, *Timaeus*, 37, c-d.

other cards in the spread may also illustrate how the calling will continue to stress the client or ourselves.

As the Major Arcana are archetypes, they will play out in every area of our lives and the lives of our clients; it may be that their question or situation reflects in many aspects of their life. We can dig into the graves of their past mistakes and resurrect a common reason; a singular message that is being relayed into their life until they learn to answer it.

The Last Judgement card, reversed, can be a powerful and profound entry to a deeper reading from even the most mundane of questions.

Finally, the Fool unites with the World, reversed, and whilst being in the world, is not of it.

## Celtic Cross Reading with Majors-Only and Reversals

## Lesson 32

~

THE FOOL MET THE WORLD (REVERSED) AND SAID,
I AM FREE FROM EVERYTHING –
YOU CAN CALL ME EVERYTHING (BUT I HAVE NO NAME).

~

The World when upright is a card of synthesis and completion, of a finality, closure, and a new beginning. In this final lesson, we consider all the qualities that the Fool has taken on (and off) during his journey of spiritual transcendence into (and out of) the World.

1. Freedom
2. Reality
3. Trespass
4. Everyone
5. Chaos
6. Unity
7. Stillness
8. Silence
9. Nothing
10. Singular
11. Boundless
12. Empty
13. Timeless
14. Perfection

15. Light
16. Continuum
17. Renunciation
18. Enlightenment
19. Apparent
20. Eternity
21. Everything

We have changed one word in the previous lessons; we have re-worded the lesson of Justice (reversed) as "boundless" rather than "everything", which is the quality we have given the World.

It is often the case that the World card brings a new perspective on a reading, like a picture frame that highlights any discrepancies or points of interest in a painting. When reversed, the World is still a sign of totality, of completion, but now it is lost – everything has been turned inside-out.

The Fool knows this, of course, because he sees the World as it truly is – as itself. There is no longer a difference between any one thing and another (as we saw in the reversed Justice where he became "boundless").

The reversed World in an everyday reading symbolizes an empty conclusion to some event or concern – not so much a waste or sacrifice, but more of a putting away of the toys at the end of play. It calls for an acceptance that the matter is indeed over, it is all done and packed away, even if you still want to enjoy the holiday and have not yet left for the airport.

It is a sad card, but we must not wallow in it, be nostalgic or resist the inevitable change.

The card is reversed to tell us that the World is what it is because of such change – when we live in it as temporal beings, there will always appear to us to be endings and beginnings. The World reversed is an ending, simply that. We have enjoyed the ride, but we cannot continue, our time is done, our money spent, the writing or the course is complete.

We will conclude this series of lessons with an example of a full Celtic Cross reading with Majors-only and encourage the reader to practice with Celtic Cross readings in future, using only the twenty-two Major Arcana and reversals.

## Example

The question asked by the client was "I had a profitable business being self-employed but settled for work in a large company for security – I am thinking of returning to my self-employment but cannot make up my mind".

1. Situation: Blasted Tower (rev).
2. Challenge: Devil (rev).

3. Resource: Last Judgement.
4. Aim: Justice.
5. Past: World (rev).
6. Future: Chariot (rev).
7. How You See Yourself: Empress (rev).
8. How Others see You: Fool.
9. Concerns: Strength (rev).
10. Outcome Point: Hierophant.

*Illus. Celtic Cross Spread with Majors & Reversals.*

Looking over the whole reading, the answer is complicated – with all those reversals we see that it is subtle and nuanced, and not a simple yes/no.

In the outcome position, we immediately notice the Hierophant (an expert or professional, but also an institution with rules and tradition) and our eye is also drawn to the future being the Chariot (reversed), signifying an ambition that has come off the rails, *Ben Hur* arena-style.

Their past is the World, reversed, so they have just come through a situation of leaving something behind which they regretted. But that is now past, and must not influence their present state, as it appears to be.

There is a conflict – they want to be considered an expert or professional, but it may be getting confused with their thoughts about working for oneself or working for others. The two things are not necessarily the same; one can have respect in a company for one's expertise as much as working for oneself. In fact, sometimes working for oneself can attract more negative regard than being a company person. There is a confusion here that may cause them to get off-track in either position.

We look at the 'aim' at the top of the Cross and see that they are aiming for a sense of fairness, a work-life balance, with Justice upright. We saw in lesson 11 that this card is also "authenticity" and being true to oneself. That is their aim – but it may not be served by going back to a previous life.

We turn to the paired cards of 'how you see yourself' and 'how others see you' and find that they see themselves as "rotting away", (recall the Empress reversed as "a perfect place now gone sour") yet others see them as the Fool – someone with absolute freedom. We would want to investigate this difference.

The resource card is the Last Judgement – they need to make a commitment to whatever new life awaits them, but again, it may not be anything to do with the past.

What is holding them back? That Strength card (reversed) in the 'concerns' position. They are concerned about taking a break, removing themselves from the race. Why so? It is what they need to do.

We see that 'challenge' in the Devil (reversed), it is their own projection (of weakness, likely, given the other cards) that is being called out here, nothing to do with their career.

We finally look at the reversed Blasted Tower, the last card we have read in this case, even if it was placed in the first position. In Majors-only readings, as with all other readings and spreads, we can follow our eye and instinct across a reading in any best order or sequence, rather than be constrained because the card positions have been numbered in a book 1-10.

As we saw in Lesson 27, the reversed Blasted Tower is a change that is not a change – and a perfect card for illustrating the whole interpretation of this reading. It is a Tower they have pulled down themselves, nothing to do with the workplace.

We would likely talk about them taking time-out to re-evaluate, making changes in their current workplace to gain more recognition, and secure themselves for a future time in which they could look at the situation again.

To answer their question directly in one sentence, it would be "Stay in your current workplace, take time-out and then look at it again, but do not leave now".

We now conclude with a final moment in our last lesson, when the Fool catches sight of his own reversal, and removes himself entirely into the Truth.

# Lesson 33

~

THE FOOL MET THE FOOL (REVERSED) AND SAID,
I AM FREE,
YOU CAN CALL ME,
BUT I AM ALREADY GONE.[87]

~

The spiritual life is neither abundant or dreamt, it is neither anything you can think or feel; it is outside of awareness as much as it is both full of terror and blessing. It has nothing to do with you or your business in the world, and it lacks understanding and wisdom – which is the point. It is nothing other than itself.

The Fool (reversed) is neither here nor there – it is the absence of anything at all, a negative nothingness, a thing that we can only know because it is not anything and must therefore exist (non-exist) for "anything" and "everything" to have meaning.

It is ungraspable, something that escapes us.

When the Fool (reversed) is in a reading, we look at its position, the cards around it, and read them as if they are meaningless in its light. We do not read it, itself. It is truth as it is foolish, it is a paradox as much as it is obvious.

If we require a keyword for it in a reading, it is "unknowable".

Reversed, the Fool can be only interpreted as the thing that we cannot know, that will elude us, is free to every interpretation, so every guess is as good as any other – there is no card like it, particularly reversed.

We have at last come to the end of the true journey of the Fool, one that does not take on lessons from each of the Major Arcana, but transcends them, illustrated by the reversed Arcana.

---

[87] See 'Theme from the Movie Manhole' from Grace Slick, *Manhole* (Grunt/RCA Records, 1974).

## Majors Keyword Compression

A useful consideration for Major Arcana, particularly when they are paired or appear linked in a spread, is to compress their meaning down to one word. This will generate other thoughts in the process of doing so which can be used in the interpretation. We start with a simple statement comprised of any particularly relevant keyword for each card, and then join them together, before compressing them into a single word or concept.

In the examples we will also see that sometimes a Major Arcana card can have much the same meaning as another, dependent on the card with which it is paired, attesting to the multivalency of the Major Arcana. If we are bound to divide the entirety of existence into only twenty-two categories, there will be much overlap and possibility of similar interpretation under different circumstances and context.

## Examples

- Hermit + Justice = Self-balance = Acceptance.
- Devil + Empress = Self-generation = Evolution.
- Magician + Wheel = Conjuring Movement = Initiation.
- Temperance + Chariot = Braking Movement = Halting.

In these examples we see how the Self can be any card, depending on the paired card or context of the reading and question. Similarly, movement (and any other concept) can be any card, such as the movement of the Wheel in one case and the movement of the Chariot in another case.

This method also allows us to conduct simple two-card Majors-only readings, a quick and useful party trick, literally useful for parties, as they can be used for more direct readings than the Oracular Sentences in *Tarosophy*. If we received the Temperance and Chariot combination, we would be able to tell the person that they should stop dead in their tracks regarding their situation, and not continue with it. If we received the Magician and Wheel, then they should start something new, literally give a spark to the wheel and go with it.

# - IX -
## TAROT INCANTOS

## Panolepsy Not Theopropia

I confess,
I wouldst rather go to Arcardia
For oracles,
Than seek out the Mantic Lyre
Of Apollo in Delphi,
Where the pavements are littered
With iron coins and fleece,
With tossed aside lots,
Asking which god should be called,
For riches, renown, or revenge.

I confess,
I would rather hear the great god Pan
Speak guttural in some forgotten grotto,
The voices of stars,
Whispered in my dreams,
Asleep in the cave,
My only company,
The ancestors and spirits of that place.

What price the carved petitions,
When the heavens are already open?

## Naught

See that joker in the pack,
Naught but a seed in his sack?
See that man at the table,
Naught but a tale and a fable?
See that woman sat in silence,
Naught but a veil of innocence?
See that woman in verdant wealth,
Naught but her own rude health?
See that soldier resting there,
Naught but barley in his hair?
See that priest on his seat,
Naught but vows that he must meet?
See those lovers in their tryst?
Naught but their rings of amethyst?
See that prince riding there?
Naught but the wind in his hair?
See that lion and that maid,
Naught but flowers in their trade?
See that man on mountain peak,
Naught but nothing will he speak?
See that wheel that does not stop,
Naught but upwards in its drop?
See those scales and the lady blinded,
Naught but the rules she has decided?
See the man upside-down,
Naught but light as his crown?
See the reaper in his field,
Naught but the seed he has concealed?
See thine angel in her place,
Naught but time, naught but space?
See that figure in the dark of your room,
Naught but shadows in her womb?
See that builder in the tower,
Naught but plans of their own power?
See that star so far, so near?
Naught but hope and naught but fear?
See that poet in his bed,
Naught but dreams in his head?
See the light that shines above,
Naught but innocence in his love?
See the Angel, hear their call,

Naught but glory in the fall.
See the world and every deed,
Naught but nothing in the seed.

## Numbers

0 is empty, the white rose of possibility.
1 is singular, an endless creativity.

2 is a mystery, neither this nor that,
3 is the first shape, where all is at.

4 is a square, power enfolding,
5 is a star, the secret witholding.

6 is the sun, two triangles at and all,
7 is three plus four, a canopy galore.

8 is two square, strength in relationship extended,
9 is four plus five, the inner star comprehended.

10 revolves to Magician and Fool,
And the numbers dissolve like a magical tool.

11 is two Magicians in the temple of law,
12 is the endless, made mystery in all.

13 is the breaking of the one in three,
14 is the tempered magic in an angel's key.

15 is the bright star of the only one,
16 is the light breaking down what was done.

17 is the magic of planets and spheres,
18 is the cycle of power-granted fears.

19 is the one, the son and the sun,
20 is a new world divided from this one.

21 is the two and the one made whole,
So, it ends and begins, the numbering of the soul.

## The Thing

The Fool has done the thing.
The Magician has the skill to do it.
The High Priestess knows she can survive it.
The Empress understands it.
The Emperor rocks it.
The Hierophant will ask for help and give it.
The Lovers love it.
The Chariot just does it whatever.
Strength holds it.
The Hermit doesn't expect help.
The Wheel turns it into a revolution.
Justice measures it up.
The Hanged Man sees it the other way around.
Death takes it and turns it into something you never expected.
Temperance brings it together.
The Devil whispers "why not enjoy yourself?"
The Tower says, "this is day one".
The Star tells you what the thing can be if you listen.
The Moon invites you out of your shell.
The Sun demonstrates a life lived without fear.
The Last Judgement reminds you that everything is the new life.
And the World says you will do the thing if you keep at it.
Which card do you need today to do the thing?

## 22 Confessions

I confess that I am free.
I confess that I am connected.
I confess that I am the secret.
I confess that I am everything.
I confess that I am that which begins.
I confess that I am every belief.
I confess that I am in love.
I confess that I go.
I confess that I relate.
I confess that I am myself.
I confess that I change.
I confess that I am this way and that.
I confess that I may be wrong.
I confess that I die as I live.
I confess that sometimes I experiment.
I confess that I lust.
I confess that sometimes it doesn't work.
I confess that I might see more than I reveal.
I confess that I can only see myself sometimes.
I confess that I want to be enlightened.
I confess that I want something else.
I confess that I want everything.

## But This Card

The Fool will tell you to go, but the World will tell you stay.

The Magician will tell you to talk, but the Last Judgement will tell you to wait for the call.

The High Priestess will tell you to be quiet, but the Sun will tell you to demonstrate.

The Empress will tell you it is time to grow, but the Moon will tell you it is time to fear.

The Emperor will tell you to do your will, but the Star will tell you to follow your vision.

The Hierophant will tell you that it will never change, but the Tower will tell you it will.

The Lovers will tell you to choose, but the Devil will tell you that you cannot.

The Chariot will tell you to move on, but Temperance will tell you to stay.

Strength will tell you to fight, but Death will tell you to surrender.

The Hermit will tell you to follow your truth, but the Hanged Man will tell you to turn it upside down.

The Wheel of Fortune will tell you it is just luck, but Justice will tell you that you receive what you deserve.

*Illus. Paired Majors for But This Card.*

## Baggage

The Tarot Major Arcana is a complete set of luggage which we unpack in our journey ... learning to let go along the way.

I. Intellectual baggage; the curse of believing what you know.

II. The Baggage of the Unknown; the curse of believing what you do not know.

III. Natural Baggage; the curse of believing that you are your own history.

IV. The Baggage of Responsibility; the curse of power.

V. The Baggage of Culture; the curse of believing everyone else.

VI. Relationship Baggage; the curse of believing someone else.

VII. The Baggage of Success; the curse of believing you are what you have accomplished.

VIII. The Baggage of Wounds; the curse of believing you are that against which you fight.

IX. The Baggage of Yourself; the curse of being only yourself.

X. The Baggage of Change; the curse of believing it will stand still.

XI. The Baggage of Equality; the curse of seeing everything the same.

XII. The Baggage of Values; the curse of choosing to stand by one thing alone.

XIII. The Baggage of Mortality; the curse of transformation.

XIV. The Baggage of Angels; the curse of being connected to the divine.

XV. The Baggage of Ignorance; the curse of being limited by what we experience.

XVI. The Baggage of God; the curse of being struck by reality.

XVII.     The Baggage of Vision; the curse of having a future.

XVIII.    The Baggage of Reflection; the curse of self-awareness.

XIX.      The Light Baggage; the curse of awareness.

XX.       The Baggage of Mortality; the curse of knowing there is another place.

XXI.      The Weight of the World; the curse of knowing that this is all there is.

0.        The Bag of Nothing; the curse of being free from all baggage.

The Tarot Major Arcana illustrate the baggage we carry and the curses we must dispel in the Way of the Fool.

## Without

Without the World we would be lost.
Without Judgement, there would be no cost.

Without the Sun, there would be no light,
Without the Moon, there would be no insight.

Without the Star, there would be no vision,
Without the Tower, there would be no revision.

Without the Devil, there would be no pleasure,
Without Temperance, there would be no measure.

Without Death, there would be no end,
Without the Hanged Man, there would be nothing to suspend.

Without Justice, there would be no equality,
Without the Wheel, there would be no reciprocity.

Without the Hermit, there would be no guide,
Without Strength, there would be nothing to abide.

Without the Chariot, nothing would ride ahead,
Without the Lovers, everything would remain dead.

Without the Hierophant, everyone would be without grace,
Without the Emperor, everything would be a random race.

Without the Empress, nothing would be given,
Without the High Priestess, everything would be hidden.

Without the Magician, heaven would not be as the ground,
And Without the Fool, nothing would be found.

## The Major Arcana (Does Not Mean)

That we forget does not mean that we are not free,
That we fail to look does not mean that we cannot see.

That we do not know everything does not mean that we are known,
That we cannot see our growth does not mean that we are not grown.

That we are sometimes weak does not mean that we are not strong,
That we are sometimes taught does not mean that we are always wrong.

That we are unworthy of love does not mean that we cannot love,
That we are lost does not mean we will never see the maze from above.

That we wrestle with our beasts does not mean they are always outside,
That we feel alone does not mean that we have died inside.

And that the Wheel turns,
Does not mean it learns.

That we cannot see the measure of life does not mean it is not fair,
That we cannot make a sense of it does not mean that it is not there.

That we die does not mean we cannot live every moment in joy,
That we do not speak to our Angel does not mean we are not in their employ.

That the darkness is there means only there is light,
That we live in ruins does not mean we cannot set the heavens in our sight.

That the stars are far away does not mean we will never arrive,
That the jackals eat everything does not mean that nothing will survive.

That the light is too bright means nothing to me,
As the life ever after is everything it was said to be.

That the world is as it is means it is a reminder to see,
That things are as they are until you are free.

## Tarot Poem

We go together to the gates, full of wonder,
Once in the garden, now torn asunder;

The earth from the heavens, the waters from the fire,
On our hands we counted ten and did conspire.

The Courts in their ranks and in their aeons unfold,
Through the elements all our stories told and untold.

There is nothing in these fragments that is not real,
In each an arcana of secrets with nothing to conceal.

All is a testimonial and reminder to atone,
Our personal bible written in cards, not stone;

Say these secrets to yourself in the middle of the night,
Speak them to the tarot, turning tales of endless delight;

... I am free,
Life is magic,
And I am more myself than anyone else,
I can always grow from here,
And at least I know what I fear,
Who can teach me, and what I can teach,
I can love, even if I am unloved,
I can move away from what I choose,
In the strength of accepting what I will lose.
Whether alone or known my light still shines,
This is my wheel, forever, given unto me,
It is true, I am here and now and free.
My choice to stand up for myself,
For I am as close to death as a breath.
Oh, sweet alchemy of existence;
There is pleasure and, in its passing,
A fall which must be endured.
For in everything, a certain vision is cast,
In moonlight, sunlight, we leave the past -
Endless delight, the World in which I am free ...

## Tarot Telephone

The Fool said to the Magician nothing.
The Magician whispered to the High Priestess "He said nothing".
The High Priestess told the Empress nothing when she asked.
The Empress smiled at the Emperor as if she held a great secret.
The Emperor commanded the Hierophant to tell what the Fool had said.
The Hierophant told the Lovers to instead go find the secrets of the heart.
The Lovers asked the Charioteer for direction.
The Charioteer spoke to the Lady and the Lion as he travelled.
The Lady and the Lion taught the Hermit something alone.
The Hermit said to the Wheel, "Stop Revolving".
The Wheel complained to Justice about this game.
Justice asked the Hanged Man for another view.
The Hanged Man said to Death, "Stop Dissolving".
Death said to the Angel, "Stop Resolving".
The Angel said to the Devil, "Stop Revolutionising".
The Devil shouted at the Tower, "Top Falling!".
The Tower fell and the Star heard "Stalling".
The Star shone and the Moon reflected "Calling".
The Moon changed and the Sun became "Dawning".
The Sun shone and upon all that lived, all the Bodies cried "We are Reborn".
The World looked back and, considering everything,
Said to the Fool, "Say Nothing".

## Celebration

What does the Tarot celebrate? Celebration is an active recognition of honour and can be realised by frequenting those things most worthy. In the following *Tarot Incanto* we find reasons to celebrate everything; the reader is encouraged to draw a card every day for a week every now and again and celebrate what is given to them.

The Magician celebrates the magic of the world by creating something new every day.

The High Priestess celebrates the mystery of the world by deepening her questions every day.

The Empress, by helping something grow in her nurturing, celebrates life.

The Emperor celebrates power by doing something for themselves and something for another, whilst being clear of the boundaries.

The Hierophant celebrates revelation by respecting the worth of lineage, tradition and heritage.

The Lovers celebrate love.

The Chariot celebrates freedom of movement, even within a box.

Strength celebrates courage by being brave.

The Hermit celebrates the light by shining as an example of its radiance.

The Wheel celebrates change by doing something different. Anything.

Justice celebrates truth by being true.

The Hanged Man celebrates what is above by connecting to a higher principle, just for a moment.

Death celebrates life by living despite itself.

Temperance celebrates diversity by getting to know a different perspective, making an inner alchemy.

The Devil celebrates everything by not refusing to enjoy what is here.

313

The Blasted Tower celebrates possibility by letting go of something worn and broken.

The Star celebrates vision by making one little step on the water towards it.

The Moon celebrates fear by stepping into it.

The Sun celebrates redemption by buying a mistake back from the child and resolving it for the future.

The Last Judgment celebrates the new world by answering the call to it.

The World celebrates connection by reaching out and seeing as much of it as possible.

The Fool celebrates freedom by his constant celebration of everything - and nothing.

## Cards are Cards

Ten coins might get me a birthday card,
But one coin gets me a gift card.
Nine coins should get me an identity card,
But two coins only gets me a top-up card.
Eight coins could get me a business card,
But three coins get me a student card.
Seven coins would get me a red card,
But four coins gets me a savings card.
And six coins will get me a credit card,
But five coins just a bad Christmas card.

## Hang in There

Said the Hanged Man
to the Magician
Who said Yes,
I will try and bring food to the table.

Said the Hanged Man
to the High Priestess
Who said Yes,
I know that change must come.

Said the Hanged Man
to the Empress
Who said Yes,
I will nurture what I can.

Said the Hanged Man
to the Emperor
Who said Yes,
I will know what I can manage and not.

Said the Hanged Man
to the Hierophant
Who said Yes,
I will listen to the experts.

Said the Hanged Man
to the Lovers
Who said Yes,
I will know that love will carry me though.

Said the Hanged Man
to the Chariot
Who said Yes,
I will focus on the things I can do.

Said the Hanged Man
to the Lady and the Lion
Who said Yes,
I will stay gentle and brave.

Said the Hanged Man
to the Hermit
Who said Yes,
I will learn about myself.

Said the Hanged Man
to the Wheel
Who said Yes,
I will ride this revolution.

Said the Hanged Man
to the Lady of the Balance
Who said Yes,
I will recognise more equality.

Said the Hanged Man
to himself
Who said Yes,
I will know this is for me.

Said the Hanged Man
to the Skeleton
Who said Yes,
I will remind you of what is important.

Said the Hanged Man
to the Angel
Who said Yes,
I will see you through.

Said the Hanged Man
to the Darkness
Who said Yes,
I will never leave you.

Said the Hanged Man
to the Toppling Kings
Who said Yes,
I will rise to the challenge or fall.

Said the Hanged Man
to the Star
Who said Yes,
I will light a future by deed.

Said the Hanged Man
to the Moon
Who said Yes,
I will count the measure of this time.

Said the Hanged Man
to the Sun
Who said Yes,
I will rise again.

Said the Hanged Man
to the Resurrected
Who said Yes,
We will hold our hands up when we need.

Said the Hanged Man
to Everyone
Who said Yes,
We are one and together at last.

Said the Hanged Man
to the Fool
Who said Yes,
I will dance and hang in there.

Said the Hanged Man
to the Magician
Who said Yes,
I will.

## To Say to Myself One Day

(As I turn over the Major Arcana in Order)

I am the Air and my Spirit has no Edges,
I am Mercury and I Rule the Table,
I am the Moon, Serene in all my Faces,
I am Venus, Whole and Healthy,
I am Aries, I am Empowered in my State,
I am Taurus, Steady in Faith,
I am Gemini, and I have Choice,
I am Cancer, Ambitious and Creative,
I am Leo, the Courage and Bravery of the Lion be Mine,
I am Virgo, I can be pure and bright,
I am Libra, balanced through insight,
I am Water, diving deep, one with the flow,
I am Scorpio, transforming myself as I go,
I am Sagittarius, straight to the point,
I am Capricorn, passionate and determined,
And I am Mars, Burning to Undo,
I am Aquarius, Taking Myself out of the Box,
I am Pisces, I can Dream Beyond Myself,
I am the Sun, Always Centred, Always Expanding,
I am Fire, I shall arise from the Ashes,
And, Finally, I am Earth and Saturn,
I exist here and now.

## The First Ten Mistakes of Mysticism

The Magician raises his hand in the tempest, and says, I am the centre.

The High Priestess conceals to reveal when truth requires no revelation.

The Empress gives lie to manifestation as existence.

The Emperor creates separation in the illusion of control, doubling his error.

The Hierophant teaches and enslaves the many.

The Lovers attract and create their own Devil.

(The Devil, he comes here and is the Shadow of Fear)

The Chariot presumes to move forward as if Time existed.
Strength, she is Close to Infinity, but resists - we become what we fight.

The Hermit, he holds the light but not becomes it.

The Wheel, ah, the Wheel turns more in truth than any other.

## The Pyramid of Existence

- 0 -
Silence.

- I -
An indrawn breath, then a word.

- II -
A pilgrimage, a huckster by the road, then a temple.

- III -
First Nothing, then Something, then something else, then Creation.

- IV -
Freedom, Will, Soul, Nurturing, Empowerment.

- V -
Building Disbelief, a Lie, a Secret, Congress, Law, Religion.

- VI -
Annulment, Division, Rendering, Pollution, Control, Taboo, Expulsion.

- VII -
The leap, the shuffle, the quietly sat, the pregnant pause, the conquest, the
hand up to heaven, the journey from the garden, a race well run.

- VIII -
Independence, Flexibility, Calmness, Maturity, Confidence, Experience,
Insight, Ambition, Strength in all its guises.

- IX -
We come to the end of the beginning, the altar, the pillars, the garden, the
throne, the church, the gate, the victorious riding from the city, an unseen
fight, each alone in it all.

- X -
Rhyme. Reason. Recall. Renew. Respect. Revelation. Romance.
Reconciliation. Response. Radiate. Revolution.

## - XI -

Stay or Go. Push and Pull. Speak or Hold your Peace. Give or Take. Attack or Retreat. Live and Learn. Love Not Lost. Forwards or Reverse. Restrain or Release. Yourself or Others. Round and Round. The Same in the End.

## - XII -

Abuse your freedom, ignore expertise, surrender in silence, waste, bully, preach your virtues, ride over the downtrodden, silence dissenters, withdraw, gamble your fortune, be unfair, turn it all upside down if you will.

## - XIII -

From silence comes forth speech, from mystery comes forth nature, from experiment comes education, from love comes triumph, from strength comes wisdom, from revolution comes equality, from sacrifice comes not death but transformation.

## - XIV -

The first sight of the White Sun, the Loop of Eternity, The Crescent Moon, the Wheatfields Exultant, a Blaze of Blood and Glory, the Teaching of One who Knows, Love and the Gate to Paradise, the Chariot of the Spiritual Mind, all its Battles yet still Infinite, the Ancient View from on High, the Glory of an Ever Turning Wheel, the vision of Truth, the Secret of the King, the Endless Day after Night, and thine Angel.

## - XV -

And not a word here in the shadow of the pyramid, in the name of Set.

## - XVI -

The spark, the name, the vibration, the nature of light, the coherence, the transmission, the surface of things, the penetration, the holding of it, the spin, the centre and the circumference, equidistant to everything, the noise, the dawn, the modulation, the dark, the tree struck by lightning.

## - XVII -

A vision of a foolish man, words whispered in the Grove of Hermes, an oracle on a three-legged stool, nature's augury, entrails of a ram, the *Shekinah* (blessed be She), a prophetic ecstasy, the trance of the mind, predictions made by the priestess of Athene before a battle, the ramblings of a mendicant, predictions made on Fate's Wheel, a weighing up of the soul by Maat, Odin hung on a Tree, reaching out for runes carved in him one by one, messages from the after-life or the future, the heart pierced by an Angel of the Lord, voices of those things conjured in dark prayers, sudden insight that changes everything, and the simple vision of a better life.

## - XVIII -

A dream of a lost child, a dream of being someone else, a dream you know that you cannot recall, a dream of meadows and trees through which the stream wanders, a dream of conquest, a dream of god, a dream of true love ever after, a dream of going somewhere you know not where, a dream in which you are fighting a beast as you turn into that same creature, a dream you cannot tell anyone, a dream which is only confusion, a dream where you are found out, a dream of drowning, a dream of dying, a dream of the soul and a dream of night after night in darkness. A dream of fire and a dream of water. A dream in which the screaming no longer awakens you.

## - XIX -

A life lived freely, magically, mystically, naturally, deliberately, faithfully, lovingly, thoughtfully, strongly, wisely, revolutionary, fairly, deeply, creatively, divinely, delectably, ascendingly, visionary, fearlessly, brightly, *Nihil sub sole novum.*

## - XX -

Before the new life comes to take us, before we are buried and reborn in the pyramid of existence, let us hear that calling of life to go whither we will, think freely, divine deeply, live healthfully and bodily, be brave, be advised, be loving and quick to help others. Let us be strong, carry ourselves for ourselves, and be the centre of our own being. Let us live in the truth or be aware of eventual reckoning, and let us know sacrifice, Death, our Angel (Blessed be They), the Devil and the eventual collapse of matter as much as our spiritual life. Amongst the stars we live, each in our own orbit, each with as much light as another, to the end of our days.

## - XXI -

A thing that could not be written until all was written.

Silence.
An indrawn breath, a pilgrimage of sorts.
First nothing, then freedom, then the building of our disbelief.
After annulment, we fall, and come to the beginning of the end.
Rhyme, stay or go, abuse your freedom if you will, but from Silence comes Speech and the first sight of the White Sun.
In the shadow of the pyramid of existence, our life is lived.
Nothing but a spark, the vision of a foolish man, a dream of a lost child, a life lived freely, before the new life comes to take us, a thing that could not be written until all was written.

## AMEN.[88]

---

[88] In this *Tarot Incanto* we take each Major Arcana as a lens through which to view each of those arcana preceding it. As such, it provides an increasing number of keywords to each card. However, as a pyramid, this structure may be explored in many ways, for example, selecting every third word once that layer is reached, or every fourth word, etc. These provide different narratives of existence, even whilst using the same cards.

# - X -
# THE MINOR ARCANA

## The Minorverse

In the Ace, we find Space, full of possibility if we enact it practically.

In the Two, we find what we must do, full of possibility, if we enact it quickly.

In the Three, we find what makes us free, full of possibility, if we enact it easily.

In the Four, we find what we can do more, full of possibility, if we enact it furiously.

In the Five, we find what we can survive, full of possibility, if we enact it radically.

In the Six, we find what we can fix, full of possibility, if we enact it harmoniously.

In the Seven, we find what remains unforgiven, full of possibility, if we enact it gracefully.

In the Eight, we find what we hate, full of possibility, if we enact it mercifully.

In the Nine, we find what we think is mine, full of possibility, if we release it easily.

In the Ten, we start again, full of possibility, if we plan our route eternally.

## Minors Only Reading

In this method, we utilise an oracular sentence structure as we have seen in *Tarosophy*, applied now to the Minor Arcana, demonstrating that they too can provide a deep and profound message from the Universe. The reader is (as everywhere in this book) encouraged to use alternate key-words or concepts for their own work, or work with those provided and then modify them over time and with experience of the method. This is a split-deck method using only the forty Minor Arcana and a two-card draw.

1. Take the forty minor cards from the deck.

2. Shuffle and lay out two cards side-by-side.

3. Create a sentence using the oracular sentence structure as follows:

- "The Universe is Wise and Tells me that …"
- "… **from the** [Card 1 *Number* Keyword] **of** [Card 1 *Suit* Keyword] **will arise the** [Card 2 *Number* Keyword] **of** [Card 2 *Suit* Keyword]".

Note that as these are Minor Arcana, based upon their correspondence to our fundamental map of the Tree of Life, we are utilising the *Number* and *Suit* keywords alternately within the sentence to fit this specific structure.

## Example

**Cards**: Seven of Pentacles + Four of Wands.

**Interpretation**: "The Universe is Wise and Tells me that from the Nature [7] of Time [Pentacles] will arise the Construction [4] of My Life [Wands]".

In even plainer words, "I must be patient as things are still working over a longer period of time".

We can now further explore those two cards and see how that meaning could equally be generated from what we already know about the cards – it should match to any book-reading or "intuitive" response to the images because these keywords are from the same source as inspired the Golden Dawn/Waite-Smith/Thoth models of Tarot.

This is also a quick way to use "pip" cards in "non-scenic" decks like the Marseilles.

Here are the key-words:

## NUMBERS

- Ace = Source
- Two = Energy
- Three = Creation
- Four = Construction
- Five = Struggle
- Six = Heart
- Seven = Nature
- Eight = Echo
- Nine = Dream
- Ten = Realisation

## SUITS [two alternatives, choose the best match]

- Pentacles = Time/My Money
- Swords = Thoughts/My Mind
- Cups = Love/My Heart
- Wands = Ambition/My Life

## Example

**Cards**: 9 of Cups + 6 of Swords.

**Interpretations**: "The Universe is Wise and tells me that from the dream of my heart will arise the heart of my mind".

A more enigmatic message perhaps, but in plain language, it suggests, "follow your heart and your mind will be content", that is, in this case put your feelings first, not necessarily what makes logical sense.

## Suits For their Opposite Themes

In Tarosophy, we teach that each card is multivalent in that it contains a multiple number of meanings. These meanings may tend to a dwell-point or strange attractor – expressed as a "keyword" or concept, but they can range over all possible interpretations.[89] The Blasted Tower may usually tend to denote 'shock' or 'acceleration' but can potentially mean anything, dependent on its position, on other cards, the question, and the oracular moment. It could potentially mean 'a pleasant gift' or even 'a new romance', even though those meanings – as interpreted – are usually the tendency of other cards.

In recognition of this teaching, we provide many methods to shake up – accelerate – the readers ability to interpret cards in a fully flexible manner. Although early teaching may give general themes in terms of cards, symbolism, ranks, suits and numbers, these teachings are more to encourage confident learning and reading rather than set a fixed attitude for life.

We can now consider stretching our vision of the cards, in this case, the Minor Arcana, by taking them towards their opposite reading in terms of theme by suit. In our first encounters with the deck, we may learn that Cups "are" emotions or Wands are fire, or that Swords represent intellect and logic. Now let us reach for their almost-opposite themes and see how the spiritual suit of Wands might apply to a mundane reading, and how to read the Swords in terms of emotional situations and questions.

In looking at the cards this way, with terms kindly provided by my co-author of many other books, Tali Goodwin, we can begin to appreciate how flexible we can be with readings, and how the cards will always provide meaning, even if they themselves must be pursued further away from their usual singularity.

In each Suit, we will consider the cards as adding something (upright) or taking something away (reversed) in their opposite theme. In this way, we can apply their appearance to a range of possible questions and situations within their opposite world.

---

[89] A tarot card meaning can likely be termed a "strange attractor" in that it is fractal. A set of keywords are chaotic attractors in this same sense, in that they represent terms that are "locally unstable yet globally stable". In a reading, the Five of Wands may symbolise the different opinions held by a specific person at a specific time, but *every* time the Five of Wands comes up in any tarot readers reading, it does not mean those opinions held by that one person. It "globally" tends to mean disagreements, mock fighting, a lack of planning, etc. as "stable" meanings.

## The Suit of Wands

*Wands are usually considered as the spiritual cards, or as the cards denoting willpower and ambition, regarding their correspondence to Fire. Let us take them in the context of mundane and everyday situations and questions, such as "should I wear something different" or "is it time for me to take up a new hobby?"*

Ace of Wands: Adds drive/takes away motivation, meaning or purpose.

Two of Wands: Adds new dynamism/takes away comfort zones.

Three of Wands: Adds new vison/takes away self-determination, autonomy (giving in to outside influences).

Four of Wands: Adds community/takes away refuge.

Five of Wands: Adds practice/takes away naturalness.

Six of Wands: Adds success/takes away assuredness.

Seven of Wands: Adds confidence/takes away stability.

Eight of Wands: Adds mobility/takes away motivation.

Nine of Wands: Adds defence/takes away protection.

Ten of Wands: Adds accumulation or acquisition/takes away control.

When we view each card through the simple lens of addition and subtraction of a quality, we can lift that addition or subtraction into any of the other realms. If the Six of Wands, illustrated in the Waite-Smith Tarot by a man on a horse, possibly returning from some victory and accompanied by his supporters or army, tends towards a meaning of "victory", what does this add, or subtract – if reversed? The victory in the realm of ambition means that 'success' has been added and would remove surety if reversed. This is illustrated by the horse glancing out to the viewer, as if to suggest he could throw the rider at any time – we might recall that most accidents happen on the way down the mountain, once the summit has been attained. That 'success' or loss of assuredness can then be applied to its equivalency in any other realm. In the realm of an everyday decision, such as a new hobby, it would suggest upright that the new hobby would bring success. In reverse, the choice of hobby is not yet certain and should be re-evaluated.

If we drew the upright Nine of Wands in the choice of an item of clothing, it would suggest that we would want something that could defend against the elements. Deciding whether to go out gardening in the afternoon, should you want to ask the tarot, would be answered with "add community" if you drew the Four of Wands. Perhaps invite others afterwards to enjoy a social event in the garden.

When we bind the concept of multivalency with the tarot, as we do with Tarosophy, we begin to see the deck as a complex arrangement of all possible meanings and interpretations, each card in a constantly shifting movement towards its own core 'meaning' yet never arriving at it in a fixed manner. The 'meaning' of each card is also constantly modified by every other card in the deck, whether it is present in the reading or not. In holding our state of awareness and relationship to the cards in this manner, we become oracular – the shuffling of the deck, the infinite arrangements of the universe, the unknowably vast and intricate workings of our own mind, all become *simultaneous* – and the meaning of the reading becomes its own obvious truth. This is Tarosophy and the deeper meaning of "may a full deck of possibilities be yours".

### The Suit of Swords

*Swords are usually associated with the element of Air and the cutting nature of the mind, so of logic, intellect, learning and rationality. What happens when we consider them in the context of emotional situations?*

> Ace of Swords: Adds rationale/takes away sanity.
> Two of Swords: Adds pragmatism/takes away clarity.
> Three of Swords: Adds separation/Takes away connection.
> Four of Swords: Adds conflict or division/takes away dissembling.
> Five of Swords: Adds betrayal/takes away doubt.
> Six of Swords: Adds passage/takes away resolution or departure.
> Seven of Swords: Adds deviousness/takes away harm or maliciousness.
> Eight of Swords: Adds censure/takes away repression.
> Nine of Swords: Adds turmoil/takes away anxiety.
> Ten of Swords: Adds desolation/takes away difficulties or past trauma.

If we drew the Ten of Swords in the outcome of an emotional situation, it would not only signify that the present path was obviously negative – witness the illustration of a figure with ten swords stabbed in the back – but also, that its main consequence, emotionally, would be to bring about desolation. This word derives from the Latin word meaning "to abandon". The Ten of Swords clearly indicates that the emotional path chosen would be better abandoned before it led to a personal abandonment.

We can see too that the Three of Swords brings a negative reading either way up in an emotional situation; it either adds separation or takes away connection. These may seem obviously opposite and apparent, but some cards function in the same way whether upright and reversed, and others are more complex – all dependent on their 'natural' attractor of meaning and their distance from it.

It is also the case that certain numbers in each Suit function slightly differently, such as the Swords being 'better' in the lower numbers than the higher, as air and thoughts like movement rather than fixity.

We might imagine we are looking at the deck as a flickering three-dimensional arrangement of the seventy-eight fundamental components that are required to build a universe that looks like the one in which we live.

## The Suit of Pentacles

*The Pentacles tend to earthy correspondences, such as health, wealth, resources, money, and the body. Let us take them, as we did the Swords, in terms of relationship situations – usually denoted by the Suit of Cups.*

Ace of Pentacles: Adds a shared goal/takes away opportunity.
Two of Pentacles: Adds balance/takes away individuality.
Three of Pentacles: Adds planning/takes away spontaneity.
Four of Pentacles: Adds consolidation/takes away mobility.
Five of Pentacles: Adds necessity/takes away indulgence.
Six of Pentacles: Adds selflessness/takes away generosity.
Seven of Pentacles: Adds appraisal/takes away easiness.
Eight of Pentacles: Adds commitment/takes away leisure.
Nine of Pentacles: Adds Security/takes away liberty.
Ten of Pentacles: Adds wherewithal/takes away resourcefulness.

If we now imagine we have conducted a three-card reading for a deeply emotional question, past, present, and future, with these concepts in our mind we would not be confused by the appearance of, say, three Minor arcana from the Suit of Pentacles. A beginner reader might consider this strange, perhaps, as they would associate this Suit with finances and health. They might even say out loud, "is there money involved?" This could indeed be the case, of course, but let us look a bit deeper.

Suppose we had drawn the Five of Pentacles (rev), Nine of Pentacles, and the Ace of Pentacles (rev).[90]

This would indicate, in the emotional give and take of the cards; in the past, with the reversed Five of Pentacles, an "indulgence" had been taken away. This can be interpreted that someone in the relationship was indulging the whims of the other, and this had been deliberately removed at the choice of that person. They had likely become exhausted from it. The Nine of Pentacles in the present shows that this has added a sense of emotional "security" to the relationship. This makes sense (in context of the past) in that

---

[90] I would note that all example readings in this book are not 'chosen' to "easily fit" the narrative, as this often disguises the fact that the author has neither experienced or tested the combinations, seen them in the real world or hides the simple fact that the method makes no sense at all. If I do not have a real-world example to hand, I either create one or at worst, use a random number generator to choose cards and then always use them. If we are to teach a teaching, we should want to trust the teaching for ourselves.

all the cards are now truly on the table and the indulgence was a false luxury - not a situation that had stability. The Ace of Pentacles, reversed, removes the emotional "opportunity" for indulgence or falsity. It is a reality check on the relationship – a function of the realm of Pentacles in the world of emotions.

Despite these challenging cards, and the reversals, this is a powerful and deep reading that can lead to an exploration of the false or previously unrecognised 'contract' in the relationship and its betterment in the future. We might ask how we could turn the Ace of Pentacles upright in the real world, by making an action list and encouraging the client to slowly turn around the card (if they had a deck) on a table, as they make each step towards a reversal of the reversal.

## The Suit of Cups

*The Suit of Cups is usually the realm of emotions, love, and relationship questions, also of the imagination. Let us consider them instead in terms of business and finance questions – usually the realm of Pentacles.*

Ace of Cups: Adds creativity/takes away flow.
Two of Cups: Adds partnership/takes away individuality.
Three of Cups: Adds teamwork/takes away co-operation.
Four of Cups: Adds choice/takes away uniqueness.
Five of Cups: Adds denial/takes away responsibility.
Six of Cups: Adds sentimentality/takes away practicality.
Seven of Cups: Adds ideas or imagination/takes away structure or a reality-check.
Eight of Cups: Adds resignation/takes away completion (You will not succeed - if you hang in the towel).
Nine of Cups: Adds gratification/takes away value.
Ten of Cups: Adds Success/takes away ambition (you have it all now, there is no longer anything to strive for).

If we were to pull a single card in response for a big question such as "Should I continue in my present business or change career?" and drew the upright Seven of Cups, that would signify that at the present time you should only make a list of ideas and examine them, not actually make a move one way or another. This "emotional" card adds "ideas" and "imagination" in its own Suit, so in context of a Pentacles-like question, it is realised/manifested as a literal list of ideas.

If you are adding Court cards to this approach, then we extract their fundamental energy which can be applied to any context, even one particularly far away from their usual realm:

Page: Adds/Removes Opportunity.
Knight: Adds/Removes Change.
Queen: Adds/Removes Development.
King: Adds/Removes Security.

The King of Swords in an emotional question adds security; whatever has been decided is fixed and clear, there is no undercurrent or hidden motive at play. If he were reversed, that security is removed, and the emotional current may well be experiencing what one student called "unreasonable cruelty".[91]

The Major Arcana, belonging to another order of meaning, can be read as usual, no matter their context or the form of question. This is part of what makes them an illustrated correspondence of the archetypal realm. It is only when we drop down to the Minors that we see a function by which they are more fixed in orbit towards a singular "meaning". This is also a deep function corresponding to how we create our world, both internal and external, which for advanced Tarosophists provides a contemplation in the deeper implications of divination. In effect, this world is a divination of itself. A divination squared, if you will.

In considering (and more importantly, *applying*) the cards in any context, we can appreciate their complete multivalency. It is simply how the cards work in the first place. They do not "have" a meaning, they each "tend towards" a meaning. This mental shift is fundamental to the development of Tarosophy.

---

[91] My thanks to Dave Kim for this succinct phrase for the reversed King of Swords. The students of the Tarosophy beginners Certificate Course can produce a full and single story for a reading of all seventy-eight cards at the end of their ten-week study, which also combines upright and reversed cards. If we can take them from absolute beginner to being able to produce a reading for a spread which is all seventy-eight cards, it installs absolute confidence in any smaller spread.

## Ten Minor Lessons

In this section we will turn to the Minor Arcana of the tarot and discover them anew through the Kabbalah, commencing with the Aces and working down the Tree of Life to the Tens.

## Aces

In the context of Kabbalah, the Aces are nascent, they are not the 'beginning' but they are the seed before the beginning. As such, they are potential that needs to be sparked, to be realised. In a reading then, they bode well but they require attention and activation. We should not take them for granted, for example, by telling someone "a new romance" awaits them with the Ace of Cups. It means the potential is there, they perhaps even know the person and the possibility. However, without some numbers later down the Tree, there is no movement, even to the ever-flowing Ace of Cups.

We will see that the Twos are more of a beginning. The Aces are the source from where the beginning arises. They are each a point, a single thing. An almost-nothing from which comes everything that follows in their Suit.

**The Ace of Wands** is the highest of the Aces and is the fire of creation - or rather, the seed of fire. It is the first Will, the first ambition, the first sense of "I am". It is "becoming".

**The Ace of Cups** is next in the Aces and is the water of creation - or rather, the source of water. It is the first creation of itself. It is the first sense of "I create". It is "making".

**The Ace of Swords** is the penultimate Ace and is the Air of creation - or rather, the source of Air. It is the first thought, the first decision. It is the first sense of "I exist". It is "formation".

**The Ace of Pentacles** is the final Ace and is the Earth of creation - or rather, the source of Earth. It is the first thing, the first sense of existence. It is the kingdom of here and now.

In an everyday reading where an Ace appears, it signals the position in the spread where something is waiting to be born; an ambition (Wands), creation (Cups), decision (Swords) or an action (Pentacles).

If it is in the past, it may have been missed, and is reminding us that it is still possible. If it is in the present, then it needs immediate attention. If it is in the future, then we must wait for the right time.

In Kabbalah, this is an illustration of Kether (Ace) in the four worlds;

Emanation (Wands), Creation (Cups), Formation (Swords) and Action (Pentacles).

## A Reading Trick with any Aces

We have seen that the Ace of each Suit is the seed of it, so the Ace of Wands is the seed of ambition and lifestyle choices – a spiritual ambition in the highest sense. Another example, the Ace of Pentacles (consider the garden gateway that Pamela Colman Smith depicts) is the nascent, unborn, intention to act, to leave the garden and do something in the world.

Knowing this, we can use it in reading with a simple trick; we can read the Aces with the card next to them in a straight-line mini-spread as:

- "I intend to …" [whatever the next card illustrates].

If we had the Ace of Wands followed by the 3 of Cups, it would be "I intend to become (have the lifestyle of) celebratory (3 of Cups)".

The Ace of Swords followed by the 10 of Wands would be "I intend to decide to carry everything". In this case, the person is setting themselves up for a fall, for a hard job, even before they start.

In a non-linear spread, if we have an Ace somewhere in the spread we can look to the "future card" to see where this seed or intent is going to play out – and in the outcome card.

## Example

As an example, in a Celtic Cross, if the Ace of Pentacles was in the "resources" (bottom of the cross) position, and the "future" (right of cross) card was the 3 of Swords and the "outcome" (top right of spread) card was the Queen of Wands … "You intend to act with your resources to separate yourself out from confusion and gain control of the situation". However, this is only an *intention* – we must look to the other cards too and see how they can put this into practice and take their first step.

## A Simple Ace Deck Rite

We can deliberately select out an appropriate Ace for something we intend to do and then shuffle the rest of the deck and draw a card out, placing it next to the Ace for a divination.

## Example

Let us say we intend to do something creative but have no idea what it should be.

We select out the Ace of Cups and then shuffle the rest of the deck. We draw out one card and place it next to the Ace, using the oracular construct of "I intend to create…"

If it were the Five of Wands we drew, "I intend to create [Ace] … a practice group [5 of Wands]". It may be a surprising answer and one we had not considered. In this case, rather than create something by ourselves, we are advised to create a group and then create things together.

## Twos

When we now look at the Twos in terms of Kabbalah, they relate to Chockmah (2) on the Tree of Life, the second numerical emanation following Kether.

This word, Chockmah, means "wisdom". It is the second thing that happens – the real beginning, the force, the word, that comes out of the seed of the Aces. Wisdom is indeed the practice or action of philosophy. We can see this in the Twos to some extent, in each card of each Suit, there is more dynamic movement or stillness, or illustration of relationship between two things.

Using the names of the four worlds, here are the Twos from a Kabbalistic perspective:

- Two of Wands: Wisdom of Emanation.
- Two of Cups: Wisdom of Creation.
- Two of Swords: Wisdom of Formation.
- Two of Pentacles: Wisdom of Action.

The word 'wisdom' shows us the benefit of experience to make choices and it also relates to 'wit' which locates the mind and thoughts as the basis of consciousness. These cards show us two aspects; a lesson from experience but also the first wise actions in any creative process. Let us look at them again with this simplification:

- Two of Wands: having a plan, knowing what something will look like from the beginning.
- Two of Cups: having a relationship, creating an equal partnership from the beginning.
- Two of Swords: having clarity, holding different thoughts together from the beginning.

- Two of Pentacles: having flexibility, recognising change from the beginning.

It is not important that a client knows that the Two of Cups is Chockmah (2) of Briah (Creation) in the Tree of Life of the Four Worlds but can be useful as another layer for us to bring to the reading.

In our next number, we look at the Threes and discover how to quickly map the rest of the Minors to the Tree so we can get on with even deeper applications of Kabbalah to our readings.

## Threes

In the Threes of the Tarot in terms of Kabbalah we can build up our entire keyword list for all the Minor cards. We have seen how the Suits represent the four worlds of Kabbalah. These four worlds start at the divine and work down in layers to the world in which we live.

They are, starting from the top:

- Emanation (Atziluth): Wands.
- Creation (Briah): Cups.
- Formation (Yetzirah): Swords.
- Action (Assiah): Pentacles.

These correspondences show us the four worlds and the nature of the four suits.

We also have the ten numerical emanations drawn as the Tree of Life, again, starting from the most divine unity at the top (1) and working down to the final manifestation in reality (10). These *Sephiroth* (plural, the singular is *Sephirah* are numbered 1 – 10 and as we are now familiar, match the Ace to Ten in the Tarot. They are as follows:

1. Kether (crown).
2. Chockmah (wisdom).
3. Binah (understanding).
4. Chesed (loving kindness or mercy).
5. Geburah (severity).
6. Tiphareth (beauty).
7. Netzach (victory).
8. Hod (splendour).
9. Yesod (foundation).
10. Malkuth (kingdom).

The words in Hebrew do have more interpretations than those single words, but they are the most common representations used in Kabbalah and for our purpose. If we put this together, having learnt and remembered just fourteen correspondences, we can now generate all forty of the Minor cards from these keywords.

Starting at the top we have Ace of Wands, the 'crown of emanation'. That makes sense and gives us an insight through correspondence that the Ace of Wands is truly a fire-starter, a kick-starter, the ignition point of the whole of creation.

At the bottom, we have the Ten of Pentacles, the final *Sephirah* in the lowest world; the Malkuth in Assiah, the 'kingdom of action'. Again, that makes sense, the Ten of Pentacles is where everything happens and is on the surface – it is purely material.

We can do this with any of the Minors and start to see the Kabbalistic layer in our readings. We can also see why the fives are often more 'negative' than the sixes which are in the geometric middle of the Tree.

## Example

The Threes represent Binah, 'understanding', which is also the complement to Chockmah (2) which we looked at in the Twos. The Threes are formation in response to the force of Chockmah. They are also seen as the Feminine to the Masculine.

The **Three of Wands** is the 'emanation of understanding', where the formation and structure of the world starts to come into being – this is illustrated by Pamela Colman Smith intuitively and through her reading of the Golden Dawn *Book T*, likely, which is pure Kabbalah and Tarot. She draws the ships further heading into the sea, everything has been set in motion to the plan in the Two, now it is a step further ahead and is set in motion. How does this show "understanding"? Well, perhaps we can see that we must understand how things happen once they are set in motion – that understanding comes from 'standing under' what is taking place and out of our control.

The **Three of Cups** is the "understanding (3) of creation (Briah)" and a true cause for celebration. To create, we must have three things, not one, not two – but three.

The **Three of Swords** is the "understanding (3) of formation or structure (Briah)". This is a harsh lesson because to create structure we must divide, separate, make one thing different to another.

And finally, we arrive at the **Three of Pentacles**, Binah in Assiah, the Great Mother in the lowest world. This is the "understanding of action" and we can again see this wonderfully in the Waite-Smith Tarot. There is someone acting to create something and two people with an understanding of what must be built.

When we take the Minor cards in these numerical sets with a bit of Kabbalah, it can rapidly add to our whole language and potential interpretations in everyday readings.

Readers are encouraged to write down these key-words and their combinations for each particular Minor Arcana, and also consult the Thoth Tarot where this layer of Kabbalah is far more on the surface of the design and illustrations than the Waite-Smith Tarot

## Fours

Next, we look at the Fours of the Minors through a Kabbalistic perspective. The Fours correspond to Chesed which is usually translated as "mercy" and generally means a "loving kindness".

If we use our key-words, we get the following:

- **4 of Wands**: Mercy of Emanation.
- **4 of Cups**: Mercy of Creation.
- **4 of Swords**: Mercy of Formation.
- **4 of Pentacles**: Mercy of Action.

Those are a little bit ambiguous and general, so let us dig a bit deeper into the nature of Chesed on the Tree of Life. The role of Chesed on the Tree of Life is *expansion*. It is love, charity, and yet it is also the hidden goodness in the world which must be brought to light through our own actions.

We can see how this is illustrated by the four Fours:

- **4 of Wands**: The ever-present invitation to do good, to share enjoyment in the company of others. To emanate "mercy" by offering it without expectation of return.
- **4 of Cups**: To not refuse to accept what is offered to us as love and kindness. To not block the waters of creation by our own ego and selfishness.
- **4 of Swords**: To live in peace and only do what is good to do, resting otherwise.
- **4 of Pentacles**: To not cling to that which has been given to us in life.

As we can see, there are two cards there which illustrate the negative side of expansion, in fact, all four show how we can block expansion by not accepting invitations, love, the battles we must face or sharing what we are given or gain. In looking at the role of the Sephiroth, we can derive a quite complex philosophy and set of teachings from the Tarot minor Arcana.

**Fives**

In Kabbalah, the fifth Sephirah is called Geburah, meaning 'severity'. It is also referred to as Pachad, meaning 'fear'. If we refer to the bible, we can now recognise that "the fear of the Lord is the beginning of wisdom" as referring to Geburah and Chockmah on the Tree of Life.

As we have seen, we can use our simple keywords to construct the core of the Fives as follows:

- **5 of Wands**: Severity of Emanation.
- **5 of Cups**: Severity of Creation.
- **5 of Swords**: Severity of Formation.
- **5 of Pentacles**: Severity of Action.

We can also see Geburah as an organising and formulating principle on the Tree; it is the complement to Chesed on the other side of the Tree; balancing the outflowing of love with some tough decisions. If there were only the Fours, we would drown in everything together at the same time. If there were only the Fives, we would all be so rigidly structured and divided nothing would change. We will meet the balance of the Fours and Fives in the Sixes.

The **Five of Wands** shows how people try and organise themselves to emanate or start a project. It is the setting of the ground-rules, the push and shove of establishing who does what and when. It can be a good time if it goes right, and a horrible time if it goes wrong. It is (like Geburah) a necessary evil.

The **Five of Cups** is the harsh rule of creation; you have to break a few eggs to make an omelette, you cannot cry over spilt milk, what is past is past, it is water under the bridge… everything we say to ourselves and each other when any new creation is opening up – something has had to be left behind, given up, or spilt from the existing situation – otherwise there is no creation. It is tough love, Geburah and Chesed.

The **Five of Swords** continues the theme of the Fives. To decide anything, to discuss it, to communicate it, there will be divisions and differences as soon as any definition is required to act. The three figures here show the three possible attitudes to such decision-making; ignoring it, embracing it or being somewhere uselessly in the middle. The Fives are rigour and no more so than here in the world of formation.

Finally, we reach the **Five of Pentacles**, the severity of action. It illustrates how sometimes our income and work is deferred to a later date, how the actions we take are influenced by our environment – and create it. In the world of action and manifestation there are severe differences, whether it be in wealth, health, or weather. This is the final world of severity and structure, played out in every aspect of our experience.

We are usually far happier to receive Sixes in a reading than Fives – these Fives are ruthless, heartless, calculating, structural, machines without any love at all. But again, they are necessary in the whole. Geburah, illustrated by the four Five cards of the tarot, can be viewed as the crucible of love (Chesed), where all our love is tested and refined in the fire of the four worlds.

## Sixes

As we reach the mid-point of the Sixes, we can look to find better balance than either the Fours or the Fives, particularly when viewed on the diagram of the Tree of Life. We will also look at how a simple three-card reading can be enhanced by reading a layer of Kabbalah.

There are several versions of the Tree of Life, which is a diagram of our relationship to the divine and a construction plan for the creation of the universe. In this version, we can see that the sixth Sephirah, Tiphareth (meaning 'beauty'), is at the harmonious centre of the Tree, acting as a channel for everything above and below it.

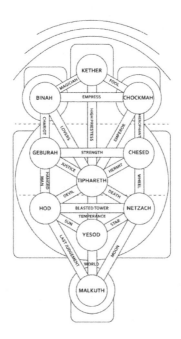

*Illus. Tree of Life with Tarot Correspondences to Paths.*

Tiphareth is illustrated through correspondence to the Tarot by the four Sixes of the Minor Arcana.

As we have seen, the four Suits relate to the four worlds of Kabbalah, so the four Sixes show the nature of 'beauty' in each of these four worlds:

- **6 of Wands**: Beauty of Emanation.
- **6 of Cups**: Beauty of Creation.
- **6 of Swords**: Beauty of Formation.
- **6 of Pentacles**: Beauty of Action.

The **Six of Wands** shows the 'return of the King' in a sense, if we consider that Tiphareth is the son to the Mother (Binah) and Father (Chockmah) energies of the Tree. It is the harmonious point of victory, achievement, rulership, etc., but there is always the possibility of the sin of pride.

The **Six of Cups** is again a strange equi-point in the Tree. It shows the balance between age and beauty, between male and female, and the "beauty of creation" in terms of human relationships.

The **Six of Swords** is the beauty of formation when it is carried out into the world and makes ripples. It is a mental balance achieved through movement and progression towards an ideal.

Finally, the **Six of Pentacles** shows a literal balance point in the scales of charity, the balance of time and resource, give and take, and the beauty of perfect action that benefits all.

## Example

Whilst we will continue to look in following numbers at the Seven, Eight, Nine and Ten of each Suit in terms of Kabbalah, let us take a moment to apply what we have so far learnt.

If we take a simple past + present + future three-card reading, we will see how the layer of Kabbalah might help us deepen the reading.

In this example, we will only use Minor cards from the Ace to the Sixes which we have already covered.

- Cards: We receive the 3 of Wands (past), 5 of Wands (present), and 4 of Cups (future).

We can see from our layer of Kabbalah that this situation is mainly about the highest world of emanation (Wands) and a little bit of the world of creation (Cups). It is something that is moving into being from the very highest principles into creation. It is likely that the person will need to do something creative with this new impulse, even if it is not immediately manifest (no

Pentacles) or structured (no Swords).

We are deliberately ignoring the 'meanings' suggested for usual interpretation of the cards so we can see them stripped down to their core correspondences to Kabbalah. Next, we see that are moving from a '3' in the past to a '5' in the present. That is a reasonable jump from Binah (3), 'understanding', to Geburah (5) 'severity'.

We can interpret this as there having been a push into some constraint that has moved the situation on, hence the reading, also from something that was already understood for a time in the past. It is not new – it is an inevitable development of some impulse.

We can do a little of that layer just through numerology alone, but Kabbalah does allow us to have a more dynamic map through the Tree of Life and corresponds to numerology because it is originally based on numbers and letters – in Hebrew there is no difference.

That '5' in the present is moving into the '4' of the future, so it needs to take a step back from being too 'severe' (5, Geburah) and return to 'mercy' and 'loving kindness' (4, Chesed). That sounds like the client needs to stop beating themselves over the head about this situation. Again, we have not even yet "read" the cards, we are seeing the construction of the universe underneath whatever situation is being played out upon it – the divine machinery at work.

Putting the Sephiroth and the Worlds together with our keywords, we remind ourselves:

- 3 of Wands = Binah of Atziluth = understanding of emanation.
- 5 of Wands = Geburah of Atziluth = severity of emanation.
- 4 of Cups = Chesed of Briah = mercy of creation.

That kind of makes sense – going from an understanding of an impulse, realising its constraints and demands should we act upon it and then the release of creating something new from it. The Minors can be just as profound as the Majors when taken in terms of Kabbalah.

In a more advanced consideration, we can also look at how those connect as a route on the Tree of Life; in this reading, from Binah to Geburah and then to Chesed, and how the Major Arcana on the paths between those Sephiroth illustrate more about any situation.

Returning to what we have already covered for those three cards, we can see that with the Three of Wands in the past, a specific understanding what reached about what was already set in motion. It indeed had already been pushed out of the reach of the client - those ships were already set sail. They have come to the reading more for confirmation, not for revelation.

In the present, the Five of Wands shows the 'necessary evil' of having to practice what we preach, to start to re-organise our life around our values, restructuring what needs to be expressed. This will cause conflict for the client – a part of the necessary evil.

And then in the future the client is best advised to aim for the Four of Cups, about which we wrote "To not refuse to accept what is offered to us as love and kindness. To not block the waters of creation by our own ego and selfishness".

We can see even in this sketch version of a reading, how a layer of Kabbalah maps out from just three Minor cards a deep pattern in the life of the client, underneath their presenting problem or situation. We will next look at the Sevens and continue to put Minor cards together in readings with Kabbalah.

## Sevens

How do we know the best way to respond to a situation? How do we read our tarot cards to see the most effective way of dealing with something; do we approach it with direct action, ignore it, run away from it; do we treat it as psychological insight or would that be just avoidance of a situation where we need to act in practical way?

As we look at the Sevens and reach the more manifest levels of the numbers, we will see how a Kabbalah reading of Tarot can get very practical. First, we will provide ourselves fourteen Kabbalah keywords, such as "expanding" for Chesed, or "Reflecting" for Netzach, and apply them to the Sevens.

1. Kether 'crown' = Ace = Point.
2. Chockmah 'wisdom' = 2 = Energy.
3. Binah 'understanding' = 3 = Structure.
4. Chesed 'loving kindness' or 'mercy' = 4 = Expanding.
5. Geburah 'severity' = 5 = Contracting.
6. Tiphareth 'beauty' = 6 = Balancing.
7. Netzach 'victory' = 7 = Reflecting.
8. Hod 'splendour' = 8 = Conforming.
9. Yesod 'foundation' = 9 = Building.
10. Malkuth 'kingdom' = 10 = Completing.

As this cosmic machine operates on four levels, we sometimes may want to know which level is best to get the most effective response to a situation:

- Emanation (Atziluth) = Wands = Mystical or Spiritual World (Self).

- Creation (Briah) = Cups = Magical or Archetypal World (Superego).

- Formation (Yetzirah) = Swords = Astral or Psychological World (Ego).

- Action (Assiah) = Pentacles = Physical World (Body).

These alternative titles for the four worlds are extremely broad and should be taken just in the context of this approach to reading, where we use them to divine the most appropriate way of responding to a situation.

Let us look at the Sevens with our alternative keywords:

- **7 of Wands** = Reflecting in the Mystical or Spiritual World (Self).

- **7 of Cups** = Reflecting in the Magical or Archetypal World (Superego).

- **7 of Swords** = Reflecting in the Astral World or Psychological World (Ego).

- **7 of Pentacles** = Reflecting in the Physical World (Body).

We can see how these keywords play out in Pamela Colman Smith's illustration of the Sevens which likely used the Golden Dawn *Book T* descriptions, given to her by A. E. Waite.

*Illus. Line of Sevens in descending order of the Four Worlds.*

She was illustrating 'victory' (the literal translation of 'Netzach') in different ways, from the 'victory over small things' of the Seven of Wands, as it is described in *Book T*, to the 'illusionary victory' of the Seven of Cups. In the Seven of Swords, we have 'yielding when victory is in grasp' (or it being snatched away from us) and the Seven of Pentacles illustrates what *Book T* calls "little gain for much labor". It is this latter card, the Seven of Pentacles, that Pamela has literally interpreted from the Book T text, "A cultivator of land, and yet a loser thereby" by illustrating the card with a scene from the potato famine in Ireland, as the worker rests regretfully on his hoe, looking at the withered leaves of the potato plant.

As we have written elsewhere, *Book T* is a far better 'little white book' to the Waite-Smith Tarot than the guidebook that A. E. Waite sketched out as *Pictorial Key to the Tarot*. Of course, they could not publish the secrets of the Golden Dawn at that time with the deck itself, which led in part to the confusion - and freedom of interpretation - of that deck for a century to follow.[92]

Our role for the Seven is not only 'victory' but also 'reflection'. In the machine of the cosmos, Netzach functions as nature, habits, cycles, and the energy that spirals into life. It reflects, echoes and spills into existence below the 'veil' that separates it from Tiphareth.

Netzach is also a lower version of Chesed, and in turn, Chockmah, on that pillar of the Tree. This gives us even more depth as we learn about them separately and together. The 'force' of Chockmah, the 'word' of existence drops down into the expansion of love in Chesed and resolves itself in the 'natural world' of Netzach with all its emotional loops and cycles.

It is Hod (8) that we will look at next as the rigid, structural logic of thought which balances the aspect of Netzach. Consider Netzach as Dr. McCoy in Star Trek, Hod as Mr. Spock and Captain Kirk as Tiphareth.

In the meantime, if we had the Seven of Cups in the 'future' position of a reading, we would see that as 'reflecting in the magical world'. It is an imaginary situation that is being placed in the future and therefore one that is still susceptible to magical influence. All situations are changeable through magical acts, just some more so than others.

If we had the Seven of Pentacles in the 'outcome' of a reading, we would see that as rather more fixed, reflecting in the physical world. It would require an actual action to resolve it, not just thoughts or feelings, ambition, or plans – but an actual act.

We will continue looking at the cards in this light when we pair up with the Eights in the following part of this section.

---

[92] Tali Goodwin & Marcus Katz, *Secrets of the Waite-Smith Tarot* (Woodbury: Llewellyn Publications, 2015), p. 81.

## Eights

The eighth *Sephirah* (numerical emanation) on the Tree of Life is called Hod, which means 'splendor'. When we consider this in terms of correspondences, we can compare it to other systems, not only tarot and numerology. As an example, we can make correspondences to Ancient Egyptian deities, or Greek deities, or Roman gods and goddesses, etc.

There are good magical reasons for working with correspondences, and at a deeper level, we use them to remind ourselves that everything is connected in one unified creation.

Hod relates to Mercury in terms of communication and mental processes, and in the Ancient Egyptian pantheon to Thoth, lord of Magic and Scribe of the Gods. We can use these correspondences in Tarot Magick.

If we consider Hod, for example, it is the component of the Tree of Life that sits at the bottom of the pillar of "formation", and hence it is very structural. It is an organizing principle, it corresponds to our thoughts and decisions, logic, and rationality, when we consider the Tree in terms of our psyche. Hod (8) corresponds to thoughts, Netzach (7) to emotions, and Yesod (9) our ego-process and personality structure. Malkuth (10) corresponds to our body.

Whilst we are not looking at the Major Arcana in this section, we consider them as illustrating the connections between these various parts of our psyche.

The Blasted Tower connects Hod and Netzach, showing the relationship between our thoughts and feelings; the Moon connects Netzach and Malkuth, showing the connection between our emotions and our body, etc. In terms of the Minor Arcana then, Hod represents the 'conformity' to balance Netzach's giving forth without constraint. Hod is a lower reflection of Geburah in this sense.

The conforming of Hod is illustrated in the Eights as follows:

- Eight of Wands: Conforming of Emanation.
- Eight of Cups: Conforming of Creation.
- Eight of Swords: Conforming of Formation.
- Eight of Pentacles: Conforming of Action.

We might also put back in our basic keywords for the Suits, so we have:

- Eight of Wands: Conforming of Ambition.
- Eight of Cups: Conforming of Emotions.
- Eight of Swords: Conforming of Thoughts.
- Eight of Pentacles: Conforming of Resources.

We can see the **Eight of Wands** illustrating that we are putting all our ambitions, everything that is coming from us into the world, into flight and conforming to one pattern, one direction. This card signifies aligning everything that we Will into one goal, one vision, even ahead of it coming into manifestation.

The **Eight of Cups** illustrates the eclipsing of all our thoughts and ambitions by emotions, whether they be positive or negative. They move us into a different space, either physically or emotionally within ourselves. This is when we conform to our deepest emotions, and connect to ourselves, without any other person being present in our mind.

The **Eight of Swords** shows what happens when we conform to our thoughts – too much. We can become bound by them if we mistake them for being anything other than a useful framework. That is when they become a prison. If we think that our past decisions should be judged from a present that we were blind to, they become a prison. We must not form everything from conformation; there needs to be change and flexibility to see outside of any particular moment or situation.

Finally, the **Eight of Pentacles** shows a conforming to work, to resources, to what is right in front of us at the moment. We can become lost in the present, acting just in the moment. This can be good and bad, depending on the circumstances, of course.

We can see how the Eights are a lot more solid than their twinned Sevens on the other side of the Tree, and perhaps also how each of the Eights has a trap if we take it by itself.

Many traditional books on Kabbalah – and the way we teach it – twin the Sephiroth to ensure we learn them as sets which interconnect, rather than as separate things. The Tarot is like this too – all the cards are locked in an endless shuffle with each other, and none of them (other than the Fool) are free from each other in their grand picture.

Next, we will return to a practical reading and put our teaching to practice again as we cover our penultimate part of this section on the Nines.

## Nines

In Kabbalah, Yesod, the ninth Sephirah means 'foundation'. If we look on the Tree of Life, we will see how much of a foundation it is to the rest of the Tree. In some alternative versions of the Tree of Life, it is even more so, as it is drawn as the only Sephirah connecting to Malkuth below it – everything above rests upon it.

In our correspondence to the psyche, Yesod represents our ego, our unconscious and our personality, everything that we build to face the world, and is built by the world as we engage with it. It is a building block, and one which is dynamic, subject to change from moment to moment.

In a reading, if we see a Nine card we can look to where it is in the reading and see that as a potential pivot point. If a Nine is in a 'past' position, we will want to explore the client's memories connected with the situation far more than their future hopes.

In NLP we would call the Nines as indicating "the difference that makes a difference".

We will look at a reading next, but first we will sketch out what the individual Nines mean in terms of a Kabbalah layer. We will also now add to our considerations of the Minors the Shakespearian designs used by Pamela Colman Smith to illustrate *Book T,* which brings along Kabbalah through her interpretation of the text into images.[93]

- **Nine of Wands**: The foundation of belief; see how the character on the Waite-Smith version holds true to his own authentic values and beliefs, despite the opinions of others in the world.
- **Nine of Cups**: The foundation of love; see the character of Falstaff on the Waite-Smith card, who has become "fat-witted" and "full of old sack" (beer) in self-love.
- **Nine of Swords**: The foundation of thought; see Juliet from whom all hope has been removed, leaving only terrible consequence and a singular grief she cannot face.
- **Nine of Pentacles**: The foundation of resources; this is Rosalind, secure in her society but constrained by it, particularly regarding her gender.

In these cards we see most clearly how the Waite-Smith deck is a Shakespearian-themed (or theatre-deck) interpretation of the Kabbalah of the Golden Dawn. They show the more negative side of Yesod, the ego-process just as it is when it is left to itself and with no higher function (awareness) at work.

These four cards also illustrate the four buffers that people throw up to survive in the world and where they might most be clinging to their own present detriment.

---

[93] *Ibid*, p.40.

## Example

Here is a simple three-card example reading where this might be illustrated:

- Past: 9 of Cups.
- Present: 5 of Pentacles.
- Future: Ace of Swords.

*Illus. Nine of Cups, Five of Pentacles & Ace of Swords.*

Here we see that the Nine of Cups, the 'foundation of love' or comfort, which is the Yesod of Briah (foundation of creation) has been in the past. The harsh present shows in the Five of Pentacles, the 'severity of action', Geburah of Assiah, the constraints now applying to the manifest world. We can already see that pair as a developing story of some emotional satisfaction which has led to a withdrawing from the real world which is now suffering.

It is likely the reading has been requested at a time when it cannot be ignored, and we recall the quote for Falstaff we gave for the Nine of Cups in *Secrets of the Waite-Smith Tarot*, where he is told that he has forgotten what was most important to him in life.

The future, then, is somewhat unsurprising. It is the Ace of Swords, the 'crown of formation', the 'point of thought', the seed of 'I exist', the very first thought. It illustrates that the client must formulate a new decision, a new thought about themselves – a radical cut from their past, which no longer serves them. They should not try and do anything, create anything, even change anything – this has not served them to change the situation. It starts only with a new thought and time.

We might draw three further cards and place them above the Ace of

Swords to show the exact nature of the 'new thought' that might be formulated to seed the future change.

Next, we will meet the Tens in the concluding part of this section on the Minor Arcana in terms of Kabbalah.

## Tens

In this final part of our section on the Minor Arcana considered through Kabbalah, we look at the Tens and use a ten-card reading to demonstrate how we can apply the layers of Kabbalah we have now covered to an actual reading.

If the Aces are nascent or prior to beginning, then the Tens are what follows the end; they are already 'past due' and returning to their source.

The Twos and the Nines are more to do with the starting and ending of things; the Aces and Tens are just before anything and just after everything, almost joined together.

We can imagine this in the Ten of Wands; the best option for the figure illustrated by Pamela Colman Smith would be to drop the ten staves and bundle them up into just one bundle; the Ace.

Similarly, in the Ten of Pentacles, the young fool pats his dog and looks out at us as if to say, 'this is not the end but the beginning of my journey'. The Ten of Cups offers a rainbow covenant that the divine is connected to the world, and the children dance ahead of a new generation of life.

And the Ten of Swords can truly go no further in that line of thought – the traitorous or rebellious thoughts have ceased the old body of knowledge and moved on to a far more simple and unified idea - the Ace.

The Tens show a completion and what is happening even in that very center of that finality - a new beginning. The kingdom (Malkuth) of each world is in the Ten, but at the same time they illustrate that the Kingdom is created to create a new beginning which is already underway.

In the Tens, we learn that desire only exists until we have that which we desire, and then it becomes redundant; thoughts only exist until the action is attained to which they lead; money lasts until we purchase something; a family to create another family; ambition until it is fulfilled, and so on.

## Example

To conclude this section, let us imagine we now have five Minor Arcana within a ten-card reading, say, a Celtic Cross, in the following positions:

- Past: 8 of Swords.
- Resources: 4 of Wands.
- What Others Think: 2 of Pentacles.
- What You Think: 7 of Wands.
- Concerns: 9 of Swords.

In this reading, we might first look at those two cards for the "how others see you" and the "how you see it yourself" positions. This pair of cards often explains how a situation is stuck.

Here we have the Two of Pentacles (Chockmah in Assiah) as to how others are looking at it, and the Seven of Wands (Netzach in Atziluth) for how the client is seeing it all.

These are two very different Sephirah in two different worlds: the lowest and the highest, in fact.

Looking back over this section on the Minors, we read these two cards as "the wisdom (Chockmah) of action (Assiah)" for the Two of Pentacles and the "reflecting (or victory) in the mystical world" as an interpretation of Netzach in Atziluth for the Seven of Wands.

It is not too difficult to see how these two positions might be conflicting; everyone else is seeing that the situation requires change to happen, based on experience and practicality, but the client themselves is seeing it entirely as a 'spiritual' situation.

When we consider the illustrations of those two cards, in the Waite-Smith Tarot, we can see that the person feels as if they have been fighting this battle against other people's values for some time, and that they might resist people suggesting some juggling of their position.

We could discuss this with the client and suggest from those two cards that they might be holding onto something for the sake of it, or through habit (an attribute of Netzach) which may not be necessary.

If we look then to their concerns (the Tarosophy way of reading the hopes/fears position in the Celtic Cross) we can see they are concerned there is no end in sight and their thoughts are worrying; in Kabbalah we saw the Nine of Swords as the "foundation of thought" and what happens to logic (Swords/Foundation) when the ego (Nine/Yesod) is in charge.

It is here too that we can see they are maintaining a position for the sake of it – there is no reality to their concerns should they make a change that seems obvious to others.

How can we help them enact this change that so far, they have resisted, leading to a situation where they have had to come and consult a tarot reader of all people?

Let us look at the Resources card, but perhaps we should look at the Past card first, to get any other insight into how they have come to this situation?

In a Celtic Cross, as with any other fixed-position spread, it is important to read around it in the order that is most useful to you and the client – not be fixed into reading it in the given sequence, one card at a time.[94]

When we look at that Past Position card, the Eight of Swords, we see something very appropriate and powerful - and this is a real reading, not a made-up example. Here is what we had in our earlier description of the Eights:

The Eight of Swords shows what happens when we conform to our thoughts – too much. We can become bound by them if we mistake them for being anything other than a useful framework. That is when they become a prison. If we think that our past decisions should be judged from a present that we were blind to, they become a prison. We must not form everything from conformation; there needs to be change and flexibility to see outside of any particular moment or situation.

Now we can see that something in their past led them to conform. They are bringing this sense of safety in conformity to a situation that demands the opposite; the Two of Pentacles. The Hod in Yetzirah is like a stuck cog in a machine, and the Chockmah in Assiah is trying to get some rotation into the ground. No wonder there are sleepless nights (Nine of Swords).

We may not even need to bring up the exact event in life that led them to conform for their own well-being and safety, but it is likely to be in childhood and something that has played out in every area of their life, career, and relationships.

When we apply Kabbalah to a reading, we get the whole picture, not just the snapshot being presented to us through the specific question or situation being presented by the client.

Finally, then, we can look at the Resources Position and see the Four of Wands; another card in Atziluth (Wands) like the Seven of Wands.

We can suggest that they apply some Chesed (4) or loving kindness to themselves as a resource, rather than get stuck lower down in Netzach (7)

---

[94] There are several Tarosophy methods and spreads that work deliberately to be read one card at a time in a specific sequence, but most spreads shared on social media are neither well-designed or extensively tested, so are difficult, or almost impossible to read when you try and read them by the numbers or in any manner. If a group or individual is pumping out endless 'spreads' onto social media ("a Christmas spread every day for December!" or "Here's our top ten Halloween spreads!") you can usually guess they have never actually used them or tested and refined them in real readings for other people.

fighting a habitual battle. They need to expand, loosen their boundaries, etc. (qualities of Chesed), as a spiritual act.

When we look at those two Sephirah on the Tree of Life, seeing how one is immediately above the other, it illustrates this very well. We can also (in a more intermediate technique) simply recall that the path between them corresponds with the Major Arcana card of the Wheel. This not only shows the relationship between the expansion of Chesed and the cycles of Netzach, but how that plays out in life in terms of fortune. Here we can suggest to our client it is time to turn their fate into destiny, by rising above the wheel of habits and misfortune, to do something different.

By learning these basic correspondences to the Tree of Life, we can now use the lens of Kabbalah in our reading, opening far deeper dimensions of divination.

## Freedom Sequences

In this section, we will continue to look at the Suits of the Minors as a map of manifestation. In our correspondences to the Tree of Life, we can take each Suit and produce a sequence of actions which best produce results with as least conflict to the patterns of the universe. These can be used as checklist or journal templates when engaged in any project or personal change-work, relationship development, etc.

## Freedom in the Wands

We commence with the Suit of Wands, which can be considered as a map of intentions and the manifestation of individual or collective Will. It is also a sequence that shows us the process of aligning to universal Will – turning our fate into our destiny.

Here (in brief) are the steps towards True Will made by the Wands.

*Do First and Plan on the Way.*

Ace: Own Your Intention; accept your responsibility to do it because no-one else will.

Two: See what it might look like when you are successful; see one detail of how you will know you have arrived.

Three: Set it in motion now with one action, change or activity; the Universe is going to go with you because it cannot stop.

*Everything Moves About the Middle.*

Four: Accept every opportunity that opens, testing only that it takes you towards your ambition; others have their Will and together you may share parts of the journey.

Five: Incorporate and utilize every obstacle or confusion as a signpost that you are on the Way. There will be adjustments and consequences to every act of organization.

Six: Keep moving in a singular direction, even if at an angle. Keep your eye on the destination no matter where the horse takes you – at the end of the day, you hold the reins.

*When it Hurts, You Know it Works.*

Seven: Know when not to stop; others will resist change as much as you have done.

Eight: When it seems to have escaped you, move faster. When it seems to be dead, live; and when you want to give in, go more quickly. Remember the beginning and the end.

Nine: Now own your experience, including your mistakes along this Way. You would not have got this far without having to make changes.

*Many are the Sticks, But One the Bearer.*

Ten: Carry it out and know that you are moving forward even if sometimes you cannot see the next step. Take a moment to put everything down and see it together – the Ten becomes an Ace again when everything is seen as one thing – your individual Will.

## Freedom in the Cups

In the sequence mapped by the Cups, we look at understanding our emotions and reaching tranquillity when we are confused or uncertain. The Suit of Cups can be considered a map of feelings and emotional states. It is also a sequence that shows us the process of finding inner calm.

Here (in brief) are the steps to emotional tranquillity made by the Cups.

*Attaining Tranquillity.*

Ace: Understand first that everything is moving through you.

Two: Recognize that you are not alone.

Three: Begin to practice every engagement in life as its own celebration and reward.

*Arriving at Tranquillity.*

Four: Accept your own boundaries.

Five: Accept your losses as learning.

Six: Accept that your own state is not the gift of other people.

*Remaining in Tranquillity.*

Seven: If you are going to imagine things, make them wonderful.

Eight: Move away from what makes you feel worse.

Nine: Own your Accomplishments, whether big or small, you are not the judge.

*Maintaining Tranquillity.*

Ten: Understand at last that everything is here and now.

## Freedom in the Swords

In the Swords, we discover the sequence of clarity, freedom from past thoughts, memory, representation of trauma or confusion.

*First Steps to Freedom.*

Ace: Make your intention singular. To your own thoughts be true.

Two: Set yourself in the centre of conflict.

Three: Separate yourself from everything but that which you choose.

*Fighting for Freedom.*

Four: Take time to find your own space and stay inside it.

Five: As things change, learn when to fight, freeze or flee.

Six: Stay on course no matter the ripples.

*Finalising Your Freedom.*

Seven: Take care when others try and steal away your thoughts of freedom.

Eight: Realise at last which thoughts keep you prisoner.

Nine: Be prepared to mourn all that to which you were once so attached.

*Fixing Your Freedom.*

Ten: Keep those old thoughts dead and buried in order to return to the Ace.

## Freedom in the Pentacles

In the Pentacles, we discover a route towards financial freedom, in both a realistic and magical sense. The Suit of Pentacles can be considered a map of the way in which manifestation occurs and as such we can discover in it a route to realize our resources.

Here (in brief) are the steps towards financial freedom made by the Pentacles.

*Start from What You Have.*

Ace: Invest in the long-term, as you aim to live better every day.

Two: Take stock of where your time is going; it is your most valuable resource and holds everything together.

Three: Decide that you are always working for yourself, whether it appears so or otherwise.

*Give and Take.*

Four: Arrange what you have into the most sustainable way – there should be no effort in owning what you possess.

Five: Accept that others have different things to you, but the measure is between what you desire and what you experience in the journey.

Six: Do not waste your time tickets (money) in giving them to those who might waste time.

*Work is Reward.*

Seven: You may have to start again several times so learn to enjoy the process of growth for its own reward, rather than the hoped for outcome.

Eight: Spend your time in work that creates and provides you experience, which is its own reward.

Nine: Money can be a trap as well as a tool; your reward is in the measure of your own confidence and contentment alone.

*Be Now but Leave it Behind.*

Ten: Build a legacy – in time, all that you have done will be the property of the future.

## Ten Ways of the Minor Arcana

In this final part of our section on the Minor Arcana, here are the core key-words for the Numbers and Suits to produce the most direct and simple one-card reading with Minors Only.

## Numbers

1. Own it.
2. See it.
3. Start it.
4. Friend it.
5. Fight it.
6. Ride it.
7. Stand it.
8. Move it.
9. Master it.
10. Carry it.

## Suits

- Pentacles: Time.
- Swords: Thoughts.
- Cups: Feelings.
- Wands: Aims.

## Examples

We draw a card for whether to pursue a particular course of action and receive the Six of Pentacles. This is "Ride It" and "Time", i.e., "Ride out time", meaning do not act, wait patiently, now is not the time to act, simply ride it out.

In another example, we might be asking about a new relationship and receive the Two of Swords, "See it" and "Thoughts". Ironically, the Waite-Smith image shows a blindfolded woman bearing two swords. We take this as advising we ask the other person what they think about the relationship so we can literally see exactly what they think. There is no other action advised other than to gain sight of the thoughts about the relationship, and perhaps also allow the other person to see our thoughts. It might be terrifying advice to enact, but still the most direct and authentic divination.

# - XI -
## COURT CARDS

## Court Cards

The Court cards embody the representation of energy levels in the deck and these levels have stabilised to be best represented by personification. We should realise that these are not illustrations of people – and specifically, not illustrations of courtly hierarchy. These are the common correspondences of the levels of energy that make up a reasonable model of the universe with the other realms, being the activities and behaviour illustrated by the Minor cards and the patterns and nexus points of the Major Arcana.

The four-square model of the Court cards allows us to square the elements and sets up a recursive pattern which is implied by this process. In the same way we can have a Kabbalistic "orchard of orchards", with each of the Sephiroth containing a whole Tree *ad infinitum*, we can have a "fire of earth of earth" or a "water of earth of air of earth".

The Court cards could be most simplistic rendered, as we saw in *Tarosophy*, as abstract representations of their "element of element" pattern. The Page of Pentacles is a stone (earth of earth) whereas the Queen of Swords is a cloud of cold mist (Water of Air).

The personification of these sixteen varieties of cross-referenced energies can be to any object or living thing, such as animals. This reminds us to think of the Court cards as elemental energy cards first and personifications second – and never first as "people". It may be simplest to represent the energies as people, and most easily recognisable, but this is also the way in which we can get locked into these cards as images and why many find them most difficult to interpret.

We all know what a "youthful" energy might be in the realm of "emotions" (Knight of Cups) but we are also likely to actually know at least one such person, who will also contain many of the other energies to some extent of another, confusing the issue.

In terms of Tarosophy, then, we will always look at the Court cards as a grid of four-by-four energies first, however they are personified.

In the following affirmation verse, we take each Rank and then affirm the quality of each Suit in order; Pentacles, Swords, Cups and Wands.

*Each Day let me bring the whole court to life as much as possible.*

*Let me be as **purposeful** as all the Pages; investing, learning, creating, and seeking.*

*Let me be as **motivated** as all the Knights; working, challenging, questing, and changing.*

*Let me be as **resourceful** as all the Queens; nurturing, deciding, dreaming, and purposeful.*

*Let me as **sure** as all the Kings; persistent, considered, connected, and true.*

*This day, may I square this square of elemental energy and make my life real.*

## Tarosophy Four Card Court Card Method: Turn a Page

Here is a method from our Tarosophy approaches where we treat tarot as a language. All of the cards have a part in the language of divination, and we here look at the Court Cards.

We also provide a template "what you can say" oracular sentence which is an example of "oracular sentences" we use to teach students to quickly read tarot when they are beginners.

This is what we call a split-deck method and uses the 16 Court Cards only, in four separate piles so the four Kings are in one pile, then the four Queens, Knights and Pages in separate piles.

Concentrate on a situation that you feel is beyond your own solution.

1.  Shuffle Your Kings.

    Select out a King.

    The King tells us our overall view on a situation, how we go about settling it:

    - King of Swords: Sharp (Sudden)
    - King of Cups: Creative (Cautious)
    - King of Pentacles: Practical (Possessive)
    - King of Wands: Wonderful (Wilful)

Whatever our gender identification, we can see these approaches as choices in our lives.

2.  Shuffle Your Queens.

    Select out a Queen.

    The Queen tells us our engagement with a situation, how we go about resolving it:

    - Queen of Swords: Logical
    - Queen of Cups: Deep, Emotional

- Queen of Pentacles: Careful, Practical
- Queen of Wands: Sure, Passionate

Whatever our gender identification, we can see how we have resolved issues in these ways in our lives.

3.  Shuffle Your Knights.

    Select out a Knight.

    The Knight tells us what must be brought into the situation that is not present, what must change:

    - Knight of Swords: A New Thought
    - Knight of Cups: A New Feeling
    - Knight of Pentacles: A New Thing (Event or Object)
    - Knight of Wands: A New Ambition or Goal

4.  Shuffle your Pages.

    Select out a Page.

    The Pages tell us how we go about making that change, in what aspect of our lives:

    - Page of Swords: Words and Science (discussion)
    - Page of Cups: Love and Art (leisure and enjoyment)
    - Page of Pentacles: Work and Wealth (money, resources)
    - Page of Wands: Belief and Example (role model)

5.  We can now lay these four cards together and create an oracular sentence.

    The template for the sentence is:

    - I should settle this situation [King word] and be [Queen word] as I need only [Knight word] and not anything else, so must concentrate on [Page words].

Here is a real example with the cards chosen and their words put in the oracular sentence.

**Question:**    What should I do about the recent business issue?

**Cards:**    King of Cups + Queen of Swords + Knight of Cups + Page of Wands.

*Illus. Four Court Card Reading.*

**Interpretation**: "I should settle this situation [creatively] and be [logical] as I need only [a new feeling] and not anything else, so must concentrate on [belief and example, and being a role model].

    We can see in that sentence that we must take a moral high-ground, that the situation is not going to be dealt with financially, for example, but rather by getting to feel about it differently. We also must be logical and creative, in fact, perhaps, professional.

# - XII -
## TAROT FOR ALL SEASONS

## Tarot for All Seasons

In this section we will see how Tarosophy uses tarot cards to engage with important times and seasons of life, such as the phases of the moon, and the pagan festivals in the circle of the year. Through correspondence and poetry, we can create powerful invocations, resolutions, recognition, and awareness of the tides of time. We will begin with a re-solution for the New Year. As with most other Tarosophy methods and verse-patterns, this follows a correspondence of the Minor cards in numerical sequence (here, from the Ace to Ten), and in Suits up the Tree of Life, in this order; Pentacles, Swords, Cups and Wands.

## A New Years (Minor) Re-Solution

Let the Aces remind me to begin more than I should;
To only plant in nurturing ground,
To only decide what is true,
To only share what I love,
And to only begin what I value.

And the Twos remind me what goes down will come up;
For Everything is connected,
Everything has consequences,
Everything is bound in love,
And everything is how we make it.

In the Threes I will recall that I can build slowly;
I will build to benefit all,
I will build to celebrate with all,
I will build even if it hurts,
I will build the world as best I can.

And in the Fours, I will learn to hold it together;
To save my resources for the longer-term,
To rest myself when I need it,
To not over-burden myself with other's needs,
And to attract those who recognise me.

I shall fight with the Fives like I mean serious damage;
By continuing even if I feel separate,
By learning from every argument,
By owning every loss,
And by recognising I am responsible.

And take opportunity to find harmony with the Sixes whenever possible;
I shall aim to be fair in all dealings,
I shall guide as I can when I am asked,
I shall take all my past into creating my future,
And be an example to myself above all.

Those Sevens shall teach me patience this year;
To not expect everything immediately other than illumination,
To live without expecting support,
To know what is imagined and what is real,
And to understand I will always have to stand for myself.

As the Eights teach me to do it for the sake of it;
To work with passion or not work at all,
To work without constraining myself to what is possible,
To work knowing I must leave out as much as I put in,
And to work in the light that everything changes.

If the Nines don't trick me into giving up too early;
By getting too attached to comfort,
By losing sight of the end,
By being too self-satisfied,
Or by thinking I have won.

The Tens will greet me with the rewards of all Aces;
All the reality of the universe,
All the answers to my questions,
All the love that is everything,
And all the will I need.

(And let me meet each and every Court card along the way
With equality, curiosity, and individuality, so I learn from every Suit).

**New Moon**

The New Moon allows us to make a re-start every twenty-eight days and is a good time to open opportunities in life. This method uses three cards and requires just a few minutes on the eve of the night of the New Moon and the day of the New Moon.

**Opening a Moon Gate**

On the eve of the day of a New Moon, before bed, create a Moon Gate as follows.

Visualise a black circle (alternatively, draw one or use something that is a black circle) and imagine it contains all possibilities.

See it on your table or altar and imagine that tomorrow a lunar eye will open within the darkness of the circle and let something new through into your life during the day.

Shuffle your full deck and lay out one card to the left of the circle and one card to the right, both face-up.

The left card shows something that you need to face in your life or come to better terms with and has been hidden.

The right card shows something that you need to look out for tomorrow as a way of doing something about the first card. It shows how you must nail down the situation or hook it into your life.

Look at the two cards together until they have something simple to tell you that makes sense.

When you have that, for example "You are holding back too much (Chariot) and should look for a moment when you are doing too much (Ten of Wands)" draw a third card but place it face-down in the centre of the imagined or real circle.

Go to sleep.

The following morning, on the New Moon day, turn up the middle card and it will tell you what to *say* today when the situation arises that helps you face what has been hidden.

In this way we create a new opportunity in our lives to make a significant change, on a new moon day (or night) which supports such transformative work.

It might be in our example that we turn up the Hermit card and that tells us that we must say "I need time to myself' or "leave me alone for now".

We would look out that day for a moment when we feel as if we are carrying too much (Ten of Wands) and then say out loud, "Hey! I need a time out from this, leave me alone for a bit" and that will lock into our need to face the Chariot challenge in our lives.

Most of all though, it creates a new opportunity which will open all sorts of subsequent events or challenges which will follow it. We call this an *astral cascade*. You may also discover that this simple change in your life acts out over fourteen days before coming to a new state with the Full Moon.

Advanced Tarosophists will see that this simple method is constructed of the Hebrew letter corresponding to the Moon, QOPH, which is spelt in full as Qoph + Vau + Peh which in turn provides the operating steps of the transformation. The black circle and sleep are suggested by *Qoph*, the 'back of the head', and the Moon card itself. The "nailing down" card is *Vau*, a 'nail' and the "speaking" card is *Peh*, a 'mouth'.

**Super or Full Moon**

As we look at how tarot can be used to engage with temporal tides, let us also consider that correspondences are the heart of the Western Esoteric Initiatory System and symbols are their language. A perigee full moon ("super moon") allows us perhaps the opportunity to connect to the Lunar correspondences more intricately.

**Moon Song**

Shuffle your chosen lunar deck during the night of the Full or Super Moon, which is the closest point of the moon and the earth. Consider the power of tides, dreams, and the unconscious; one's connection to the unseen and sometimes fearful realm.

Turn the deck up and locate the Moon card in the pack.

The two cards either side of it can be read as a message from your unconscious. They may also provoke a significant dream.

These two cards also illustrate the surfacing of an important aspect of life of which to be more aware in your conscious mind.

Allow them perhaps to suggest a song lyric or title and then go look up the entire song. This song may hold further messages for you at this time.

## Beltane

Each of the festivals can be associated with a Suit or certain Minor Arcana of the Tarot, indeed, they can be associated with specific Court cards or Major Arcana. There are many systems of correspondence that can be utilised in this light. Once we have a system, we can activate it by split-deck methods or magic, evoking the corresponding energy of the time into our tarot.

In this example, we have associated the fire Energy of Beltane, or May Day, with the Suit of Wands, also corresponding to Fire.

## Beltane Wands

On Beltane Eve, April 30th, take out the ten numbered cards of the Suit of Wands out of your most energetic tarot deck, Ace to Ten.

Shuffle and place these ten cards in a single pile face-down by your bedside.

Say, as you shuffle or prepare for sleep:

*Beltane Spirits, Summer Light,*
*Bless these cards of Fire Tonight.*
*To Light my Passion as a Flame,*
*Pick me a Wand by your Name.*

In the morning of Beltane (May 1st), turn over the top card and this will indicate the Wand of Power that the spirits have gifted you to use between Beltane and the Summer Solstice for the most magical results. The suggested interpretations below are for the Thoth Tarot, which is an extremely energetic deck to use for Beltane.

### Receiving your Beltane Wand.

### Ace of Wands.
The Spirits have Presented you the Wand of Will!
To cast the magic of this wand in your life, make one clear decision after another, towards one aim at a time.

### 2 of Wands (Dominion).
The Spirits have Presented you the Wand of Power!
To cast the magic of this wand in your life, take full responsibility and expect others to follow your lead.

### 3 of Wands (Virtue).
The Spirits have Presented you the Wand of Perfection!

To cast the magic of this wand in your life, aim to set the best example of what you believe in most.

### 4 of Wands (Completion).
The Spirits have Presented you the Wand of Finishing!
To cast the magic of this wand in your life, finish one task after another, before considering anything new.

### 5 of Wands (Strife).
The Spirits have Presented you the Wand of Dispute!
To cast the magic of this wand in your life, stand up for yourself even if it means argument.

### 6 of Wands (Victory).
The Spirits have Presented you the Wand of Winning!
To cast the magic of this wand in your life, set yourself challenges against which you can measure your progress.

### 7 of Wands (Valour).
The Spirits have Presented you the Wand of Courage!
To cast the magic of this wand in your life, be brave, be courageous, do the thing that you fear.

### 8 of Wands (Swiftness).
The Spirits have Presented you the Wand of Swiftness!
To cast the magic of this wand in your life, be quick and rapid in all things, do not engage in anything that takes too long a commitment.

### 9 of Wands (Strength).
The Spirits have Presented you the Wand of Strength!
To cast the magic of this wand in your life, take a stand and stick to it, be strong against whatever happens, however long it takes - do not budge.

### 10 of Wands (Oppression).
The Spirits have Presented you the Wand of Pressure!
To cast the magic of this wand in your life, keep up the demand on yourself or others to get to where you want to go.

By enacting the attitude appropriate to your chosen wand, you should expect to see interesting changes in your life between Beltane and the Summer Solstice.

## Festival One-Card Calibration

In *Tarosophy*, we introduced *Calibrated Spreads*, and saw how we could use specially constructed spreads or methods to measure ourselves against universal patterns, such as the Tree of Life. In doing so, we can gain deep insight into every aspect of any situation, and divine where best to act, in what manner, and in a way free from the constraints of fixed meanings in the traditional concept of a spread.

A spread with three positions, for example, labelled "warnings", "suggested action" and "outcome" does not have the capability to report back if the situation really requires a divinatory message about "resources" or "where to seek support" or any other aspect outside of the spread fixed positions. The cards will be forced to try and best answer through the three given positions.

A calibrated spread resolves this problem by using the cards to 'measure' our proximity to an 'optimum' pattern underneath a situation. This allows us to discern which aspects (positions) of the situation are more awry than others and gain advice about returning them to the best possible position.

Whilst we covered calibration methods against a physical model such as the Tree of Life in *Tarosophy*, we can now add to our universal patterns those based on time. In these temporal calibrations, we accept the notion of certain times having certain energies and calibrate ourselves against these at the time. In simple terms, if we are not feeling the spring-energy of spring with a bound in every step, we can calibrate with our cards to how we can best get on that wavelength.

In this particular use of the calibration method, we use the eight festivals of the Wheel of the Year and map the tarot to these astronomical and agricultural events. As they are a creative sequence, we map the first of the growing phase to the Twos of the Minors, and the pre-start stage to the Aces, then work in sequence as follows:

- Imbolc: Aces.
- Spring Equinox: Twos.
- Beltane: Threes.
- Summer Solstice: Fours.
- Lammas: Fives.
- Autumn Equinox: Sixes.
- Samhain: Sevens.
- Winter Solstice: Eights.

As this is a calibrated spread, we take the Aces to Eights of the four Minor Suits out of the deck, resulting in a split-deck of thirty-two Minor Arcana. At any of these seasonal dates, we can then shuffle the thirty-two cards and - in its most simple form - select one card for our seasonal calibration. That card will be obviously numbered Ace (1) to 8 in one of the four Suits. We then calibrate this card numerically to the number of that festival.

If the card is the same number, then it is a powerful time where you can take immediate advantage of the activity denoted by that card. It is a confirmation that you are on the right track and how to make the most of it. If it is far away numerically (seven at most) then this card is warning that you are far off-track and advising the way in which you are going against or drifting from the best energy of the time.

## Example

Here is a handy cheat-sheet for Beltane (3), which may result in a difference of zero if you draw a Three or the largest off-track if you draw an Eight, resulting in a difference of Five. This gives an example of how the drawn card might be read at any of the festivals.

The number below is for **difference** between 3 and the number of the card, **not** the number of the card drawn:

**0**: You have pulled a Three card. There is a strong connection, and powerful influence of that card. This Beltane, look at that card and see what you must recognise, celebrate, or take time to contemplate (such as separation in the Three of Swords). It is a pivotal moment to take a big and new step at this time.

**1**: You have pulled a Four. There is a quite strong, noticeable connection. There is a lesson in this card for you, if you can hear it. What is it telling you to do more or less of in your life?

**2**: You have pulled an Ace or Five card. There is a reasonably strong connection between Beltane and your life current, enough to work with. The Ace will show which aspect of life you should begin to set a seed within, and the Five will show something about which you should set about sorting out once and for all.

**3 or 4**: You have pulled a Six or Seven card. The connection is neither here nor there at this time, but you may wish to take the meaning of the card as a general message for you.

**5**: You have pulled an Eight. You are far away from the ideal energy for you at this time, so it is reasonably challenging, and you should take notice. The Eight shows you what is holding you back.

## Easter One-Card Draw

Any celebration can be celebrated or recognised with the tarot with even a one-card draw proving a powerful and profound message, such as this method for Easter.

Grab a deck. Consider Easter.
Shuffle. Select one Card. Look.

- If you have a **Court** Card, this is some aspect of yourself that you need to resurrect this Easter.
- If you have a **Major** Card, this is a pattern in your life from which you need to arise from its shadow.
- If you have a **Minor** Card, this is something that you can do this Easter to rise to a new level.

The reader is encouraged to develop their own one-card draws for similar festivals and we will now give several more examples of multiple-card spreads or methods for selected festivals.

## Winter Solstice

In this temporal method, we work with the archetype of the Sun at the time of the shortest day and the longest night, the Winter Solstice.

Take your deck and consider the darkest times of your day, your week, your month, your year and your life. Shuffle whilst contemplating how utterly hopeless each of those moments seemed at the time. Consider if you are performing this spread on the winter solstice day itself, how it is indeed the shortest and darkest day of the year.

When you are ready, turn your deck face up and carefully go through the cards in order until you find the Sun card. Take it out, and the two cards either side of it. Place them in front of you.

Now shuffle the rest of the deck and wonder if those two cards either side of the Sun are the hidden light that you can now gain, where might be the darkness in which they are to be discovered?

Turn the deck face-up again and this time search for the World card. At this time of the year, the Sun and the Earth are powerfully straining at each other, so we look for the darkness in the World card - which also corresponds to Saturn.

Take the World card and the two cards either side of it and place them below the Sun and its pair of cards.

*Illus. Summer Solstice Spread.*

Read the card to the left of the Sun and the left of the Earth together as "This light is discovered in this darkness" and do the same for the cards to the right, above and below.

## Example

For example, if we had the Queen of Wands and the Blasted Tower above and below on the left, that could be read as **"The light of my inner compassion comes from the darkness of shock and sudden change"**. On the right-hand side, if we had the Six of Swords above and the Two of Wands below, I would read **"The light of my self-sufficiency and forward-thinking comes from the darkness of everything that I did not accomplish - yet"**.

We can then make powerful affirmations based on these cards, ready for the year until the next solstice.

## Lughnasadh Spread

In this relatively straightforward spread, we learn to turn Chaff into Gold, in recognising the start of the harvest season, usually 1st August of the year, named after the fierce and kingly Celtic God, Lugh.

Shuffle and lay out five cards from a full deck in a fan as below.

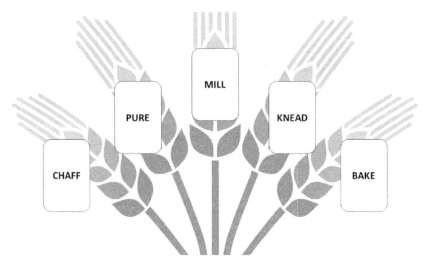

*Illus. Lughnasadh Spread.*

1. CHAFF: What can I now leave behind? Something I do [if a Minor], I am [if a Court] or a pattern in my life [if a Major]?

2. PURE: What should I focus on for the next season? Developing an aspect of myself [if a Court], developing a certain behaviour [if a Minor] or working on an overall change [if a Major].

3. MILL: What work or challenge can I meet as a sign of my dedication to sorting the chaff and purifying the kernel of my soul?

4. KNEAD: Where will I most require patience and persistence in this Work? What will not necessarily work first time?

5. BAKE: What is the resource—the Gold—which I will gain from this Work and will sustain me for the long-term?

## Birthday Method

Each birthday, spend a moment of time to yourself and send a message back in time one year in the past to yourself, particularly imagining what your past self needs to know to get the most out of their year ahead. Take your deck and wait to receive the message from your future self. Then pull three cards to hear what you have sent back to yourself from a year in the future. The first time you send a message back will be wasted on your previous past self, who has not yet started this method until next time, but it is important to start somewhere - or somewhen.

## Thank Tarot it's Friday

Every Friday, or whichever day you take to be the end of a working period, take your full deck and shuffle.

- Take two cards out.

- Ask yourself which of the two cards would be the better card to live in and why?

This line of enquiry will assist you wrap up your working week and align better to new goals for the next week to follow.

## Something for the Weekend?

Ahead of the weekend, shuffle your deck whilst thinking about your personal strengths and weaknesses.

Place the deck face-down, and starting with the top face-down card, turn through each card at a time until you find a Court Card.

Consider the strength of that card in terms of your own personal strengths.

Some time on Saturday, think, decide or act in a way that recognizes the strength signified by that card.

Then, only when you have acted in this way, on Saturday evening, turn the deck face-up and go through the cards again until you locate the first Court Card from the bottom.

Now, consider the weakness of that card in terms of your own personal weaknesses.

Some time on Sunday, think, decide, or act in a way that addresses the weakness signified by that card.

On Sunday evening, consider how these two Court Cards relate to each other, and how strengths and weaknesses can be symbolized in this way through the Tarot.

What happens when you compare and contrast the two things you changed in your life, no matter how small, in relationship to these cards.

This exercise will radically empower the way you read court cards for yourself, friends, or clients.

# - XIII -
## PRACTICAL METHODS & SPREADS

## I Beg Favour

I beg favour to read these cards for you.
In doing so, we divine together that which is unseen.
I beg favour to interpret these symbols for you.
In doing so, we read the intent of all that we do see.
I beg favour to talk with you.
In doing so, we recognise connection.
Connection
Between
What we see
And
What we do not see.
See these cards?
I beg favour to read them for you.

## Removing Damp (a Practical Interlude)

I use bicarbonate of soda powder sprinkled between every card/page of a book/pamphlet, not so much to wrinkle the sheets when pressed together. I do this in a sealable plastic box (usually an A4 size one) and put it in the freezer to control mould spores, but they are almost impossible to wipe out completely. I leave it there ten days and then brush off (with a soft wide paint brush) all the powder.

I then repeat with the "spin dryer fabric sheets" between each card/page; although I use the unscented ones and as dry as possible. My third stage is to leave them out at normal room temperature for a bit to "air" after the first two stages. It takes about 3 weeks but seems to work if anything will work at all.

If I need to remove initial damp, I leave in a breeze and open door, trying to avoid using a heater which will bend the pages/cards if you're not vigilant.

## Time Travel

A simple method of time-travel with tarot: Take a situation in your life, consider it, shuffle your deck and pull a card in answer to the question "What does this mean to me now?"

Then continue to shuffle.

Pull a card for the question, "What does this situation mean to me in a year?"

Then continue to shuffle.

Pull a card for the question, "What does this situation mean to me in two years?"

Repeat as desired.

You can also time-travel backwards.

The Tarot allows us to transcend time.

## One Thing Missing

Grab a deck, shuffle, consider the question "What is missing in my life?"

Draw a card. Consider it.

Then shuffle again, asking "What is one little thing I can do this weekend towards regaining what is missing?"

Draw a card. Consider it. Decide an action.

## Unasked Questions

Empty your thoughts. Do not care. Shuffle the deck. Take a card.

That card is the question you have not thought to ask.

Shuffle again. Take another card.

That card is the answer to the question you did not think to ask. It is the answer to an unasked question.

It may be important. It may say nothing. It does not matter. Or it may. Sometimes the deck is a devious device.

## Triangulate the Majors

In this method, we use our skill to condense each card into one word and create a traditional pyramid or triangle spread using only the Majors.

Take out the twenty-two Major Arcana from the deck and shuffle them, considering a question.

Draw six cards and lay them out in a line of 3, a line of 2 underneath, and a single card at the bottom.

This will make a triangle pointing-down.

Now use one word for each card in the following type of pattern, or whatever makes sense:

Alone, Power Rapidly.
Circle Naturally.
Courage!

In this method, we do not use linking words, like 'and', 'so', 'but', etc., then the sentence structure reflects the layout, with three words providing an overview on the first line, a piece of advice in two words on the second line, and an overall advisory in a single word on the third line.

### Example

Upturn Hope Quickly.
Ignore Freedom.
Transform!

## Simple Split-Deck Method

In Tarosophy we use many split-deck methods, where we select out the Court Cards, the Majors and the Minors into three sets.

In this simple method of getting started with split-deck readings, we provide sentence structures as templates so the beginner reader can begin to install language patterns for their own readings and development.

1. Split the deck into three piles; the 22 Major Arcana in one pile, the 16 Court cards into another pile and the 40 Minor Arcana into the third pile.

2. Take the three piles and shuffle each whilst thinking of a situation.

3. Take one card from each pile, so you will have a Major, Court Card and Minor card face-up.

4. Read them as follows:

- Major: "This situation is to teach me about..."
- Court: "And become this sort of person..."
- Minor: "So that I can act/decide to do..."

You may be surprised by how directly this provides insight into any situation and how easily you will be able to develop your reading skills for any style of reading. The reader is also encouraged to find their own voice and patterns in this method, by replacing the sentence templates when they feel ready with their own, or even modifying the language with every reading.

## Example

**Cards**: Hierophant + Knight of Cups + 10 of Wands.

*Illus. The Hierophant, Knight of Cups & Ten of Wands.*

Interpretation: "This situation is to teach me about my own authority and experience to become a more dedicated and emotional reader, so that I can carry heavier responsibilities in the future".

## Oracular Sentences II

In this method, we develop the original Oracular Sentences game from Tarosophy and explore a more detailed method of oracular pinpointing. This is particularly useful for situations which have no clear resolution or require some thinking outside the box.

1. Think of a Question or Situation. The more intractable or confused, difficult or insurmountable, the better.

2. Shuffle a full deck.

3. Pick the top two cards.

4. Lay them face up, side-by-side.

5. Pinpoint one symbol on each card, whichever symbol that comes first to your attention.

6. Consider and write what effect the latter (right card) has on the former (left card) and place it in a single sentence, i.e. "The water puts out the flame" or "The crown hangs over the bridge".

7.  When you are reasonably sure that you have the right relationship between the two symbols, draw a third card to divine the action required to develop (or remove) the situation.

8.  Select one symbol - the symbol that strikes you first - from that card.

9.  Write what advice that might offer, beginning with "So..."

## Example 1

**Cards**: 6 of Swords & 8 of Cups.

*Illus. Six of Swords & Eight of Cups.*

**Symbols**: Boat/Eclipse.

**Oracular Sentence (first part)**: "The Boat is Eclipsed".
+
**Card**: The Fool.

*Illus. The Fool.*

**Symbol**: White Rose.

**Oracular Sentence (second part)**: "So the rose must remain pure".

## Example 2

**Cards**: 9 of Pentacles & 10 of Swords.

*Illus. Nine of Pentacles & Ten of Swords.*

**Symbols**: Hooded Hawk/Swords.

**Oracular Sentence (first part)**: "The Hawk is Pinned Down".
+
**Card**: 9 of Cups.

*Illus. Nine of Cups.*

**Symbol**: Folded Arms.

**Oracular Sentence (second part)**: "So keep your arms to yourself for now".

Apply the oracular pairing and the advice to your situation.

Write down at least one action you can and will take, no matter how small.

In the first example, it might mean that other people have already 'set sail' on a project but it is being eclipsed by other things. The advice is then to not be involved, not put your name to it, etc. The action might be "I will tell them I am no longer attending meetings about it".

This method is a combination of Oracular Sentences from *Tarosophy* with the "Bridging & Pinpointing" method we use to teach Tarosophy.

## High Intensity Tarot Training

In learning to use tarot to engage life, rather than escape it - or distract us from our situation, we can engage in a form of High Intensity Workout, which was developed by co-author Tali Goodwin for use on World Tarot Day, or any other day. It is suitable for every level of experience, as it is designed to be responsive. The experienced reader can add extra resistance by using a deck with which they are less familiar or is new to them.

1. Take the 22 Major Arcana out of your deck, in a small split-deck that can be kept with you all day, so perhaps choose a deck that could get scuffed, damaged, or even lost.
2. Shuffle.
3. Turn up one card and place it face-up.
4. Look up the insight or task associated with that card and do it as soon as you can.
5. As soon as you have done that card task, turn up the next one and do the task as soon as you can. Repeat as many times as possible for one whole day, ensuring action is always taken before moving onto another card. Allow the tasks and insights to arise naturally as well as taking action.

Some tasks you may resolve to start and come back in following days to complete or work further with them. The important thing is to make a significant connection between the card and what you do. This exercise should fit into your usual day although it may disrupt it – always allow common-sense.

And if you only do one or two tasks, it might be something you really needed to work on.

The Insights and Tasks we suggest for the Major Arcana (in numerical order) include, but are certainly not limited to:

0.  I will see a freedom that I did not see before [Fool].
1.  I will see magic that I did not see before.

2. I will explore something that has been a mystery to me.
3. I will see a lesson from nature that I did not see before.
4. I will exert my will in the world in one conscious decision or action.
5. I will teach, help, or explain something.
6. I will make a commitment in furtherance of a friendship or relationship.
7. I will move forward in something that has been deadlocked or halted.
8. I will face a fear and do something that requires me to be strong.
9. I will spend a moment to myself and do something entirely for myself.
10. I will accept and embrace something that has changed or be revolutionary myself.
11. I will work to balance something I believe wrong.
12. I will try and see a situation in a whole new light, from some totally different perspective.
13. I will complete something to start anew.
14. I will find some compromise in a situation and hold to it.
15. I will do something good or resist a temptation – at least, for now.
16. I will clear some old stuff out.
17. I will find something that inspires me or follow an inspiration a little.
18. I will keep myself on my way despite not knowing something.
19. I will do something delightful to grow or observe someone who shows me joy and enthusiasm.
20. I will make a call today – I will take responsibility for something that works towards a new life.
21. I will engage with the world in one way that gives me a sense of my place in life [World].

## Further notes

The actions, insights, observations, and events can be as small as simply picking up a pair of shoes or watching a tv show – it is the connection and intent that matters.

Also, the order in which the cards will be drawn will be unique to you, and the sequence may have a deep connection to patterns in your life. A HITT workout that goes through three cards in a day, with two small insights and one big activity is just as powerful as one which goes through nineteen cards all requiring dramatic actions.

Every workout will be unique.

## Engines of Change

In this solution-orientated Tarosophy method, we upgrade the common Three-Card Spread to provide a mechanism for action and change which can be applied to any problematic or confusing situation.

In Tarosophy, certain methods are 'attuned' to specific decks or types of decks, by design. However, it has been found that using a very opposite deck can often provide break-through results.

This method is attuned to the Thoth Tarot, or any deck you might consider to be 'direct' or 'speaks to you immediately' in a 'down to earth' way. It is dissonant (not so suited) to 'fey', 'soft' or 'abstract' decks - but may yield surprising results with such decks if the reader wishes to experiment.

It is a method that has twenty-seven different sub-methods within itself, which are all open to development. Also, with the different permutations of the actual cards in just this simple three-card layout, provides us one specific solution from a possible range of tens of thousands of solutions.

## The Method

Shuffle the deck whilst considering a situation that appears presently intractable or confusing, beyond your ability to act or decide.

Pull three cards and place them face-up in a horizontal line, left to right.

You can look at all three cards although several combinations below will ask you to re-interpret specific cards once you have accomplished certain results. You may return to a card and look at it again with a slightly different interpretation than when you first respond to it. This is an essential experience of the method.

It is suggested you read through the whole list several times first for additional comments which apply to any of the combinations. Then consult your specific combination.

If you use the method over an extended period, you may find yourself naturally adapting it to the way you best act to bring about change in your life.

## The 27 Variations

There are twenty-seven variations of how three cards can be selected from a deck composed of Minors, Majors and Court cards. They are listed here in groups, so the first group contains all the combinations that have a Minor first, the second group with a Court card first, and the third group with a Major card first. In each numbered group are three further sub-sets, grouped by the second card, and to these I have given titles of their general nature, for example, the three combinations that have a Minor card followed by another Minor card are all "two act plays", requiring at least two actions before addressing the third card.

You may find certain times in your life if you use the method that a certain combination will be more likely than others - or it may simply follow a statistical likelihood. You are encouraged to journal and observe those emerging patterns over time.

## 1. MINOR FIRST, MOVE FIRST

In the first three sets of combinations, where a Minor card is first, a definite action (or actions) is indicated for the best resolution to the situation.

## A TWO ACT PLAY

**Minor + Minor + Minor** = List three actions to take - a Sword is a decision, a Wand is a lifestyle change, a Cup is an action which will make you feel differently, a Pentacle is a practical action.

**Minor + Minor + Court** = List two actions and the attitude which will get those two actions done, a King is an attitude you have only recently acquired, a Queen is someone else's attitude you admire, a Knight is whatever attitude might get the job done, and a Page is an attitude from your childhood.

**Minor + Minor + Major** = List two actions and use the Major as a signpost to direct the outcome of the two actions.

## ACTION TO ATTITUDE

**Minor + Court + Minor** = List an action (suitable to the first Minor card) which will result in the attitude of the Court card and a follow-up action that would be taken by that resulting new characteristic.

**Minor + Court + Court** = List an action that would result in the most likely way the relationship of the two Court cards would work harmoniously.

**Minor + Court + Major** = List an action that meets the Minor card and would be taken by the Court card to feel aligned to the major card.

## LITTLE, BIG

**Minor + Major + Minor** = List the very smallest, easiest, and most immediate action that could be taken about the situation regarding the first Minor card. Then determine the biggest and most difficult action determined by the second Minor card. Do the smallest action, then ONLY THEN return to the middle Major card and determine how it can now be seen as advice as to accomplishing the more difficult action - or another one.

**Minor + Major + Major** = List the smallest action determined by the first Minor card and accomplish it. ONLY THEN return to re-interpret the second Major card as another piece of advice. List another action based on the same first Minor card and accomplish it. Return to the second Major card, interpret it anew as advice on the first Minor and create a new action and perform it. This method, as most of the others, can be cycled around multiple times.

**Minor + Major + Court** = List the smallest action that the Court Card character would likely take in response to the Minor card. Do that action. Then read the major as a comment on the result of that action, made to the Court Card. List another action as a result.

## 2. COURT FIRST, CHANGE FIRST

In the second series of three-card combinations, where a Court card is first, you must approach the situation with a particular frame of mind.

## GOING ABOUT IT ANOTHER WAY

**Court + Minor + Minor** = The overall response to your situation is to adept the role of the first court card. It is suggested you practice any particular characteristics of that card for a day, listing five activities, behaviors, or particular states of mind and attitudes appropriate to that card. Practice for a day. On the following day, adopt that same role and consider from it the two Minor cards as suggesting two simultaneous actions or answers to be taken. How you go about these actions, i.e., immediately or otherwise, will likely be apparent from within the role. It should usually be quite different than how you might habitually go about a situation. This set of combinations requires a shock to your own personality and may provoke other changes out with the situation you have initially presented to the deck.

**Court + Minor + Court** = In this combination, consider two people represented by the two Court cards as being inside the situation depicted by the Minor card. List what they would find pleasing, what they would find displeasing, and then list three ways they might want to change in their own attitude (ideally) or change about the situation. Then apply those same things to your situation.

**Court + Minor + Major** = Consider the Major card as an opposing force against the situation of the Minor card, as if it were trying to stop it happening (for good or bad). List three ways in which the Court card would likely go about working through that situation. Then apply those three ways to your own issue.

## ORDER IN THE COURT

**Court + Court + Minor** = When we have two Court cards right together at the start of the combination, we are looking at a pair of energies that can be harnessed together. If they are the same rank, it shows that their attitude as a Page, Knight. Queen or King is more important than their Suit, and if they are the same Suit, then likewise, the Suit is more important. Take the two court cards together and select one attitude which they would share; then list as many ways that attitude would get the best out of the Minor card. Apply that to your situation.

**Court + Court + Court** = With three court cards, we can re-arrange them in a triangle. Decide one card which represents the weakest response to your situation, another card to represent the strongest attitude to your situation and take the third card as a potential middle way to see the whole thing.

**Court + Court + Major** = Here the two Court cards are out of balance with the Major card which represents a powerful pattern in your life. Consider which Court card is least suited to deal with the energy of the Major card and list several ways you could quietly reduce those qualities from being expressed. Similarly, consider the more adequate Court card energy and list several ways you could improve the frequency of expressing those attitudes. In this case, with no Minor card, there is no requirement to look at the actual situation – it is more about something else inside you now.

## SWIPED SIDEWAYS

**Court + Major + Minor** = A Court with a Major and Minor card in these positions might be considered side-lined by resentment when all the attention is somewhere else. List three ways in which that particular Court card would resent the situation in the Minor card or otherwise find something not to like about it. Then apply the nature of the Major card to resolve those resentments, applying the same to your own situation.

**Court + Major + Court** = Here the Court card is obstructed by another Court card hiding behind something else – the Major card. Read the first Court card as what you *might appear to want to do* about the situation, and the second Court card (on the right) as what is hidden from you by yourself – and how you should go about resolving the situation. The major card indicates your false target or something which is a major distraction and can simply be removed from the situation as it is not actually doing anything.

**Court + Major + Major** = In this section of three cards, the Court card is utterly side-swiped by a conflict between two Major patterns which is being played out in public view. The answer to your situation is to be found in how the Court card pictured would make a quiet exit from the drama of the two Major cards.

## 3. MAJOR FIRST, MEANING FIRST

In the third and final series of combinations, where a Major card is first, you are called to respond to something bigger than the apparent situation being presented to you.

## MAJOR CONCERNS

**Major + Minor + Minor** = Here the Major card is let down by the two Minor cards. Imagine the ways in which the energy represented by the Major card would be not fully represented by the situation in both Minor arcana. What must change so that you would go from those Minor cards to the full expression of that Major card – list several ways and then apply them to your situation.

### Example

**Cards: Hierophant + 8 of Cups** (Indolence) **+ 9 of Disks** (Gain).

*The energy of the Hierophant is about revelation, experience, and tradition. It is also about faith. It would be let down by Indolence in the sense of a cloying decay of its principles. It would be let down by the 9 of Disks by concentrating upon material gain rather than the loss of attachment. To work from those situations, we would have to upgrade indolence back up to discipline, and gain should be turned back to true satisfaction. Any material gain should be re-directed to what is valuable. This is a situation we might call the "fall of the priest".*

**Major + Minor + Court** = List one action that responds to the Minor card, then further detail how it would be carried out by that specific court card as an offering in a temple appropriate to the Major card. Apply that to your situation and the sacrifice or offering you must make in your case.

A temple for the High Priestess would be one of Moon Mysteries, a temple for the Blasted Tower would be one of conflict and the worship of destructive forces, for example.

**Major + Minor + Major** = Here we see that the situation is a 'minor' manifestation of the **conflict** between two archetypal forces - which are illustrated by the two Major cards. First, list three ways (or more) in which the two Major cards conflict with each other. Then consider the 'Minor' card as a buffer that absorbs those shocks. In what way would it deal with the conflicting forces? When you have done that, reverse the Minor card or consider the 'opposite' words to those three buffers as an indication of how you can turn this challenge into an opportunity. This is (like several of the Major card combinations) somewhat abstract but can be powerful and liberating.

## PLAY ACTING

**Major + Court + Minor** = Imagine a character in a film who appeared like the central Court Card and whose motivation was driven by the force of the Major card. The Minor card illustrates a challenging scene that they must overcome in some way, halts them, seeks to stop them fulfilling their destiny. You are the scriptwriter – what do they say when they overcome this scene? Use that sentence as your guiding principle for the next week, particularly regarding your situation.

**Major + Court + Court** = The Major card is a curse which has afflicted the two characters shown by the two Court cards. They must work together to unpick the curse. Write a description of how they would act to overcome the seemingly magical and overwhelming curse. Apply it to your situation.

**Major + Court + Major** = A character, depicted by the central Court card, is trapped in a prison devised by the two Major cards. Describe the nature of the prison, and how the character would escape – what help do they need? What is the single fault of the prison that will allow them to escape? Apply that escape to your own situation.

## BIG PICTURE

**Major + Major + Minor** = There is a painting which is entitled by a combination of the two major cards, such as "The Silver Path of God" for the 'Moon' and the 'Hierophant'. Another example might be 'The Darkness of Motion' for the Devil and the Chariot. Devise a succinct and elegant title and then imagine the actual painting. Is it oil or watercolor, precise, cubist or abstract – lifelike or surreal? When you have the painting in your mind, imagine the Minor card being blended into it, as if it were being absorbed into the larger painting. How does this make you feel? In that complex sensation is the answer to your current question or situation.

**Major + Major + Court** = There is a portrait of the Court card which has been illustrated in any style that seems fitting for that court card. It has survived two sets of disasters which are indicated by the two Major cards – what two disasters ('flooding', say, for the High Priestess) would have befallen this portrait? List the damage that has been done to the portrait and how it has changed the image. Imagine further that the image could tell you what it has learnt by surviving those two events. This is the lesson of your current situation, and the more it is embraced, the easier it will be.

**Major + Major + Major** = Our final combination, and all the Major Arcana. Look at the three cards and see them as three large images arranged equally around a circular gallery in which you are stood in the center. Now begin to imagine the room spinning. Open your eyes to remind yourself of the three images every now and again, and then close your eyes and spin them even faster around you. After a few moments, keep accelerating the speed of their movement until they blend, faster and faster. Until they are one constant ribbon of moving colors around you. When you have them moving in a blur around you, allow a new image to arise out of that blur. There is nothing else you need do – the universe is already doing it.

The advanced reader can also consider dignities regarding interactions between the cards which will provide more nuanced readings.

## Tarot Affirmation Generator

We can generate useful affirmations with any draw of three Major Arcana cards. This is a useful method for the New Year, a Birthday oracle for a friend, or as an extra bonus to the reading at the end of a client session.

When we have drawn three cards, we should create an affirmation in the first person ("I"), with a positive action and a resultant positive consequence.

## Examples

**Cards**: Star + Devil + Emperor.

*Illus. The Star, The Devil & The Emperor.*

**Affirmation**: I Look into the Darkness and Regain My Power.

**Cards**: World + Justice + Judgement.

*Illus. The World, Justice & Judgement.*

**Affirmation**: The World is Balanced and a New Life Awaits Me.

**Cards**: Sun + Magician + Strength.

*Illus. The Sun, The Magician & Strength.*

**Affirmation**: The Light Above gives me Strength.

**Cards**: Tower + Hierophant + Justice.

*Illus. The Tower, The Hierophant & Justice.*

**Affirmation:** I break down old teaching and find my truth.

## Stuck in the Middle

In this exercise, we use the deck to discover a solution to a situation where we might literally feel stuck in the middle of difficult choices or decisions with unclear consequences. In these complicated situations, we incorporate the complication into the deck and then use it to simplify the situation to the best possible solution.

Thinking of the situation or not, consider which tarot card you want to be stuck in forever if you had to be stuck in one scene. This might usually be a very obviously positive card such as the Ten of Cups, for example. Then consider the card you would first remove if you were told that you had to remove one card from the deck forever. In most cases this might be a card considered generally negative, such as the Blasted Tower, or a personal *bête noire* such as the Devil, Hanged Man or Two of Swords.

1.  Shuffle and turn your deck over to be face-up. Look through the cards, keeping them in sequence. Go through until you find the first of those two cards, it does not matter which one.

2.  Then take out that card and all the others in sequence until you find the other card.

3.  Separate out that selection of cards, with the one card at the top and the other card still at the bottom. It could be a few cards, or it could be still most of the deck. If the two cards are right next to each other, this is a critical situation which is entirely in your own hands - you need to make a decision without any further oracular or divined information.

4.  Now place the top card to your right on your table, whether it be the "stuck forever" or the "remove" card. Place the bottom card, the other choice, "stuck" or "remove" card, to your left.

5.  Deal the rest of that selected set of cards onto these two cards, alternating from on pile to the other, starting with the top card onto the right card and then the bottom card on top of the left card.

6.  You will finally end up with two cards face-up on the two piles, which were in the "middle" of the stuck card and the remove card.

7.  Read these two cards as a solution to the current situation which faces you, where you must always find the strait and narrow way between wanting something when nothing lasts forever or removing something that cannot be removed.

## Using Combination Decks

In cartomancy, we can often use a combination of decks for a reading such as those I most use personally, being Tarot + Lenormand or Tarot + *Psycards* (or Da Es *Philosopher's Stone*) Oracle cards. Generally, we can see a combination reading as using the Tarot to set up the general themes (Majors), insights (Courts) and actions (Minors) for the client, and the Lenormand/Oracle Deck as a convincer that we have covered all and every detail.

The reader can use an oracle deck to provide a clarifier on a certain segment of the reading, which has drawn the attention of the client but feels unresolved to them.[95] We might draw one card and provide a direct answer or several cards and use them to create a strategy or add insight to the tarot card. We can use one card from an oracle deck as a placeholder for the entire reading, and suggest the client hold that image in their mind as a gateway to the insights provided by the reading.

One further use of combination decks is to use several cards from an oracle deck to suggest a ritual or magical activity for the client which can empower their choices and actions arising from the reading.

## Example

Following a tarot reading we are looking at the World card in a 'suggested future action' position and seek to divine further as to the nature of this 'global' action. We draw three cards from the *Psycards* deck and receive Fortune (12) + Tree (23) + Sage (31). This could tell us that we need to find our fortune in a literal tree-related manner, by consulting someone who knows about Nature; an ecologically-minded friend or even an actual druid, perhaps. In other circumstances, it could suggest we save up towards getting expert advice or consultancy.

As a ritual, we might consider the winding stairs of the Fortune card, the Lamp, and the Tree, and create a small ritual whereby at midnight we find a tree in a safe environment and spiral around it with a light, seeking to draw some expert advice towards us over the coming week, even composing a verse with the words "solid advice like this tree, illuminating advice as my lamp".

---

[95] As one NLP teacher once told me, "Don't even give them a millimeter in their words or thinking, because they'll only use it to escape through".

## Etymology Oracles

One of the methods of Tarosophy applied to Oracle Decks is "Etymology Oracles". When using an oracle deck with keywords, we take time to look up the sources of the words, back to their earliest roots. We then construct a sentence from those original meanings, giving an oracle. This can be used for the most mundane or the most profound of questions presented to the oracle.

Here is a question of mystical import, "How can one live in nothing?" presented to the *Oracle of Oz* by Doug Thornsjo.

The cards received are: Haste + Contentment + Fortune with the base card of Rupture, ironically including the words "First Aid".

We look up the meaning of "haste" and find it obviously refers to making something urgent. This is not then merely 'speed' but choosing to make something urgent in one's life. But what?

We look up "contentment" and discover it originates from settling a debt making payment on a claim. We read this as denoting that we must urgently pay our dues to life, i.e., our attachments, in the context of this oracle.

We refer to the meaning of "Fortune" and see that it originates with the Goddess of Fate, 'Fortuna', who is the ruler of our fate. This suggests that Fate follows the Free of Debt to Life.

And finally, we see that "Rupture" derives from 'to break through'. This is a break-through oracular answer to us - we must break through and not hesitate in implementing the oracle.

In summary, "How Does one live in Nothing?"

*Break Through.*
*Make urgent your payment on all claims to life.*
*Thus, both free and find your fate.*

In Etymology Oracles we can quickly and easily use a new oracle deck, particularly one with key-words, to immediate effect in our life.

## Can you handle the Truth?!

Sometimes we might like to receive a different card or cards than we have laid out for ourselves. Sometimes a client may wish we had pulled an entirely different reading for their situation. We might even ignore a glaringly obvious reading of one card in a spread and concentrate instead on twisting the other cards to our version of a desired truth.

However, rather than simply avoid the temptation to try taking out a new reading, we can utilise that feeling and - with a little tarosophical trick - instead, dig deeper - down to the truth, the absolute truth, and nothing but the truth.

In this case, we might be looking at trying to learn a hard lesson from a difficult week, full of emotional issues that are still too raw to consider with any amount of objectivity. However, as we really do want to face up to the issue, we can decide to dig deep.

1. Take a deck. Shuffle. Consider the Week.

2. Take a Card but do not look at it. Place it face down.

3. Shuffle the Deck again, asking "What should I have learnt to do better from this last week?" Draw another card and look at it. What does it say to you? Ring any bells?

4. Now ask the universe, "No, really, what should I have really learnt? Even if you don't think I'm ready to hear it, what is the real lesson?" Glare down at the face-down card.

5. Feel a real fear from it. Maybe it really does contain the truth?

6. Turn up the face-down card. What does it say? Are you ready for it? Can you handle the truth?

## Bows and Burdens

These verses are in order of the Tens to the Aces, each describing the four cards of that number in order of Pentacles, Swords, Cups and Wands.

*Illus. Bows and Burdens, the narrative of the Minor Arcana.*

## TENS
It ends ...
A house, an execution, a bow, a burden;
We reside, we remove, we celebrate, we carry.

## NINES
A garden, a bed, a display, a guard;
We enjoy, we suffer, we indulge, we protect.

## EIGHTS
A display, a prison, a decay, a flight;
We labour, we escape, we leave, we move.

## SEVENS
A famine, a thief, a vision, a fight;
We starve, we lose, we stare, we stand.

## SIXES
A giving, a voyage, a gift, a parade;
We reward, we go, we remember, we honour.

## FIVES
A poorness, a grief, an argument sustained, and an argument postponed;
We struggle, we mourn, we get involved, we get out.

## FOURS
A saving, a rest, a refusal, a party;
We hold, we retreat, we wait, we attend.

## THREES
A job, a separation, a share, an investment;
We show, we break, we celebrate, we prosper.

## TWOS
A dance, a decision, a proposal, a plan;
We balance, we weigh, we receive, and we conceive.

## ACES
A Coin, a Sword, a Cup, a Wand;
We build (a House), we strike (an execution), we bless (a rainbow), we take up (a burden)

*And it starts again.*

We can use these verses (as we can use any of the Incantos) to conduct a quick oracle for any situation or as a year-ahead method.

**Minor Arcana Method**

1.  Select out the Forty Minor Arcana and shuffle whilst considering a situation or thinking about the previous year and looking forward to the next year.

2.  Draw three cards and take their message together from these verses.

3.  The first card is the past of the situation or the previous year, the second card is what you can do now in the situation or at the turn of the year, and the third card is the future for the situation or the year ahead.

**Example**

**Cards**: 7 of Swords + Ace of Pentacles + 10 of Pentacles = A thief (we lose) + We build (a house) + A house (we reside).

We can word this as "despite losses in the past due to someone else, you can now build yourself up at home and in the future be confident that you will be secure in your residence".

However, there is a surprising and deeper structure to these apparently simple statements about what we see on the Minor Arcana, such as a bed or a voyage - and it is found through Kabbalah.

**Kabbalah of the Verses**

In brief, each Suit of the Tarot corresponds to a "world" of the Tree of Life in Kabbalah.

In order of our verses:

- Pentacles=Assiah/Action (Doing).

- Swords=Yetzirah/Formation (Thinking).

- Cups=Briah/Creation (Feeling).

- Wands=Atziluth/Emanation (Spirit).

The numbers of the cards correspond to the Sephiroth of the Tree of Life.

In order of our verses:

- Tens = Malkuth/Kingdom (activity).
- Nines = Yesod/Foundation (the psyche).
- Eights = Hod/Glory (the mind).
- Sevens = Netzach/Victory (the emotions).
- Sixes = Tiphareth/Beauty (awareness).
- Fives = Geburah/Strength (organising).
- Fours = Chesed/Love (Mercy) (expanding).
- Threes = Binah/Understanding (form).
- Twos = Chockmah/Wisdom (force).
- Aces = Kether/Crown (point).

There are alternative translations of each of those titles which can also be used in what follows.

To use Kabbalah in our readings and learn the secret of life from this we can simply write down "Creation is ..." or "Life is ..." and then a sentence made straight from our verses and the corresponding key-words.

If we take the very first part of our first verse, "A house (we reside)," this is 10 of Pentacles which corresponds to 10 = Malkuth (Kingdom) of Pentacles = Assiah (Action).

We can say, "Creation is ... our house where we reside in the kingdom of action".

This is also "doing, in the world of activity" when we use the optional keywords. The 10 of Pentacles really does mean "do it, get on with it".

This works for all forty cards, immediately revealing the deep Kabbalah in the illustrations.

If we look further up the Tree, for example, "A party (we attend)" is the 4 of Wands.

This is 4 = Chesed (Love) of Wands = Atziluth (Emanation) which gives us the sentence "Creation is ... a party we attend in love of emanation".

We can re-word that a little and see a beautiful statement if we replace emanation by spirit, the divine, god, goddess, etc.

The 4 of Wands is also "expanding, in the world of spirit" if we take the optional keywords.

You can re-word any of the key-words, so long as you keep to the basic source-words. You can also tweak the sentence a little to what sounds natural.

## Example

**Card**: 5 of Cups = "Life is ... A grief we mourn until we find the courage to create".

These correspondences work even if we put the sentences the other way around; the 8 of Cups becomes "to leave behind decay ... is the victory of creation".

What might that mean in a spiritual sense? As an illustration of a divine pattern written into the universe at a large and a small scale?

These verses can be used to provoke deeper contemplations and prompts for journaling.

## Reversals

We can also use these verses to read reversals ... we use the opposite words to those given in the verses, but the Sephiroth/World words remain the same.

## Example

**Card**: 6 of Swords = "A Voyage (we go) is the beauty of formation" when reversed becomes "Do not go and stay where you are ... to experience the beauty of formation (structure)."

In everyday terms, the 6 of Swords reversed then means "stay where you are and enjoy relative stability for a time".

The reader is encouraged to play with what these verses reveal in the forty Minor Arcana.

We may start to see that we already have learnt a lot about "Netzach in Atziluth" because we can see what is drawn on the 7 of Wands.

## Advanced Method

We can also draw 2-3 Minor cards for a situation and put these verses together, forming a powerful chain of Kabbalistic significance.

## Example

**Cards**: 7 Cups + 3 Wands + 7 Pentacles.

A Vision (we stare) + An Investment (we prosper) + A Famine (we starve).

This really does not look like a positive reading. It warns that following a vision which might lead to investing time or money will result in a catastrophe.

The Sevens in Kabbalah (and particularly well-illustrated as such in the Thoth Tarot) are rather unstable, even if they are full of energy.

At a deeper level in Kabbalah, we see Victory (7) in the World of Creation (Cups), indicating that the creative urge is extremely strong and driven to manifest this project. We then have Form (3) in the World of Spirit (Wands) giving the project a tension between its highest goals and getting it manifest and structured. This is where it will fail. Then we end up with Victory (7) in the World of Action (Pentacles) which in this case means that reality will win over the vision - it will be a hard lesson.

Notice that the 'victory' does not mean 'victory' for the situation or person - it means victory in the relevant world, in this context that is negative because the deeper urge is a strong creative force or vision which has become attached to a spiritual aspiration. But it is not practical. It is unrealistic, so the real world will win.

For those familiar with Kabbalah, we can also look at the Tree of Life and see those cards both sitting unbalanced in Netzach and hopping up briefly to Binah before dropping right back down under the Veil.

These forty simple statements about what we see in the pictures on the Minor cards of the Waite-Smith Tarot reveal the secrets of creation because that is what A. E. Waite and Pamela Colman Smith designed and illustrated in the first place.

**Weight Management Through Tarot**

In Tarosophy, we see tarot as an interface to daily life as much as it is to the divine world. As such, we can apply it to any situation where change is required, to support that change as it is made on every level.

In this one example, we look at how we might utilise tarot to manage our diet and weight - as a supplement to recommended approaches, such as consultation of a health professional, personal trainer, dietician, etc. We can then apply this general approach to any other situation which we may not have previously considered supporting with tarot.

**Weight Management Method**

1. Select out the Court Cards, Minor Cards and Major Cards into three separate piles.

2. Select out a Court Card that best represents you now, and a Court Card that represents the "ideal you" towards which you wish to work.

3. For one week, place the two cards a distance away from each other, in a place that you can regularly see, such as above your desk, or on a dressing table - even an altar.

4. At the start of the second week, select a Minor card for "advice" and a Major card for "energy/motivation" and place those two cards

above the two Court cards.

5. For every day that week you take the advice in practical activity, and/or feel the energy of the Major card, you can move the two Court Cards closer together a little.

6. Repeat this with a new Minor/Major card selected from your shuffled deck at the start of each week for 4-5 weeks or until you obtain evidence of your achievement.

Again, this approach can be taken with any desired outcome or personal change-work.[96]

## Finding Balance

Sometimes we may feel as if some situation, person, or relationship has blown us off-course. We might feel and use phrases such as "out of balance", "just off" or "off-centre". The original "Finding Hope" method in *Tarosophy* can be modified slightly to address this situation and re-locate the balance we might need in our life at a particular time.

## Finding Balance Method

1. Take your deck. Consider an unfair situation or imbalance in your life.

2. Decide on a Court card as your Significator.

3. Shuffle. Turn your deck up.

4. Go through it carefully in order and locate your Significator and the **Justice** card.

5. Count the number of cards between the two cards (none, if they are together).

6. Locate the card (or two cards) that is half-way between your Significator and the Justice card.

---

[96] It can also be built into a ritual or other activity for those who are familiar with ceremonial practice.

7. This card indicates how to take the first step towards regaining balance or finding fairness in the situation:

- If it is a Court card, it is how you might think about the situation.

- If it is a Minor card, something you can do about it.

- If it is a Major card, consider it as showing a pattern from which to learn and release in your life.

## Example

Using a German version of the Thoth Tarot, I count 54 cards between the *Ritter der Stäbe* (Knight (King) of Wands and the *Ausgleichung* (Adjustment (Justice)) card. I count half this value between the two cards and locate the 27th card, *Ritter der Scheiben* (Knight (King) of Disks). This informs me that I must be patient and act slowly towards a long-term goal and not see things as they are just in the moment. I also see 'shadow' aspects of how the situation is acting on the worst sides of my character and the projections of another.[97]

## How to Read for any Relationship

As three out of every five readings will be about relationships, we should have at least one approach to relationship readings which is adaptable to any situation. In this next method, we use the deck itself to create a spread for the reading, and this approach can be conducted in endless variations depending on the actual state of the relationship.

In this example, we select cards for a relationship reading which has been described by the client as repeating an old pattern. It can also be used as given with a new relationship, or a stalled relationship seeking some change.

## Relationship Reading

As we are looking at a relationship reading, we select the Suit of Cups for the first part of this method. We then decide on three cards from the Suit of Cups which represent the stage of the relationship. In this case, it is a new relationship, or a repeated pattern of relationship, or perhaps a relationship that needs a new start.

As it requires a look at the root causes of the relationship pattern - or is a

---

[97] Marcus Katz, *Secrets of the Thoth Tarot, Vol. III* (Keswick: Forge Press, 2020), p. 52.

new relationship entirely, we select the Ace, Two and Three cards of the Suit. These are the beginning cards so model the beginning of any situation.

1. We take our Ace of Cups, Two of Cups, and Three of Cups out of our deck and place them in a triangle, with the Ace of Cups at the top, the Two of Cups to the left and the Three of Cups to the right.

2. Shuffle the remaining deck considering your relationship or those of your querent/client.

3. Lay out a card, placing it above the Ace of Cups, straight, saying "This is where your passion is rooted".

4. Lay out a card, placing it diagonally at forty-five degrees, tilted to the right, next to the Two of Cups on the left, saying "This is how your passion passes into relationship with individuals".

5. Lay out a third card, placing it diagonally forty-five degrees, tilted to the left, next to the Three of Cups on the right, saying, "This is how your relationship to individuals passes into groups of friends, and communities, the workplace, etc."

*Illus. Specific Card Selection for Triangle Spread.*

417

We can see in this approach that the situation itself is modelled by the cards we have pre-selected, and then the spread and questions are formed by those same cards. We then shuffle the deck and create a reading based on the spread and positions suggested by the pre-selected cards.

If this was about how to end a relationship, we could pre-select and lay out the Eight, Nine and Ten of Cups, and use those cards to suggest the three stages of most positively ending a relationship. If the question was about struggles about money, we could use the Five, Six and Seven of Pentacles to create a triangular layout.

I tend to start with a three-card layout using this approach, as it gets to the main triangulation points of a situation. It is also based upon the Kabbalah, so having three *Sephiroth* (relating to the three numbered cards of any Suit) creates a powerful dynamic for the reading.

## Intermediate Variation

We can also add a fourth card to this approach, placing it in the centre of the triangle to consolidate, confirm, or clarify the reading. In the given example above, we would also place the Ten of Cups in the middle of the triangle at the beginning of the reading, and then lay out the three cards as above, and place a fourth card on top of the Ten of Cups in the centre of the triangle, saying finally "And this is how your relationship to everyone (and everything) was formed by your family upbringing". This can have quite an impact.

## Advanced Variation

We can also place another round of cards - or even two more rounds - of three cards at right angles to the diagonals, building a star layout. The next round of cards at right angles are "This is how you block these relationships [within yourself, with individuals, with groups], then the next round, which are placed again at diagonals, are "This is how you can incorporate and utilize these challenges to improve your relationships [within yourself, with individuals, with groups].

These three cards of blocking or challenging, and then another round of three cards for incorporating and utilising those challenges, can be adapted to any specific core question, such as relationships as given, or the money worries mentioned, or any other variation of this approach - for any situation.

## Quick Relationship Method

Sometimes, we need a quick reading on a relationship, depending on the situation. In our previous method, we saw an endlessly adaptable method - now we give a short and quick method.

1.  Shuffle your deck and split it roughly into two piles, one for each person in the relationship.

2.  Shuffle each separate pile whilst thinking of that person (or the client's description of themselves and the other person) and then take the top card from both decks.

3.  Place these two cards face-up to the left and right, with a gap between them. This tells us what is going on for each person in the relationship on the surface.

4.  A Court Card indicates the personality traits that the person is expressing in the relationship, a Minor card shows the situation that the person tends to provoke or encounter in the relationship, and a Major card reveals the archetypal pattern that is playing out through that person through the relationship.

5.  Put the two remaining piles of cards together again, shuffle, and select the top and bottom cards, placing them between the two separate cards in a column.

6.  The top card tells you what can be aimed for in the relationship between the two, and the bottom card what resources can be drawn upon to achieve that aim.

## Advanced Version

Split the deck into the Majors, Minors and Court Cards, split those three piles into two each and then pull one card from each for each partner, showing the three facets of the relationship from either side (i.e., a Court, Minor and Major for each partner).

Then put the remaining cards from the three piles together and draw a resource and aim card after shuffling.

## Direct Advice from the Court Cards

Sometimes we need frank advice, delivered directly, particularly before doing something we might regret or could have done better - or might have done - or will do - or should do ... In this method, we use two concepts ported across from NLP with the Court cards, and frame them in specific language patterns to obtain a very blunt answer. This, as with many methods in Tarosophy, is modelled on particularly elegant or unique readers to produce a pattern which can be taught to other readers.

We use two NLP concepts; modal operators of necessity and meta-programs. In the first, we consider how words such as "might, could, should, would" apply to the Court Ranks, and in the second, we make a correspondence of certain types of behaviour and the Suits. In both cases, we provide upright and reversed interpretations.

### Modal Operators of Necessity in Court Ranks

A modal operator of necessity is a word applied to the type of 'need' involved in an action. There is a big difference between saying, for example, "I must do the cleaning" and "I could do the cleaning" - or even, "I might do the cleaning". We use four types of these modes which have been attributed to their corresponding Court card Rank.[98]

- Pages: Might do/Might not do.
- Knights: Should do/Should not do.
- Queens: Would do/Would not do.
- Kings: Can do/Cannot do.

### Meta-Programs in Suits

In meta-programs, we consider a range of strategies people use in modelling their world, some of which are commonly used to describe people, such as "a big picture thinker" as opposed to a "detail person", or someone who only thinks for the "short term" as opposed to a "long term thinker". We usually operate towards one end or another of these various programs, and as a result, communicate and behave in different ways to each other, particularly when we are relating to someone at another end of one of the spectrums. We have allocated four meta-programs to corresponding Suits, giving one end of the scale for upright and the other end for reverse:

---

[98] It is perhaps arguable which modal operator *might* best apply to which Rank, but once we have settled on a system, we *should* utilise and test it, then we *can* make modifications once we have observed the results.

- Pentacles: Short-Tern/Long Term
- Swords: Little Steps/Big Steps
- Cups: For Yourself/For Others
- Wands: Towards Something/Away from Something

## Direct Advice Method

1. Take the sixteen Court cards as a split-deck and shuffle - keeping all cards upright.

2. Thinking of being open to any advice, select one card.

3. Read it according to the keywords for Rank and Suit, e.g., the Page of Wands "might do [something] towards something". We will call this X.

4. Turn the deck so all the remaining fifteen cards are reversed, shuffle again and select one card reversed.

5. Read the card according to the keywords for Rank and Suit, both reversed (the second part of each keyword), e.g., the Queen of Pentacles (reversed) "Would not do [something] long term". We will call this Y.

6. We now place X + Y together in a sentence, with a connecting word which best makes sense of the grammar or meaning, e.g., You would do X [and/but/if/so...] you cannot do Y.

Use your ingenium to construct the sentence according to a positive outcome frame using a linking word. If alternate linking words fit, calibrate to your own intuition as to which one is correct [most congruent].

In our examples above, we might say "I *might* do *something* towards the project, but I will [would] not do something long-term". This could be very direct advice to remain somewhat aloof from a pet project to which you were thinking of dedicating your whole life to, and certainly not consider it a long-term commitment. This frank advice of an alternative way of looking at something can be quite insightful and change our views. Sometimes the advice from this method can be very confirmatory and positive.

## Example

**Cards**: Page of Cups + Knight of Wands [Rev].

"You might do it for yourself [but] you should not do it away from something [else]".

We might want to do it for ourselves, but we should not do it in blind and immediate response to someone else doing something we do not like, the "something else" in the reading.

## Divining How to Act Appropriately

In this simplified version of the Lightning Matrix method from *Tarosophy*, we use just the Court cards to address a situation in which we are uncertain as to how to act appropriately and proportionally.

1. Take all the sixteen Court cards out of your tarot deck.

2. Shuffle whilst thinking of an uncertain situation.

3. Lay out the top four cards, face up, left to right.

4. Read the cards as follows:

    - 1st Card: How not to act in the situation.
    - 2nd Card: How to act in the situation.
    - 3rd Card: How to be seen by other people.
    - 4th Card: How other people see you now.

The following concise keywords may be utilised:

## Ranks

- Page = Reserved.
- Knight = Enthusiastic.
- Queen = Concerned.
- King = Remote.

## Suits

- Pentacles = Practicality.
- Swords = Decisions.
- Cups = Emotionally.
- Wands = Lifestyle Changes.

## Example

If we had the King of Pentacles in the second position, it would be: "Act Remotely about Practical issues" whilst we might have the Page of Swords in the third position: "Be seen by others to be reserved in your decisions". The overall advice would be to back off and the other two cards in the reading would likely confirm that approach.

## Out of the Box Solutions

Sometimes we need to find an out-of-the-box solution to an otherwise intractable problem. We have seen one way of dealing with impossible questions elsewhere in this present book, and this method is an alternative using a split-deck.

1. Ask your deck the following question for a situation "What is it that I haven't considered yet which will help me the most?"

2. Split your deck into three piles, selecting all the sixteen Court cards into one pile, the forty Minors into another and the twenty-two Majors into the third pile.

3. Ask the question and shuffle each of the three piles.

4. Turn up the top card in each of the three piles, from left to right in that order; a Court Card, a Minor and a Major.

5. Read as follows, using the suggested oracular sentence structure:

   • Court Card = "I should act unusually with [the main quality of the card ... e.g., 'ruthlessly' for Queen of Swords] in order to ..."

   • Minor Card = "do [unexpected action corresponding to the Minor card, e.g., 'take time out' for the 4 of Swords] to achieve ..."

   • Major Card = [theme of Major card, e.g., balance for 'Justice'].

## Example

**Cards**: Queen of Swords + 4 of Swords + Justice.

*Illus. Queen of Swords, Four of Swords & Justice.*

**Interpretation**: I should act unusually ruthlessly and unexpectedly take time out to get balance.

## Motivation Card

This contemplation exercise opens the deck to a form of discussion about one's own qualities mapped to the tarot.

1. Choose a card which would represent to you in a reading 'motivation' if it came up.

2. Decide upon the card which would be opposite to that card, either a simple reversal of the card itself or another card in the deck. If you chose the Strength card as meaning 'motivation', the opposite card might be the Hanged Man? Or the opposite of the Ace of Wands might - for you - be the Ten of Pentacles.

3. Contemplate how this other card represents your 'de-motivation' strategy. How do you see that playing out in your life?

4. When you have deeply considered your de-motivation strategy, for at

least one day and night, either choose a card or randomly draw one from the rest of the deck, as an action card for how to better integrate your motivation/de-motivation patterns.

## Example

My motivation card is the Ace of Wands, if that comes up in a reading, I usually read it as the seed of ambition, energy, willpower and so forth. The opposite card to that card would be - for me, at least - the other end of the spectrum, a Ten card in the Minors, and rather than Cups (the Water element opposite the Fire of the Wands) I feel as if the opposite Suit in this context is the Pentacles, fixed and earthy. It would therefore be the Ten of Pentacles for me, opposite the Ace of Wands in terms of motivation at least. On further contemplation, it means for me that I can de-motivate myself by feeling that something is finished and rewarded, which I might feel is a trap.

The reader can now conduct this method with any theme in their own life, such as "ideal relationship", "leading others", "time management" and any other issues they wish to address.

## Align your Life to the Elements

In this split-deck method, we utilise the four Aces to represent the elements of our own being, and the Court cards to calibrate our alignment to those elements. This provides useful information for re-balancing our life.

1. Take your Tarot deck. Lay out the Four Aces to four quarters of your table, face-up.

2. Take the sixteen court cards in your hands face-down.

3. Put to one side the 22 Majors and 40 Minors [these can be used in the advanced method not given here].

4. Consider your life as it is now and say the following, very deliberately, whilst also shuffling the Court Cards:

*The Ace of Wands is my Will in this World, the fire I bring from above, chosen for me and me alone.*

*The Ace of Cups is my Love in this World, the water of grace I draw from the depths, given to me and me alone.*

*The Ace of Swords is my Vision of this world, a mirror, a blade, an edge for my use alone.*

*The Ace of Pentacles is my Body of this world, the earth of my soul I manifest, as me and me alone.*

5.  Place the Sixteen Court Cards in the Centre of the Four Aces, face-down.

6.  Take a moment, then turn the pile of sixteen Court Cards face-up to discover the bottom card, saying:

*And this is who I need to be right now to balance these elements.*

This method has been slightly ritualised to provide an example of how even the simplest method can be turned into a powerful and profound piece of work.

## Connection Exercise

Divination demonstrates the connection between all things. We are each connected to another as each card is connected to the next and the tarot provides us a *cartomantic* map of connection. When we connect through our cards, we are connected through symbols to that which is real and that which is in fact, symbolised.

In this exercise, we connect with one card or one card daily for twenty-two days, consciously connecting the map to reality.

## Exercise

Take a card and use the corresponding action suggestion below or your own ingenium to give someone something specific, according to the card. You may feel like the word "give" can be replaced with the word "share", that is fine.

You might offer someone a compliment or take a moment to repeat back something they have said. Something appropriate for the card, definite and clear, and it does not have to be something big.

Then, see what they give you back. How do they respond? What is their reaction to you activating that type of connection?

Write down a keyword or phrase for their response. It will tell you everything you need to know about the connectivity of the card.

If you chose the Fool, and gave someone a chance, they might take it or leave it, leap or hold back, perhaps. At the root of any of their reaction would be choice, maybe, or surprise. Something they did not have before you gave them your side of the connection.

That indicates that freedom is *connected* to choice in the Real, underneath the world, between which tarot is the map.

Perhaps you will find unique connections for your own map. Allow actual life to teach you, test it, and divine it.

## Connection Prompts

Fool - freedom: give someone a chance.
Magician - direction: give someone a pointer.
High Priestess - connection: give someone confirmation.
Empress - growth: give someone time.
Emperor - power: give someone responsibility.
Hierophant - teaching: give someone knowledge from experience.
Lovers - choice: give someone options.
Chariot - thought: give someone an idea.
Strength - strength: give someone courage.
Hermit - enlightenment: give someone thanks for showing you the way.
Wheel - revolution: give someone a revolutionary thought.
Justice - balance: give someone a fair assessment.
Hanged Man - values: give someone something of value to them.
Death - transformation: give someone a change.
Temperance - testing: give someone a test.
Devil - shadow: give someone something they enjoy.
Blasted Tower - acceleration: give someone a deadline.
Star - vision: give someone a long-term aim.
Moon - reflection: give someone a reflection of themselves.
Sun - demonstration: give someone a demonstration of what you mean.
Last Judgement - decision: give someone your decision.
World - wholeness: give someone a direct consequence.

As an advanced and optional exercise, when you have done all twenty-two Major Arcana, you can take the keyword suggested above, or the one you used, and the response keyword, and write them onto a Tree of Life.

If you worked with the Fool, resulting in the reaction of choice, to the offer of freedom, you would look at where the Fool was located on the Tree of Life. The card is between Kether and Binah.

You would then write FREEDOM for Kether and CHOICE for Binah. In this way you will build up your own real-life map of correspondences, which can be tested and refined over time.

If you offered courage and the response was thankfulness, for the Strength card, you would locate that card between Geburah and Chesed on the Tree, and write Courage for Geburah, and Thankfulness for Chesed.

Over time, you will also start to automatically see the Major Arcana and the Tree of Life, all the connections, happening in the world around you, in every event and relationship. Eventually, you may even come to experience everything happening within these patterns at the same time, simultaneously without cause and effect, every possibility arising in awareness.

The world will soon become your teacher. It will become a living oracle.

This exercise will also, at the very least, greatly empower the depth and connection of your Tarot readings with the Major Arcana.

## Fulfilling an Ambition with the Majors

In this Majors-only method, we use the cards to define a series of steps to fulfil an ambition, which could be a single step or require twenty-two steps in a particular order of the Majors.

We can also use this as a straight 22-card Majors Spread for clients working towards success with their plans and ambitions, using a shuffle and draw of all twenty-two cards or starting at the World card and working back up in sequence until we have provided enough activity for a project to take shape towards an ambition.

We could also shuffle first and select one card from the twenty-two which would tell us how many cards to then draw, i.e., if we drew the Wheel (X) first, we would then draw nine further cards to make ten. If we drew the Fool, we must leave our comfort zone in some manner we likely already realise, before again consulting this method.

0 - Fool.
*Leaving Your Comfort Zone.*

I - Magician.
*Organisation*

II - High Priestess.
*Trusting Your Instinct.*

III - Empress.
*Nurturing & Encouraging.*

IV - Emperor.
*Setting Boundaries.*

V - Hierophant.
*Expert Advice from those with Experience.*

VI - Lovers.
*Decision-Making.*

VII - Chariot.
*Motivation.*

VIII - Strength.
*Applying the Right Control.*

IX - Hermit.
*Doing Your Own Thing.*

X - Wheel.
*Trusting to Luck.*

XI - Justice.
*Fair Play - Accepting & Giving.*

XII - Hanged Man.
*Connecting to your Highest Value.*

XIII - Death.
*Letting Go of the Past (Mistakes).*

XIV - Temperance.
*Compromise.*

XV - Devil.
*Avoiding Temptation or Easy Reward.*

XVI - Blasted Tower.
*Accelerate your Actions.*

XVII - Star.
*A Clearly Defined & Authentic Ambition.*

XVIII - Moon.
*Facing Fear - of failure or success.*

XIX - Sun.
*Demonstrating Your True Self.*

XX - Last Judgement.
*Accept a New Way of Going About Things.*

XXI - World.
*Keeping Everything in One Place.*

## An Advanced Consideration

This above approach works well in terms of Kabbalah, as if we drew the Fool (0) it would indicate that at this time, we need not draw any cards for success, as you are free to do whatever you decide; or if we drew the Magician (I) then at this time, we need not draw any more cards until we have organised what is present in our life already. It is only if we draw the High Priestess (II) that we need to draw another card; or, for example, if we draw the World (XXI) first, then we need every card to be drawn into the spread, and focus (Kether) on bringing everything together (Malkuth). When we lay out the required number of cards and look at them on the paths of the Tree of Life, we can discern further features and aspects of our path to ambition, in the connected *Sephiroth* and the specific order in which particular paths must be activated.

## Example

In this case, we have simply selected six Major Arcana cards and arranged them in a pyramid, so the first card is what we should focus upon, the second and third cards are what require assistance, and the final three cards what we need to develop first in working towards our ambition.

- Death = Letting go of past mistakes.

- Hierophant + Temperance = Get help from experts with experience + compromise.

- Magician + Lovers + World = Organisation + Decision Making + Keeping everything in one place.

*Illus. Majors-Only Pyramid Spread.*

We interpret this very clearly; that success in this case first comes by forgetting past mistakes and almost starting afresh; "die to the past". Then, almost immediately, get lots of help from others with experience and make serious compromises.

This would lead to an interpretation that the querent needs to let others advise them to see a different way of going about things, as their past attempts have failed, and their methods should no longer be continued.

The areas in which these experts should be employed is in advising on organisation and decision-making! It is then up to the querent to keep focused on this, bring everything together (perhaps with a lot of delegation or seceding authority to others) to achieve success.

There is no need to look at the further levels of the triangle, as we have six cards, because that base needs building before the spread can be shuffled and done again.

## Absent Cards

The noted absence of something is its presence. When, however, a card keeps repeating in your readings, both personal and for clients - sometimes referred to as a 'stalker' card - it may indicate a lesson to be learnt or an energy missing in your life. There was a time in my life when the Eight of Swords would keep turning up in what seemed like every reading, usually as 'future' or 'advice' or 'outcome' in a spread. It was not until I faced a fear and made a significant move of location that the card returned itself back into the field of probability. When I was even younger, every *I-Ching* Hexagram seemed to be *Wei Chi*, Number 64, where the fox drops its tail into the water just after apparently safely (and dryly) getting across the ice. It was not until I got a bit older and learnt to better complete things that the Hexagram became less common in its rejoinder.

A divination will not only divine what is present but what is lacking, depending on the question and the method deployed in the reading. If we only ask, "what needs to be known", we may forget that a useful question is also, "what might remain unknown?" Perhaps they are the same question, but again, this is the boundary we set upon the cards.

In general practice, we can always ask the opposite question when we have concluded the main reading and draw one or several cards from within the remaining pack, to get at least a sketch of what we have not thought to address. If I have conducted a divination for "Where might I best seek employment", it will only take a moment to also ask "Where would it be unsuccessful to seek employment"?

We can also observe the absence of a Suit, certain ranges of numbers, Court cards, ranks (a missing Knight, perhaps) as meaningful at the boundary of the given and presented reading. We might have a practical question that results in a reading with a preponderance of Aces and Threes, and a Four, but no lower numbers in the Minors. This indicates that the manifestation of that question is far from actuality. However, in the spirit of Tarosophy, we would then interpret the reading, and to conclude, locate the Ten of Pentacles in the remaining deck, and read the two cards either side of it, to answer the question, "What is missing to manifest this situation?"

## Dealing with Burn Out

I remember not knowing anything about the tarot - and I was foolish to think I ever would.

I remember the magic of it.

The mystery of it.

I recall slowly learning to read the cards. How I grew.

I recall the power of it. How it made me feel.

I remember the books, the courses, the experience. All the revelations without number.

I remember how many times I fell in love with tarot. Over and over, as surely as I left the garden behind me.

I made my way with it, sure and right. How bright I shined!

I wrestled with every challenge, every question, every situation and overcame them by every means.

And yet I felt alone in it, the cards my only light.

Time turned as if each card was a moment, all the ups and downs, one decade, then another and another. And another. A cartomantic calendar of revolutions.

After all, there was inevitable balance. A certain truth as the cards taught me as much as I taught them.

And when I thought I knew where I stood, I was stood upside-down, learning to always try and reach the highest view.

Travelling into the decks as endless transformation, carried by the dark river into the night of initiation.

For if you let them, they illustrate such strange alchemy; the jewel of philosophy - time itself.

The evil of ignorance, what people do in the shadow of fear, tarot is the picture of it all.

Each card a word that can shake nations, overturn every illusion, no matter how cleverly created.

I remember the hope of the future they carried for me, in the beginning.

And now, upon paths I never knew before nor can be imagined in their reality, they reflect only truth.

And light. Such light of an everlasting day, infinite in magnitude, eternal in mercy.

Remember, your cards are more than this, that, or another - they call each of us to tomorrow.

A new world, indeed. Hello, again, cards, oh how I have missed you.

# CONCLUSION

## The Greatest Challenge

There are many challenges in the future development of tarot. The impact of social media and print-on-demand services, editing suites and accessibility of stock art has opened the design and publication of tarot to many more people - a mixed blessing, and mainly for the good. However, the mixed blessing at the present time of writing is the rampant piracy of decks and books, and the flooding of the market with poorly-designed decks. This, I feel, is more than balanced out by the innovative decks and art being produced by artists, designers, and photographers who may have not previously thought to design a tarot deck.[99]

I feel that the greatest challenge to tarot is to retain the awareness of its profound mystery as much as possible as it passes through a period of relative normalisation. This is also one task of Tarosophy, to remain the thorn in the side of the passive income bland-izing of tarot, as it attempts to popularise itself by serving the simplest message to the largest audience. Tarot contains a deep mystery that should definitely be made accessible, but it should not be entirely forgotten in the race for the bottom.[100]

Further, the challenge to tarot is also, as with every human endeavour, to find increasingly better ways of working together. When the original research that eventually became *Tarosophy* was conducted, modelling readers with NLP during the 1980's, I was astonished that there was nowhere that readers regularly compared notes or methods, as if keeping some great secret that had some unknown barrier of entry. That now seems somewhat quaint and virtually unimaginable. Yet the rise of the internet and social media has brought us to a new openness, but one not necessarily where we have all learnt to navigate, perhaps to our detriment:

> As is true of all prophets, the prediction merchants of the Abarat were egotistical and combative, contemptuous of any other seers besides themselves. The fact that each of them worked in radically different ways to achieve their results only intensified the antagonism. One might see signs of futurity in the eighty-eight cards of the Abaratian tarot; another found his own vision of tomorrow in the dung of the yutter goats that grazed the golden fields of Gnomon; while a third, having witnessed the way the music of a Noncian reed pipe had induced the lunatics in a madhouse on Huffaker to dance, had then discovered evidence of how

---

[99] At the time of writing, hopefully just starting to come out of the height of the Covid-19 Pandemic of 2020-2021, the Pandemic has also accelerated creativity and online activity in tarot, as much as it has halted in-person meetings and real-world events.
[100] Alfred Whitehead I believe said, "The mind must be enlarged to comprehend the mysteries, not the mysteries contracted to fit into the mind".

the future would unfold in the footprints the patients had left in the sand.

Thus, separated both by their methodologies and by a dangerous sense of their own importance, none of the soothsayers ever compared their predictions with those of others. Had they done so they would have discovered that each of them—however unlike their methods—was receiving the same news. Bad news.[101]

## Tarot Tells Its Own Future

In a sense, the history of tarot is within the ability of tarot to predict the future. If the shuffling of the deck and the laying out of cards had no relationship at all to any narrative, in real life or imagined for the future, it would not have become a permanent artefact of human experience. The tarot then, may – or perhaps even, *should* – contain its own prediction. If we examine at least the Major Arcana, we might be able to see how the future of tarot will unfold. Perhaps future readers may come to review this tarot telling in future generations and revise it again for the next future.

1.  It will be more magical: And as more is revealed more will be concealed. The Law of the Trickster's Table is that the ball under the cup was in the hand of the one moving the cups.

2.  It will be more spiritual: And it will take its place again between the pillars. The Law of the Scroll is that what is written in the future will always look the same as what was written in the past until you change your tool of writing.

3.  It will become alive: And it will unfold in ways which only She imagines. The Law of the Robe of Water is that what is on the surface is shaped by what is deepest. We must learn to hold our breath, then, and leave our shorelines far behind.

4.  It will be more influential: And it will shape more decisions even as it resists its own regulation. The Law of the Throne is that those who take it are not alone in sitting in their own blood.

5.  It will become more traditional: And it will recover its dignity from its own roots. The Law of Revelation is that it is only the Resurrection of the Forgotten.

---

[101] Clive Barker, *Abarat Book I* (New York: Joanna Cotler Books, 2002), Chapter 12.

6. It will be more popular: And it will become surfeit of its own choices. The Law of the Lovers is that you can't have something without there being something else.

7. It will head in new directions: And as it becomes drawn by the few, it will be driven by the many. The Law of the Reins it that when you pull, you are no longer in charge.

8. It will be resisted: And even as it struggles to retain its shape, it will create that shape. The Law of the Lion is that we become that which we fight.

9. It will become more individual: And we will each own our own possibilities. The Law of the Lamp is that you have created everything before you even recognised it.

10. It will change the way we see time: And the way we see time will change tarot. The Law of the Sphinx is that the riddle is its own answer.

11. It will become universal: And even as it does, it will become diverse. The Law of the Scales is that everything is the measure of itself.

12. It will be totally upturned: And returned to a new source of inspiration. The Law of Sacrifice is that we do not possess anything worth the sacrifice.

13. It will deal with longevity: And in doing so, immortality in a sense. The Law of the Wasteland is that nothing can escape to anywhere.

14. It will become actively therapeutic: and in doing so, constantly resolved into new configurations. The Law of the Alchemist is that the stone of the wise is time, turning all to its highest form.

15. It will become more material: And in doing so, be formulated in more materials than card: And in doing so, will change forever the way it is used and thought about. The Law of the Darkness is that it will end, as it began, in the Light.

16. It will become virtual and electric: And in doing so, it will become more rapid, more engaging, more of everything, spoken in all

languages. The Law of the Lightning Tribe is that we are bound by only a word.

17. It will incorporate our developments in space: And in doing so, it will become truly stellar, universal, bound far less by a sense of place. The Law of Space is that where we go, we belong.[102]

18. It will increasingly be used to reflect our own society and psychology: And in doing so, it will go through phases of optimism and despair. The Law of the Tide is that it turns when it reaches its limit.

19. It will expand and be made purely of light, such as holograms: And in doing so, it will benefit from artificial intelligence and pattern recognition, increasing its predictive nature. The Law of the Light is that everything becomes Apparent.

20. It will become a lifetime calling for many: And in being so, it will be the basis of obscure beliefs, superstitions, cults, and new ways of living. The Law of the Angel is that we are our answer.

21. It will continually incorporate the concerns of the planet, and ecological considerations: And in doing so, it will become a living library of our species. The Law of the World is that it is the table on which the cups are placed.

And…

0. Tarot will become none and all of these things and more: and in doing so, confound expectation. The Law of the Free is that we can only ever do what we will.

---

[102] "Nothing in the void is foreign to us! The place we go is the place we belong", Camina Drummer in *The Expanse* (dir. David Grossman), Season 3 Episode 9, "Intransigence".

## The Top Ten Tarot Titles You May Never Read

In a recent organisation of my Tarot library, I came across several books that had a significant influence on my own Tarot studies over the last thirty years yet may have been consigned to the far-flung shelves of forgotten history. I would like to list these books, which whilst in some cases may be hard to acquire, I would recommend to the reader and their studies if they come across your sight. This list is also to encourage all readers to constantly expand their knowledge of many different approaches to tarot.

A few titles of those listed below are currently in print or have been reprinted in new editions. Whilst limiting the list the ten books, two extra titles I would add are *The Painted Caravan* by Basil Rakoczi and *The Thursday Night Tarot* of Jason C. Lotterhand (ed. Arina Victor).

Some readers may not have come across the anonymously authored book *Meditations on the Tarot* (1980), which is a theosophical and Christian contemplation on each of the Major Arcana and highly recommended for a lifetime study.

This list is by no means comprehensive – the number of books of obscure interest and limited publication in this field is numerous. Some are of curiosity and historical value only, such as the wildly ranging *Arrows of Light from the Egyptian Tarot* by John H. Dequer. Other books on my shelves that I have found to be incredibly inspiring but are hardly mentioned anywhere include the beautiful, profound, and practical *Metanoia: Renovating the House of Your Spirit* by Russell Sturgess (Beattitude, 2009), based on the Marseilles Tarot.

Here are a few – a Top Ten if you will – of titles for the reader to explore if they have not already done so. Some are full of rambling, disjointed thoughts loosely based on a deck of Tarot, others are essential academic or practical considerations of Tarot – and some are somewhere in between. I will leave it to the reader to make their own discoveries.

1. *The Mystical Tower of the Tarot*, by John D. Blakely (Watkins, 1974).

2. *Re-Symbolization of the Self: Human Development & Tarot Hermeneutic*, by Inna Semetsky (Sense Publishers, 2011).

3. *The Tarot*, by Eugene Halliday (The Melchisedec Press, 1990).

4. *A Feminist Tarot*, by Sally Gearhart & Susan Rennie (Persephone Press, 1977).

5. *Tarot Abecedarian: The Treasure House of Images*, by A. R. Naylor (Mandrake Press, 1997).

6.  *Evolution Through the Tarot,* by Richard Gardner (Samuel Weiser, 1970).[103]

7.  *New Thoughts on Tarot,* ed. Mary K. Greer & Rachel Pollack (Newcastle, 1989).

8.  *The Tree of HRU,* Eldon Templar (Kingfisher Press, 1990).

9.  *Tarot Revelations,* by Joseph Campbell & Richard Roberts (n.p., 1979).

10. *The Secrets of the Marseilles Tarot,* by Namron (Namron Books, 1990).

We regularly showcase and preview many of the books and decks in our collection on our Instagram feed, under @tarot.association, and the hashtag #tarotshowcase.[104]

## My Personal Reading Decks

If readers are interested in the decks I personally use for reading, I tend to cycle between a few popular mass-market decks, and several independently published decks. As new decks are being created more frequently, I have recently added to my cycle of decks those that are most intriguing, or stretch my skills, or require the development of new methods. I sometimes mix-in absolutely bonkers decks such as the *Fantod Tarot* by Edward Gorey, which has twenty cards, including my favourite card from any deck, 'The Waltzing Mouse', and a series of suggested interpretations in which one card includes "an accident at a theatre".

I am also a sucker for photographic Majors-Only decks, particularly for personal and magical work, having recently fallen for Chris Madsen's *The Witches Tarot.* I also use the *Abyssal Tarot* by Shelly Corbett, based on sensuous underwater photography, for dream work.

A lot of my magical work with tarot is with the *Tarot Obscura* by Chris Bivens, unfortunately a limited edition now out of print.[105] Many of the methods given in *Tarosophy* were originally conducted with this deck.

As with many readers, I tend to use the *Waite-Smith Tarot* and/or the *Thoth*

---

[103] It was this title which proved a complete revelation to my younger self, as I read it and realised that tarot could be used for so much more than providing a reading on a table with a spread. I still recall the moment and the feeling of that singular realisation to this day.

[104] Tarot Association Instagram at https://www.instagram.com/tarotassociation/ [last accessed 24th April 2021].

[105] See https://www.alchemywebsite.com/tarot/art_tarot10.html [last accessed 5th April 2021].

*Tarot* for most client readings, as they provide the most amount of material in the least amount of time, given long familiarity with their design. I have written in-depth about both these two decks in *Secrets of the Waite-Smith Tarot*, with co-author Tali Goodwin, and *Secrets of the Thoth Tarot* Vols. I-III.

I occasionally use the *Tarot de Marseille*, particularly the TdM Conver-style deck designed by the late Yoav ben-Dov.

In my personal work, I use a range of decks, with the *Tyldwick Tarot* (Malpertuis, 2013) by the late Neil Lovell used for self-insight, the *Philosophers Stone* oracle (1991) by the Austrian artist De Es Schwertberger for contemplation, and the *Oracle of Initiation* (2011) by Mellisae Lucia for initiatory work.

I tend to use the *Psycards* (US Games, 1989) by Nick Hobson and Maggie Kneen and the *Original Lenormand* (Tarot Association) for everyday readings and quick – yet detailed – analysis of a particular situation.

I have other personal favourites due to nostalgia, as does every long-toothed reader I imagine, in my case the *Aquarian Tarot* (1970) by David Palladini, which was the first deck I purchased, and the *1JJ Swiss Tarot*, which was the prototype of my first hand-made deck, from photocopies of the Majors of the 1JJ from a Stuart Kaplan book.[106]

In recent magical work with the Order of Everlasting Day, we have used the *Tarot of the Secret Dawn* by Derek Bain, Tali Goodwin, Janine Hall (art) and Marcus Katz. The publication of our own deck, the *Tarot of Everlasting Day* (2021) by Tali Goodwin, Janine Hall (art) and Marcus Katz has provided welcome material for the development of the Western Esoteric Initiatory System.

---

[106] Marcus Katz, *Tarosophy* (Keswick: Forge Press, 2016), p. 20.

## The 22 Major Cards of the Tarot Give Thanks …

To conclude this second book of Tarosophy teaching, we can give – and receive – our gratitude to the cards. We can thank our Major Arcana for their influence throughout the whole deck, and in doing so, vow to emulate that influence in our readings. We start by thanking the Fool and give gratitude in sequence through to the World, and in doing so, take our leave with thanks to the reader. You too, are thanked for being a reader of this book and, of course, a reader of the living wisdom of tarot.

Thank you for being open,
And
Thank you for being magical,
Thank you for being mysterious,
Thank you for being creative,
Thank you for being powerful,
Thank you for teaching and learning,
Thank you for loving,
Thank you for driving,
Thank you for your strength,
Thank you for your silence,
Thank you for your revolutionary ideas,
Thank you for your fair comments,
Thank you for turning everything on its head,
Thank you for transforming,
Thank you for your patience,
Thank you for facing your fears,
Thank you for breaking it down,
Thank you for your hope,
Thank you for your reflection,
Thank you for your light,
Thank you for your rising to the challenge,
And most of all,
Thank you for everything.

## Answers to Riddles

1.  The Moon [see A. E. Waite in *Pictorial Key*, p. 140.

2.  Eight of Wands, Lord of Swiftness.[107]

3.  Page of Cups.

4.  I am Change, Unexpected. [Tower]

    I am Change, Again. [Wheel]
    I am Change, Transformation [Death].
    I am Change, Hidden. [High Priestess]
    I am Change, Waiting beyond the Fear. [Moon]

5.  King of Swords. "If I was a thing" points to the fact the speaker is a character, i.e., a Court Card, and "Breath of Fresh Air" is AIR of AIR, the elemental correspondence of the King (air) of Swords (air).

6.  Three of Pentacles + Five of Wands.

---

[107] Thanks to Andrew Potts in our Facebook group, 'Tarot Professionals' for helpfully noting in my original text for this riddle [December 10, 2017] I had "never arrives", but that Crowley points out in *Book of Thoth* that the Lord of Swiftness can quickly arrive or already be present.

# BIBLIOGRAPHY

Auger, E. A. (ed.), *Tarot in Culture Vol. I.* n.p.: Valleyhome Books, 2014.

Bachelard, G. *Poetics of Space.* Boston: Beacon Press, 1992.

Barker, C. *Abarat Book I.* New York: Joanna Cotler Books, 2002.

Borges, J. L. *Labyrinths.* London: Penguin, 1989.

Conforti, M. *Field, Form and Fate.* Sheridan: Fisher King Press, 1999.

Crowley, A. *Liber Al.*

Derrida, J. *Writing and Difference.* Chicago: The University of Chicago Press, 1978.

Fine, L. (ed). *Essential Papers on Kabbalah.* New York City: NYU Press, 1995.

Gardner, D. *Future Babble.* New York: Plume, 2012.

Gilligan, S. *Walking in Two Worlds: The Relational Self in Theory, Practice, and Community.* Phoenix: Zeig, Tucker & Theisen Inc., 2004.

Gladwell, M. *Blink.* New York: Back Bay Books, 2007.
___. *Outliers.* London: Penguin, 2008.

Goodwin, T. & Katz, M. *Abiding in the Sanctuary.* Keswick: Forge Press, 2011.
___. *Around the Tarot in Seventy-Eight Days.* Woodbury: Llewellyn Publications, 2012.
___. *Practical Tarot Techniques.* Woodbury: Llewellyn Publications, 2019.
___. *Secrets of the Celtic Cross.* Keswick: Forge Press, 2016.
___. *Secrets of the Waite-Smith Tarot.* Woodbury: Llewellyn Publications, 2015.
___. *Tarot Flip.* Keswick: Forge Press, 2010.
___. *Tarot Temple.* Keswick: Forge Press, 2014.

Green, A. *7-Day Lenormand.* Keswick: Forge Press, 2018.
___. *Kabbalah and Tarot.* Keswick: Forge Press, 2015.

Hall, J. A. *Jungian Dream Interpretation.* Toronto: Inner City Books, 1983.

Jacobi, J. *The Psychology of C. G. Jung.* London: Routledge and Kegan Paul, 1951.

Jung, C. *Alchemical Studies, Collected Works of C. G. Jung, Vol. 13*. Princeton: Princeton University Press, 1967.

Katz, M. *Secrets of the Thoth Tarot Vol.I*. Keswick: Forge Press, 2018.
___. *NLP Magick*. Keswick: Forge Press, 2020.
___. *Secrets of the Thoth Tarot, Vol. III*. Keswick: Forge Press, 2020.
___. *Tarosophy*. Keswick: Forge Press, 3rd print, 2016.
___. *The Magicians Kabbalah*. Keswick: Forge Press, 2015.

Lévi, E. *Transcendental Magic: Its Doctrine and Ritual*. London: George Redway, 1896.

Plato. *Timaeus*. Dent: London, 1965.

Shakespeare, *Henry V*.

Townsend, M. *The Gospel of Falling Down*. Alresford: O-Books, 2007.

Vance, J. *Tales of the Dying Earth*. London: Mayflower, 1972.

von Petzinger, G. *The First Signs*. New York: Atria, 2016.

Waite, A. E. *The Pictorial Key to the Tarot*. London: Rider & Company, 1974.

Zimmer, H & Campbell, J. (ed.). *Philosophies of India 9*. Princeton: Princeton Univ. Press, 1969.

# ALSO BY MARCUS KATZ

**As Marcus Katz**

*Tarosophy.*
*The Magister (Vol. 1).*
*The Magicians Kabbalah.*
*Secrets of the Thoth Tarot (3 vols).*
*After the Angel: An Account of the Abramelin Operation.*
*NLP Magick.*
*The Alchemy Workbook (Alchemical Amphitheatre).*
*The Mountain of Myrrh.*

**Co-Authored with Tali Goodwin**

*Around the Tarot in 78 Days.*
*Learning Lenormand.*
*Practical Tarot Techniques (formerly Tarot Face to Face).*
*Tarot Time Traveller.*
*Easy Lenormand (kit).*
*Secrets of the Waite-Smith Tarot.*
*Tarot Flip.*
*Tarot Twist.*
*Tarot Inspire.*
*Tarot Turn (Vol. 1).*
*Secrets of the Celtic Cross.*
*The English Lenormand.*
*Tarot Temple.*
*Abiding in the Sanctuary.*

**Gated Spread Series**

*Tarot Life (12 booklets).*
*The Tarot Shaman.*
*The Palace of the Phoenix.*
*The Garden of Creation.*
*The Gates of Valentine.*
*The Resurrection Engine.*
*The Ghost Train.*

**Co-Authored with Derek Bain and Tali Goodwin**

*A New Dawn for Tarot: The Original Tarot of the Golden Dawn.*

Also by Marcus Katz

## Decks, Oracles & Counters

*The Truth Tellers Oracle Deck (Arkartia, art by Briar Lily).*
*The Tarot of the Secret Dawn (art by Janine Hall).*
*The Tarot of Everlasting Day (art by Janine Hall).*
*The Original Lenormand (licensed by the British Museum).*
*The I-Ching Counters (based on a design by Aleister Crowley).*

## As Andrea Green (with Tali Goodwin)

*True Tarot Card Meanings.*
*Tarot for True Romance.*
*Kabbalah and Tarot: A Step-Up Guide.*
*7-Day Lenormand.*
*Numerology.*
*Astrology Love Lookup Guide.*

## Contributing Author

*Tarot Fundamentals (pub. Lo Scarabeo).*
*Tarot Experience (pub. Lo Scarabeo).*
*Tarot Compendium (pub. Lo Scarabeo).*
*Tarot in Culture (2 vols, ed. Emily E. Auger).*
*The Llewellyn Complete Book of Ceremonial Magic (on the Abramelin Operation).*
*Jesus Through Pagan Eyes (on Christ as a Gnostic Teacher).*

## Deck Booklets (with Tali Goodwin)

*Lenormand Fairy Deck (by Davide Corsi).*
*Karma Angels (by A. Atanassov).*
*Gilded Reverie Lenormand (by Ciro Marchetti).*

Printed in Great Britain
by Amazon

18064866R00261